Ultimate Java Design Patterns

Master Creational, Structural, Behavioral, Concurrency, and Architectural Patterns for Scalable Enterprise Java Applications

Ricken Bazolo

www.orangeava.com

First Published: May 2026

Published By: Orange Education Pvt Ltd, AVA®

Address: 9, Daryaganj, Delhi, 110002, India

275 New North Road Islington Suite 1314 London,
N1 7AA, United Kingdom

ISBN (PBK): 978-93-49887-90-9

ISBN (E-BOOK): 978-93-49887-70-1

Scan the QR code to explore our entire catalogue

www.orangeava.com

Get a Free eBook

We hope you're enjoying your recent book purchase! Your feedback is incredibly valuable to us and helps other readers discover books that truly make a difference.

If you found this book useful or enjoyable, we'd greatly appreciate it if you could leave a short review with a 5-star rating on Amazon. Your review supports our work and allows us to reach more learners worldwide.

As a thank-you, we're happy to offer you a **free digital copy of this book** plus a **30% discount code** for your next purchase on our official websites:

www.orangeava.com

www.orangeava.in (For the Indian Subcontinent).

☑ **How it works:**

Leave your review on Amazon, take a screenshot of the confirmation or use the following link to submit the claim and email it to **info@orangeava.com.** Once received the required detail, we will send your rewards within 24 hours, **along with one month free subcription to the book on AVA SkillShelf!**

Claim Form
https://rebrand.ly/4d2477

Thank you for your support–it truly means a lot to us.

Downloading the code bundles and colored images

Please follow the links or scan the QR codes to download the ***Code Bundles and Images*** of the book:

https://github.com/ava-orange-education/Ultimate-Java-Design-Patterns

The code bundles and images of the book are also hosted on ***https://rebrand.ly/0bb0fa***

In case there's an update to the code, it will be updated on the existing GitHub repository.

Errata

We take immense pride in our work at **Orange Education Pvt Ltd,** and follow the best practices to ensure the accuracy of our content to provide an indulging reading experience to our subscribers. Our readers are our mirrors, and we use their inputs to reflect and improve upon human errors, if any, that may have occurred during the publishing processes involved. To let us maintain the quality and help us reach out to any readers who might be having difficulties due to any unforeseen errors, please write to us at:

errata@orangeava.com

Your support, suggestions, and feedback are highly appreciated.

Dedicated To

My Beloved Parents:

Judith Nzamba,
Pamphile Bazolo.

And

My Wife, Benjamine, as well as My Children,
Gad and Emiliana.

About the Author

Ricken Bazolo is a senior Java technologist, full-stack developer, and tech entrepreneur with over a decade of experience designing and delivering scalable software systems. He has held key technical leadership roles, including Technical Lead and CTO, working on enterprise platforms, cloud-based solutions, and high-impact applications across multiple industries.

His expertise spans software architecture, Java ecosystems, and the practical application of design patterns to solve complex engineering challenges. Ricken has extensive experience with modern architectures such as microservices and distributed systems, as well as cloud platforms, including AWS and Microsoft Azure. Recently, his work has focused on integrating artificial intelligence into business applications, particularly through Retrieval-Augmented Generation (RAG), Large Language Models (LLMs), and frameworks such as Spring AI and LangChain, enabling the development of intelligent and context-aware systems.

Beyond his professional work, Ricken is deeply committed to knowledge sharing and community building. He has led technical training programs, mentored developers, and contributed to open source projects within the Java ecosystem. Through his writing, speaking, and hands-on projects, he helps engineers bridge the gap between theory and real-world applications.

In this book, Ricken shares practical insights drawn from real-world experience, enabling developers and architects to design scalable, maintainable, and future-ready systems. His goal is to empower engineers to think beyond codes, and embrace design as a core discipline in modern software development.

About the Technical Reviewer

Chandni Prasad is a Product Manager at Google, currently leading Material Design for iOS and AI UX roadmaps to standardize cross-app user experiences across the Google ecosystem. With a strong background in highly regulated and air-gapped infrastructure, she previously spearheaded the product strategy for Google Distributed Cloud (GDC), where she launched the platform's first disconnected Console UI and its developer-facing CLI unblocking critical multi-billion dollar contracts.

Prior to Google, she owned feature roadmaps for Cisco's SD-WAN and network security portfolio, driving SASE strategy and subscription license optimizations. She holds an MBA from Cornell University, where she won the Cornell FinTech Hackathon. Outside of the tech world, she is an avid sailor and RPG gamer.

Acknowledgments

I would like to express my deepest gratitude to my wife for her unwavering support throughout the writing of this book. Her constant encouragement made this work possible, and I could not have completed it without her by my side.

My sincere thanks also go to the editorial team at Orange Education Pvt. Ltd. for their continuous support and flexibility throughout the development of this book.

Preface

Java continues to play a central role in modern software development, powering systems that range from enterprise platforms to cloud-native applications. Building such systems requires more than technical expertise; it demands a deep understanding of design principles that enable scalability, maintainability, and resilience. This book was written to help developers and architects master these principles, and apply them effectively in real-world projects.

The book is organized into 11 chapters, guiding you progressively from foundational concepts to advanced design practices. It begins with the essential categories of design patterns: Creational, Structural, and Behavioral, illustrated through practical Java examples. As you move forward, the book explores advanced topics such as concurrency and architectural patterns, providing the tools needed to design high-performing and scalable systems. It also addresses the key aspects of software quality, including testing, debugging, and writing robust and maintainable codes.

Beyond the fundamentals, this book focuses on real-world challenges. It demonstrates how design patterns integrate with modern Java frameworks, how they support distributed system design, and how they contribute to building secure and scalable applications. It also looks ahead to emerging trends such as microservices, cloud-native architectures, and the growing role of AI in software engineering.

By the end of this book, you will not only understand design patterns– you will think in patterns. You will be able to design and build adaptable and high-quality systems with confidence, leveraging the full power of the Java ecosystem in a constantly evolving technological landscape.

Chapter 1: This will introduce Java design patterns and their fundamental concepts. It explains what design patterns are, their history and evolution, as well as their categories and classifications. It also covers their benefits, best practices, and includes case studies as well as examples to understand how they solve the common software development problems.

Chapter 2: It will explore creational design patterns, focusing on object creation mechanisms. The chapter covers Singleton, Factory Method, Abstract Factory,

Builder, and Prototype patterns, along with practical examples and real-world scenarios for each pattern.

Chapter 3: This will examine structural design patterns, and how they define relationships between entities. It covers Adapter, Bridge, Composite, Decorator, Facade, Flyweight, and Proxy patterns, with implementation examples in Java.

Chapter 4: It will explore behavioral design patterns, focusing on algorithms and object interactions. The chapter covers the Chain of Responsibility, Command, Interpreter, Iterator, Mediator, Memento, Observer, State, Strategy, Template Method, and Visitor patterns with Java examples.

Chapter 5: This will focus on concurrency design patterns in Java for building efficient and thread-safe applications. It covers Thread Pool, Producer-Consumer, Read-Write Lock, Future, and Fork/Join patterns, along with Java concurrency utilities and best practices.

Chapter 6: It will discuss architectural design patterns that define the structure of Java applications. It covers MVC, Microservices Architecture, Layered Architecture, Event-Driven Architecture, and SOA, including their implementation in Java.

Chapter 7: This will explain how design patterns support testing and debugging in Java applications. It covers Test Stub, Mock Object, Singleton in testing, Strategy for testing variants, Decorator for test data setup, and best practices for testing and debugging.

Chapter 8: It will examine how design patterns are used in popular Java frameworks. It covers Spring (Dependency Injection and AOP), Hibernate (DAO pattern), JSF (Front Controller), and Struts (Intercepting Filter), with practical examples.

Chapter 9: This will address design patterns for distributed systems. It covers Client-Server, Broker, and Peer-to-Peer patterns used to build scalable and reliable applications.

Chapter 10: It will explore design patterns for security and scalability. It covers security design patterns and scalability design patterns to address common challenges in building secure and scalable systems.

Chapter 11: This will present future trends in Java design patterns. It covers reactive programming, microservices architectures, cloud-native development, integration of AI and machine learning, along with security enhancements.

DID YOU KNOW

Did you know that Orange Education Pvt Ltd offers eBook versions of every book published, with PDF and ePub files available? You can upgrade to the eBook version at **www.orangeava.com** and as a print book customer, you are entitled to a discount on the eBook copy. Get in touch with us at: **info@orangeava.com** for more details.

At **www.orangeava.com**, you can also read a collection of free technical articles, sign up for a range of free newsletters, and receive exclusive discounts and offers on Print Books and eBooks.

PIRACY

If you come across any illegal copies of our works in any form on the internet, we would be grateful if you would provide us with the location address or website name. Please contact us at **info@orangeava.com** with a link to the material.

ARE YOU INTERESTED IN AUTHORING WITH US?

If there is a topic that you have expertise in, and you are interested in either writing or contributing to a book, please write to us at **business@orangeava.com**. We are on a journey to help developers and tech professionals to gain insights on the present technological advancements and innovations happening across the globe and build a community that believes Knowledge is best acquired by sharing and learning with others. Please reach out to us to learn what our audience demands and how you can be part of this educational reform. We also welcome ideas from tech experts and help them build learning and development content for their domains.

REVIEWS

Please leave a review. Once you have read and used this book, why not leave a review on the site that you purchased it from? Potential readers can then see and use your unbiased opinion to make purchase decisions. We at Orange Education would love to know what you think about our products, and our authors can learn from your feedback. Thank you!

For more information about Orange Education, please visit **www.orangeava.com**.

Table of Contents

CHAPTER 1
Introduction to Java Design Patterns

Introduction

Java programming is central to modern software development due to its robustness and flexibility across various contexts. However, writing efficient, readable, and maintainable applications requires knowing the fundamental concepts that guide good development practices. Design patterns are one of these essential concepts, providing proven approaches to solving common software challenges cleanly and effectively.

In this chapter, we will explore the foundational principles of design patterns in Java, their purpose, historical roots, classification, and their role in simplifying complex development scenarios. We will further examine how these patterns facilitate the resolution of real-world problems by offering proven, reusable solutions.

Structure

This chapter is organized into the following sections:

- Understanding Design Patterns
    - Defining a Design Pattern
    - Why Design Patterns Matter
- History and Evolution of Design Patterns
- Categories and Classifications
- Benefits and Best Practices
- Use Cases and Examples

Understanding Design Patterns

Let us imagine that we decide to build a house. We call upon an architect to avoid fragile walls or poorly arranged rooms. The architect then offers us a plan to follow, which helps us select the right materials according to the size of the land, the preferences of the inhabitants, and other essential details. This plan is not a rigid rule, but rather a guide that can be adapted. A mansion and a cabin follow certain shared principles to ensure that they are sturdy, yet they are built in very different ways.

In the same way, Design Patterns are not fixed rules. They are standard solutions developers can use and modify according to the needs of their project, the size of the team, or the expectations of the user. Just as an architect adapts plans to each house, a developer selects and adjusts Patterns to solve specific application problems.

Defining a Design Pattern

A Design Pattern is a proven approach to solving common software design problems. Just as an architect relies on universal principles to design a staircase or a roof structure, a developer applies Design Patterns to organize code optimally.

Let us imagine we need to organize a kitchen. Without prior thought, we might place the knives far from the cutting board, store the spices in hard-to-reach cupboards, and position the stovetop near an open window.

The result: An impractical and potentially hazardous kitchen.

An experienced cook would instead apply simple yet effective principles of organization:

- **Problem**: How can we make the kitchen both functional and safe?
- **Solution**: Group tools by area of use (cutting, cooking, storage), keep the most frequently used items within easy reach, and isolate heat sources.

Design Patterns follow the same logic. They are not rigid rules but adaptable principles, like a chef adjusting the layout of the kitchen according to the menu of the day.

They transform code into a structured space where every line has its place, every interaction is predictable, and every change can be made without dismantling the whole system.

Why Design Patterns Matter

In a technological landscape where applications must constantly evolve, Design Patterns serve as a strategic compass. Imagine software as a growing city without any urban planning; adding a new district (a feature) could risk blocking existing roads (previous functionalities). Design Patterns act like urban planning regulations, allowing one part of the system to be modified without compromising the whole. For example, the Strategy Pattern allows an algorithm (such as a search engine) to be swapped out like a module in an electric vehicle without altering the rest of the car.

Beyond flexibility, these patterns transform human collaboration. Consider a team working on an online booking system. If a developer mentions using the ***Factory***

Pattern to create booking objects, their colleagues immediately understand the underlying structure. This shared language eliminates hours of technical explanations, accelerates code reviews, and reduces misunderstandings. It is as if everyone speaks the same dialect within an international project.

Finally, Design Patterns foster a mindset of active learning. Each pattern mastered becomes a new key to unlocking complex problems. Take the example of a developer who discovers the ***Observer Pattern***; by applying it to a notification system, they suddenly realize that the same model could simplify user interface update management. This revelation creates a virtuous cycle: the more patterns we master, the more use cases we identify, and the sharper our technical creativity becomes.

And what if we ignored these models? We would end up with fragile software, where each update becomes a puzzle, and teams spend more time debugging than innovating. Design Patterns are not a theoretical luxury but a pragmatic investment in sustainability and efficiency.

History and Evolution of Design Patterns

The concept of design patterns did not originate in computer science, but rather in architecture. In the 1970s, architect Christopher Alexander introduced, in his seminal work A Pattern Language, a method for designing urban and domestic spaces based on recurring patterns of quality. Each pattern represents a proven solution to a common design problem, contextualized within a specific environment. The goal was to document these solutions in order to transmit them and to build a shared language among designers. This approach profoundly influenced other disciplines, notably software engineering, which, a decade later, would draw inspiration from it to address its own challenges.

By the late 1980s, the rise of object-oriented programming had revealed practical limitations for developers. Software architectures became rigid and inflexible, code redundancy increased, and modularity struggled to take hold. In response to these issues, four experts Erich Gamma, Richard Helm, Ralph Johnson, and John Vlissides published in 1994 Design Patterns: Elements of Reusable Object-Oriented Software, a foundational work. This now classic guide formalized twenty-three design patterns aimed at optimizing the construction, organization, and maintenance of software systems. These patterns are grouped into three major categories:

- **Creational**: Govern object creation mechanisms;
- **Structural**: Define the hierarchical arrangement of components;
- **Behavioral**: Orchestrate the dynamics of interaction between entities.

Each pattern is described using a methodical framework, a problematic situation, its context of application, a generic solution, and its technical implications. This rigorous formalization not only enables the accumulation of collective experience, but also establishes a common language among professionals, thereby accelerating the resolution of recurring challenges.

In the years that followed, design patterns would no longer be limited to a mere catalog of solutions. Communities began to form to discuss, enrich, and adapt them to diverse contexts. The PLoP (Pattern Languages of Programming) conference, launched in 1994, established a rigorous peer review process. At the same time, the *Portland Pattern Repository* became one of the first technical wikis, encouraging the exchange of concrete use cases.

This movement contributed to the emergence of specialized patterns, particularly in areas such as concurrency and software testing. The very notion of a pattern thus evolved into a tool for structuring thought, one that extends well beyond object-oriented programming.

Toward Large-Scale Architectures

With the rise of web and distributed applications, design patterns are no longer confined to solutions at the class or component level. The *Model-View-Controller* (MVC) pattern, though a veteran, exemplifies this conceptual elevation by offering a clear separation between business logic, presentation, and data management.

As early as 1996, the book Pattern-Oriented Software Architecture formalized this extension by introducing patterns applicable to entire system architectures, such as:

- **Layers**: A layered structure for organizing responsibilities (user interface, business logic, data access, and so on).
- **Broker**: An intermediary that facilitates communication in distributed systems.

In 2002, Martin Fowler expanded upon this approach with *Patterns of Enterprise Application Architecture*, where he described solutions tailored to complex enterprise architectures, such as the Unit of Work or Repository patterns, designed to optimize the organization of data access and transaction management.

The Era of Microservices and Cloud Computing

The emergence of microservices architectures in the 2010s, combined with the rise of cloud computing, introduced a new set of challenges, resilience, scalability, and inter service communication. In response to this context, patterns tailored to such environments began to emerge or gain wider adoption. Among the most well-known are:

- **Circuit Breaker**: This acts as an advanced protection mechanism within your architecture. In the event of a service failure, it steps in to isolate the issue, thereby preventing a domino effect that could potentially cripple the entire system. It is a proactive approach that ensures resilience and continuity of operations.

- **Saga**: This is a distributed transaction management strategy that favors the coordination of compensating actions over the use of global transactions. It maintains data consistency by orchestrating a sequence of reversible operations, thereby offering greater flexibility in managing partial failures.
- **Command Query Responsibility Segregation (CQRS):** This introduces a clear separation between read and write operations within a system. By isolating these responsibilities, each path can be optimized according to its specific requirements, thereby enhancing both performance and scalability. It is a modular approach that encourages a more robust and adaptable architecture.
- **Event Sourcing:** This relies on recording every change as a distinct event, thereby creating a comprehensive history of modifications. This method facilitates traceability and enables the current state of data to be reconstructed from past events, offering enhanced visibility into the evolution of the system.

These patterns, often promoted by cloud providers or open-source communities, serve to enrich the toolbox of the modern architect.

A Thought in Constant Evolution

From streets and buildings to modern distributed systems, design patterns embody a method for structuring complexity. They offer a shared vocabulary, facilitate technical decision-making, and allow us to build upon decades of collective experience. Some critics argue that patterns sometimes compensate for inherent limitations in programming languages, yet their relevance remains unshaken; they help model recurring problems with clarity. More than a mere catalog, design patterns express a way of thinking about software engineering, a bridge between theory and practice, between reusability and adaptation. For the developer, they represent far more than technical solutions: they are a lever for designing robust, coherent, and scalable systems.

Categories and Classifications

When one begins studying design patterns, it is common to feel overwhelmed by their variety. Therefore, it is necessary to understand how these patterns are classified into categories. This organization not only facilitates memorization but also helps one better grasp their role within a software architecture. We shall explore the main families of patterns and the modern extensions that have emerged from the evolution of software technologies.

Foundations, the Classic Classification

This classification distinguishes three main families:

Creational Patterns

These patterns address a simple yet fundamental concern: how to create objects with flexibility, efficiency, and control. The objective is to decouple client code from direct object instantiation and introduce a level of abstraction that facilitates maintainability and extensibility.

- Singleton
- Factory method
- Abstract Factory
- Builder
- Prototype

Example:

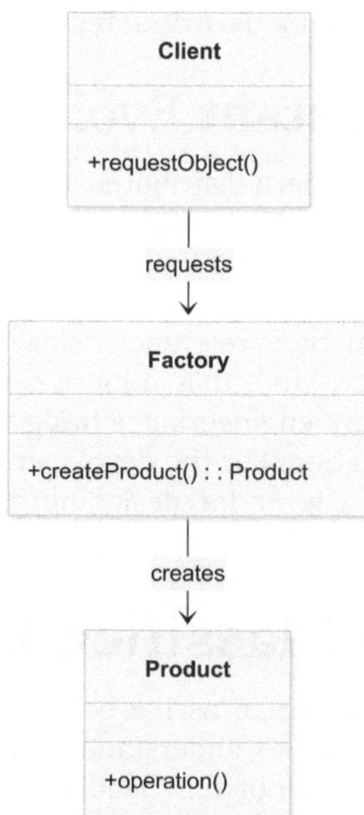

Figure 1.1: *Factory - Creational Pattern*

The following diagram clearly illustrates the operation of a creational design pattern: The Client requests the **Factory** by invoking the **`createProduct()`** method, which generates an instance of the **Product**. This object executes the intended operation through the **`operation()`** method.

Structural Patterns

This category of patterns addresses how classes and objects are organized to form robust and extensible software architectures. It promotes object composition while reducing tight coupling, thereby enhancing flexibility and maintainability.

- Adapter
- Composite
- Decorator
- Facade
- Proxy
- Bridge
- Flyweight

Example:

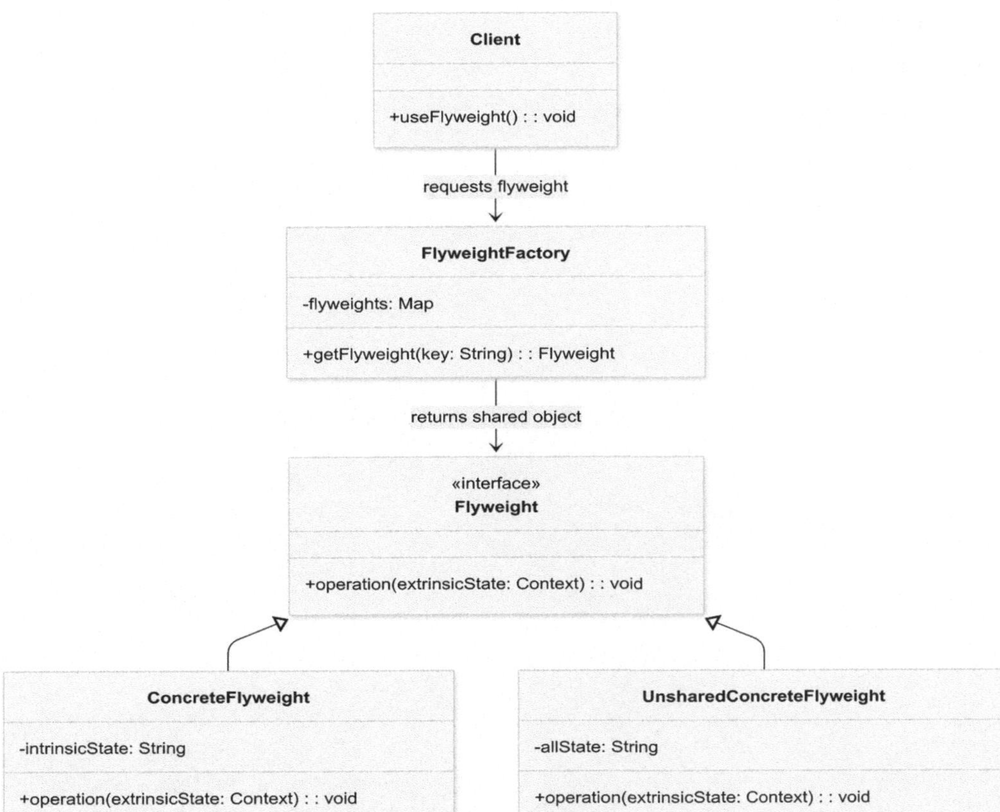

***Figure 1.2**: Flyweight - Structural Pattern*

The diagram above illustrates a structural pattern through the example of character management. The `Flyweight` defines a standard interface for objects that can be shared, such as the letters "A" or "B." The `ConcreteFlyweight` stores the intrinsic state and the shared information, such as the shape of the letter. The `UnsharedConcreteFlyweight`, on the other hand, represents objects that are not shared, such as a word with specific formatting. The `FlyweightFactory` centralizes the creation and management of shared instances to avoid duplication. Finally, the **Client** completes each object by providing the extrinsic state, such as position or color at the use time.

Behavioral Patterns

Behavioral patterns focus on the interactions between objects and the distribution of responsibility. They optimize communication, enable dynamic behaviors, and enhance flexibility.

- Observer
- Strategy
- Command
- Template Method
- Iterator
- State
- Chain of Responsibility
- Interpreter
- Mediator
- Memento
- Visitor

Example:

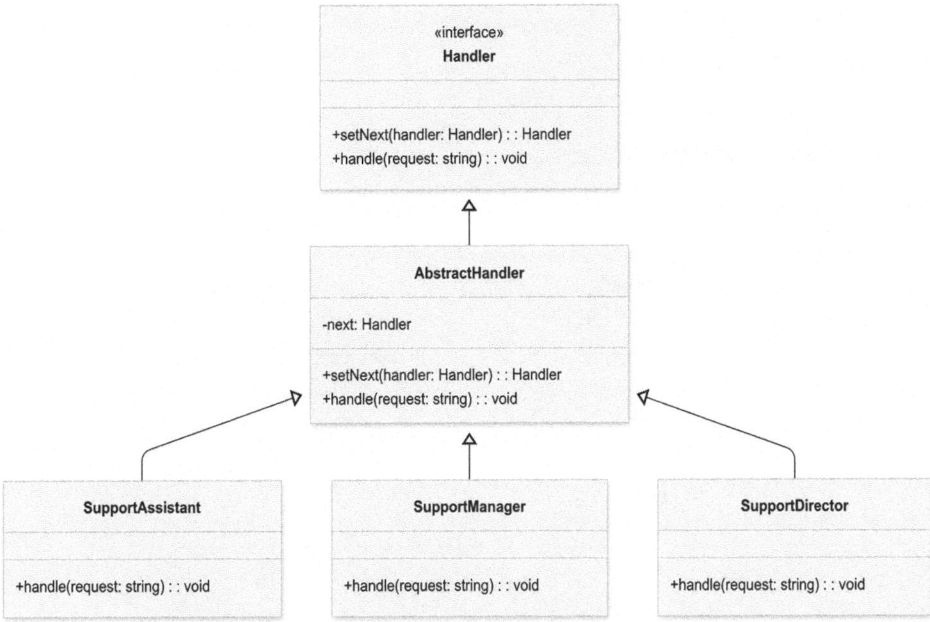

***Figure 1.3**: Chain of Responsibility - Behavioral Pattern*

The diagram above illustrates a behavioral design pattern. The role of the Handler is to provide a standardized interface for each element in the chain, while the **`AbstractHandler`** manages the forwarding logic through the **`setNext`** method. The concrete classes (**`SupportAssistant`**, **`SupportManager`**, and **`SupportDirector`**) can either handle the request directly or pass it on to the next link in the chain. Furthermore, the chain can be configured dynamically for instance, the assistant can be linked to the manager, who may, in turn, forward the request to the director if necessary.

Specialized Patterns for Distributed and Cloud Architectures

As software systems have evolved with the advent of the web, distributed applications, microservices, and cloud computing, new needs have emerged. This evolution has led to the development of complementary categories of design patterns.

Concurrency Patterns

These patterns make it possible to better leverage the multithreading capabilities of a system while ensuring consistency in a concurrent execution environment.

Examples:

- Thread Pool

- Producer-Consumer
- Read-Write Lock
- Future
- Fork/Join Framework

Example:

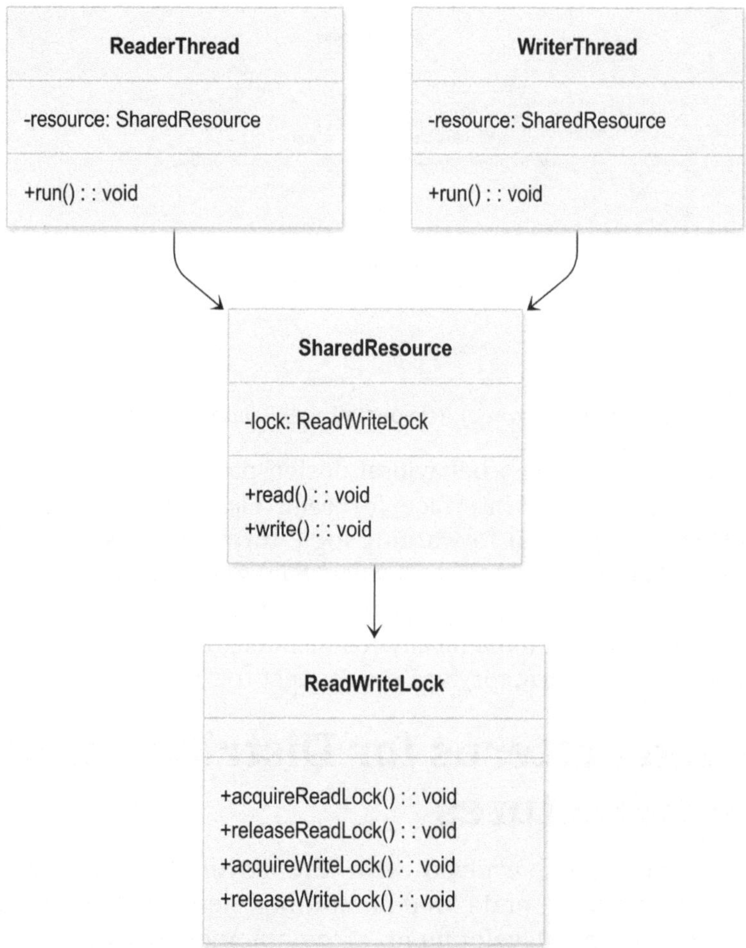

Figure 1.4: *Read-Write Lock - Concurrency Pattern*

The diagram above illustrates a concurrency pattern for managing simultaneous access to a shared resource. The role of **`ReadWriteLock`** is to control who can read from or write to this resource to prevent conflicts. **`SharedResource`** represents the shared data, accessible for both reading and writing. The **`ReaderThread`** and **`WriterThread`** threads represent read and write operations, respectively, while adhering to the rules enforced by the lock; multiple reads can occur in parallel, but a write operation requires exclusive access.

Architectural Patterns

They structure application design at a broader scale than classes and objects by organizing the system into modules, layers, or services.

Examples:

- Model View Controller (MVC)
- Microservices Architecture
- Layered Architecture
- Event-Driven Architecture
- Service-Oriented Architecture
- Repository

Example:

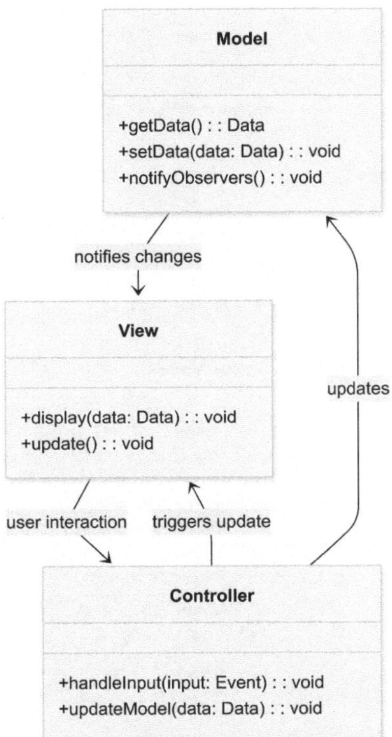

***Figure 1.5**: MVC - Architectural Pattern*

The diagram above illustrates an architectural pattern. The **Model** contains both the data and the business logic of the application. When a change occurs, it automatically notifies the **View**. The View is responsible for displaying this data to the user and may call upon the **Controller** to relay user actions. The Controller, in turn, plays a central role: it interprets user interactions, updates the Model if necessary, and then instructs the View to refresh itself to reflect the updated information.

Relying on architectural models that ensure resilience to failures, isolate faults effectively, and support eventual consistency across components is essential in distributed and event-driven systems.

Distributed Systems Patterns

These patterns are designed for applications distributed across multiple nodes or servers. They ensure efficient communication and decentralized role management.

Examples:

- Client-Server
- Broker
- Peer-to-Peer

Example:

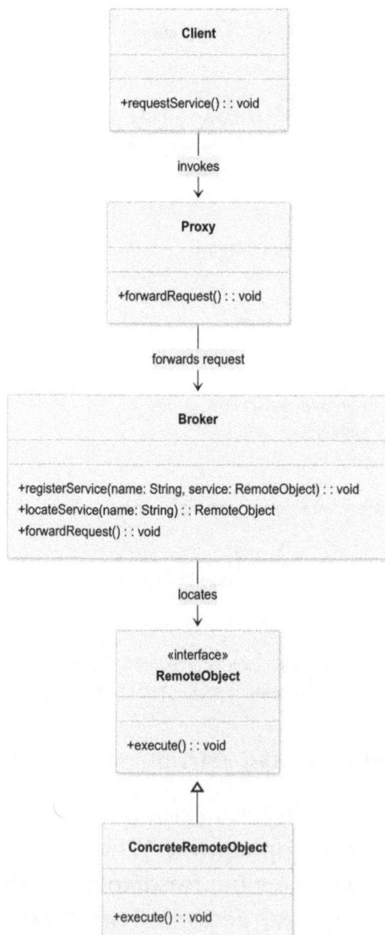

Figure 1.6: *Broker - Distributed Systems Pattern*

The diagram above illustrates the operation of a pattern specific to distributed systems. The **Client** does not interact directly with the remote object; it communicates through a **Proxy**, which acts as a local representative. This Proxy forwards the request to the **Broker**, who is responsible for locating the appropriate remote service and transmitting the request. The remote interaction relies on the **`RemoteObject`** interface, which defines the available operations. On the server side, the **`ConcreteRemoteObject`** class provides the actual implementation of the service and executes the requested operation.

Benefits and Best Practices

Design Patterns provide a common language that facilitates understanding and communication among developers. The following are overviews of their benefits and best practices for using them effectively.

Benefits

- **Improved Maintainability:** Using standardized and well-recognized structures makes code easier to understand, modify, and evolve.
- **Reusability of Solutions:** Design patterns are generic templates that can be applied to various projects. They help avoid "reinventing the wheel" and save time and effort.
- **Clear Communication:** Pattern names and concepts (Factory, Singleton, Observer, Strategy, and so forth) form a common language among developers. A simple pattern name can easily convey the intent and role of a code segment.
- **Better Code Organization and Decoupling:** Most design patterns are designed to separate responsibilities or reduce tight coupling, resulting in more modular and scalable code.
- **Enhanced Testability:** Code structured according to design patterns is generally easier to test, as patterns often encourage behavior isolation and the definition of clear interfaces.

Best Practices for Using Design Patterns

- **Do not overuse Design Patterns:** The goal is not to force a pattern into every line of code. Excessive use can make the code unnecessarily complex. It is better to choose a pattern only when it genuinely addresses an identified problem.
- **Understand the problem before choosing a pattern:** The best results come from starting with a concrete need or difficulty. A pattern should solve a specific issue rather than simply be used because it is *in fashion*.

- **Favor simplicity:** Even if a design pattern seems appealing, choosing a more straightforward solution is sometimes wiser when the problem is simple. Code readability should remain a top priority.
- **Master the core concepts of each pattern:** Design patterns are based on SOLID principles (Single Responsibility, Open/Closed, and the like). Understanding why and how each pattern works makes implementation easier and helps avoid common mistakes.
- **Combine patterns with discernment:** Multiple patterns can sometimes complement each other (for example, combining Observer and Factory). However, one should avoid adding layers of complexity without a valid reason.
- **Document and share:** When implementing a design pattern, clearly indicate in the documentation why it was chosen, what problem it solves, and its limitations. This transparency facilitates maintenance and knowledge sharing within the team.

Use Cases and Examples

We will now examine two concrete cases in which several classic design patterns are effectively combined to address common challenges in enterprise applications. These practical examples demonstrate how to structure code to maximize flexibility, testability, and maintainability.

Case 1: Payment Processing System with Factory Method and Strategy

Context: An e-commerce platform commonly manages various payment methods (credit card, PayPal, cryptocurrency, Mobile Money, and the list continues). Each method requires specific rules for execution and validation.

Problematic: How can we efficiently manage the instantiation of different payment processors while making the amount validation logic dynamic?

Proposed Solution:

- **Creating Payment Processors with the Factory Method Pattern**

  Common Interface: A sealed interface is defined to allow only specific classes to implement it. This ensures that only predefined implementations (in this case, for credit card or PayPal) will be used.

```
public sealed interface PaymentProcessor permits CreditCard
Processor, PayPalProcessor {
    String process(double amount);
}
```

Concrete Implementations: Each class that implements this interface provides its version of the *process method* tailored to the corresponding payment method.

- **PayPal Processor**

```
final class PayPalProcessor implements PaymentProcessor {
    @Override
    public String process(double amount) {
        return "PayPal payment: %s".formatted(amount);
    }
}
```

- **Credit Card Processor**

```
final class CreditCardProcessor implements PaymentProcessor {
    @Override
    public String process(double amount) {
        return "Credit card payment: %s".formatted(amount);
    }
}
```

This design approach relies on two key principles: **separation of concerns**, where each payment processor contains autonomous logic dedicated to its specific function, ensuring modularity and simplified maintenance and **extensibility**, which allows new payment methods to be integrated easily by simply creating additional implementations of the **`PaymentProcessor`** interface, without affecting existing systems. This structure promotes code clarity by avoiding complex interdependencies and supports flexible system evolution to meet future needs.

- **Implementing Dynamic Validation with the Strategy Pattern**

Defining the Validation Strategy: A functional interface represents a payment validation strategy, allowing validation rules to be defined interchangeably and flexibly.

```
@FunctionalInterface
public interface PaymentValidationStrategy {
booleanvalidate(double amount);
}
```

`PaymentEngine` Class: The **`PaymentEngine`** class receives a validation strategy through its constructor. It then uses this strategy to verify whether the amount is valid before delegating the processing to the selected payment processor.

```
public class PaymentEngine {
    private final PaymentValidationStrategyvalidationStrategy;
```

```
    public PaymentEngine(PaymentValidationStrategy strategy) {
this.validationStrategy = strategy;
    }
    public String executePayment(PaymentProcessor processor,
double amount) {
        return validationStrategy.validate(amount) ?
processor.process(amount) :
                "Validation Failure";
    }
}
```

The modular design isolates the validation logic within a dedicated interface, providing the flexibility to modify validation rules without impacting the core processing logic. This separation of concerns also enhances the system's reusability: a single instance of **PaymentEngine** can be adapted to different scenarios by associating it with various payment processors, depending on the strategy or specific requirements, without requiring any structural overhaul. This approach combines simplified maintenance with operational versatility.

Usage Example: We demonstrate how to assemble the system by defining a control strategy *in this case, a simple anti-fraud check* and executing payments using different processors.

```
public class PaymentProcessingSystem {
    public static void main(String[] args) {
       var fraudCheckStrategy = (PaymentValidationStrategy)
amount -> amount < 10_000;
        var engine = new PaymentEngine(fraudCheckStrategy);
System.out.println(engine.executePayment(new CreditCardProcessor
(), 500));
System.out.println(engine.executePayment(new PayPalProcessor(),
15_000));
    }
}
```

Console Output

```
Credit card payment: 500.0
Validation Failure
```

The Factory Method isolates the processors' instantiation logic, while the Strategy pattern allows business rules to be modified dynamically without affecting the main processing flow. This highlights the system's flexibility and adaptability to different validation policies.

Case 2: Notification System with the Observer and Decorator Patterns

Context: A banking application is looking to develop an adaptable notification system that supports *email*, SMS, and in-app *notifications*. This system should also have the capability to integrate advanced features like encryption and logging.

Problematic: How can we structure a modular system where observers react to events and cross-cutting features can be easily added without complicating the core business logic?

Proposed Solution:

- **Implementation of the Observer Pattern**

  Defining a Listener for Notifications: An interface is defined for notification listeners so that each listener class implements an update method.

```
public interface NotificationListener {
    void update(String recipient, String message);
}
```

  Notification Service: This class manages all subscribers and dispatches notifications to each.

```
public class NotificationService {
    private final List<NotificationListener> listeners = new Array-
List<>();
    public void subscribe(NotificationListener listener) {
listeners.add(listener);
    }
    public void notifyAll(String recipient, String message) {
listeners.forEach(listener ->listener.update(recipient, message));
    }
}
```

- **Enhancing Notifications with the Decorator Pattern**

  Notification Interface: A sealed interface that enforces the use of specific components for notification.

```
public sealed interface Notification permits BaseNotification,
LoggedNotification {
    void send();
}
```

  Basic Implementation: The basic notification contains the content and provides a simple sending mechanism.

```
public record BaseNotification(String content) implements
Notification {
    @Override
    public void send() {
System.out.printf("Send: %s%n", content);
    }
}
```

Decorator for Logging: The decorator adds additional functionality (in this case, logging) while preserving the sending logic of the basic notification.

```
public final class LoggedNotification implements Notification {
    private final Notification wrapped;
    public LoggedNotification(Notification n) {
this.wrapped = n;
    }
    @Override
    public void send() {
System.out.println("[LOG] Sending started");
wrapped.send();
    }
}
```

The `LoggedNotification` class ensures the separation of concerns by focusing exclusively on logging without altering the sending logic of `BaseNotification`. At the same time, feature stacking allows decorators (for example, encryption) to be added dynamically as needed without affecting existing code.

- **Concrete Execution (Main Class with a Listener)**

  Implementation of a Specific Listener for Emails:

```
public class EmailListener implements NotificationListener {
    @Override
    public void update(String recipient, String message) {
        new LoggedNotification(new BaseNotification("Email to %s:
%s".formatted(recipient, message))).send();
    }
}
```

Final Assembly: The service is instantiated, the listener is added, and a notification is triggered.

```
public class NotificationSystem {
    public static void main(String[] args) {
        var service = new NotificationService();
service.subscribe(new EmailListener());
service.notifyAll("client@bank.com", "Transfer approved");
    }
}
```

Console Output

```
[LOG] Sending started
Send: Email to client@bank.com: Transfer approved
```

The combination of patterns allows the listener to use the decorator to enrich the notification, while the Observer service handles distribution without knowing the details of the enhancement. The modular design ensures that each component, the decorator, the listener, and the service, can be tested or extended independently.

Conclusion

In this introductory chapter, we have discussed design patterns, their historical context, and their role in software development. We have also explored their classifications, benefits, and best practices, complemented by practical examples.

The next chapter focuses on creation patterns, which aim to delegate instantiation logic to promote flexibility, decoupling, and code reuse. Here, we detail Java implementations of the *Singleton*, *Factory Method*, *Abstract Factory*, *Builder*, and *Prototype patterns*.

Points to Remember

- Patterns provide structure and clarity in software design.
- Choosing the correct pattern requires analyzing the specific problem.
- Design patterns improve code reusability, scalability, and maintainability.

Multiple Choice Questions

1. Amongst which of these options do Design Patterns provide?
   a. Ready-to-use code snippets
   b. Template solutions to common problems
   c. Language-specific functionalities
   d. Debugging techniques
2. The Singleton Pattern falls under?
   a. Creational Patterns
   b. Structural Patterns
   c. Behavioral Patterns
   d. Architectural Patterns

3. Who introduced design patterns to software engineering?
    a. Alan Turing
    b. James Gosling
    c. Gang of Four (GoF)
    d. Dennis Ritchie

Answers

1. b
2. a
3. c

Questions

1. How does the Observer pattern enhance event handling?
2. Compare Singleton and Factory patterns. When would you use each?
3. How does the Adapter Pattern promote code reusability in legacy systems?

Key Terms

- **Design Pattern:** Reusable solutions for common software problems.
- **Gang of Four (GoF):** Authors of the foundational book on design patterns.
- **Creational Patterns:** Deal with object creation mechanisms.
- **Structural Patterns:** Manage the composition of classes or objects.
- **Behavioral Patterns:** Define communication between objects.

CHAPTER 2
Creational Design Patterns

Introduction

Creational design patterns provide structured solutions to object instantiation challenges, striking a balance between efficiency and adaptable system architecture.

This chapter will be examining five core patterns: ***Singleton***, ***Factory Method***, ***Abstract Factory***, ***Builder***, *and* ***Prototype***, focusing on their core mechanisms, Java-based implementations, and practical use cases. Through clear explanations and useful code examples, you will learn how these patterns decouple and modularize object creation from core system logic. This separation promotes code reuse, maintains system integrity, and simplifies adaptation to evolving requirements, ensuring robust and future-proof architectures.

By the end of this chapter, you will be equipped to choose and apply the optimal creational pattern for scenarios that demand scalability, maintainability, and a clean separation of concerns.

Structure

In this chapter, we will cover:

- Singleton Pattern
- Factory Method Pattern
- Abstract Factory Pattern
- Builder Pattern
- Prototype Pattern
- Comparative Analysis

Singleton Pattern

The Singleton is a design pattern which guarantees that a class has only one instance and provides global access. Imagine a configuration manager that loads a file only once or a connection to a shared database; the Singleton avoids costly duplication and ensures consistency.

The Singleton meets a critical need: controlling the instantiation of a class. Without it, creating multiple instances of a shared resource, such as a configuration file, results in:

- **I/O Overload:** Repeated file reads.
- **Memory Wastage:** Redundant loads.
- **Inconsistencies:** Different values between instances.

Let us consider a real-life scenario in which a lack of control over instances leads to critical malfunctions.

Case Study

Let us consider the case of a video streaming platform serving over 1 million active users. This platform utilizes a **`config.properties`** file to orchestrate essential features in real-time. This file allows:

- **System Configuration:** Control of simultaneous connections, cache optimization, and log settings.
- **Secure Integration of Third-Party Services:** Management of API keys requiring frequent updates.
- **Dynamic Video Adaptation:** Automatic adjustment of quality (HD, 4K), bitrate, and codecs based on user bandwidth.

These parameters are constantly accessed by various components, such as the *video player*, API *middleware*, and *monitoring tools*, making the configuration file a central element of the infrastructure.

Note: *In this case study, we will focus on the implementation of useful classes in order to apply the concept of the design pattern.*

Initial Problem

We have a **`ConfigLoader`** class that focuses on loading the initial **`config.properties`** file.

```
public class ConfigLoader {

    private final Properties config = new Properties();
```

```
    public ConfigLoader() {
// Load file at EACH instantiation
try (InputStream input = getClass().getClassLoader().
getResourceAsStream("config.properties")) {
config.load(input);
        } catch (IOException e) {/*...*/}
    }

    public String get(String key) {
        return config.getProperty(key);
    }
}
```

The current **ConfigLoader** implementation suffers from several shortcomings that can degrade overall performance and compromise system consistency:

- **Resource Saturation:** Each instantiation of **ConfigLoader** reloads the **config.properties** file, which, at high frequencies, can saturate the hard disk and consume unnecessary memory, compromising overall system performance.
- **Configuration Inconsistencies:** Updating the **config.properties** file can lead to inconsistencies, as some instances retain the old version, which can cause malfunctions and unpredictable system behavior.

Using **ConfigLoader** to get configuration parameters:

```
public class SingletonPatternInitialProblem {
    public static void main( String[] args ) {
// Uncontrolled use of the ConfigLoader class
        // performance issues, especially if the configuration file
is large
String apiKey = new ConfigLoader().get("youtube.key");
        String quality = new ConfigLoader().get("video.quality");
    }
}
```

How can the **Singleton pattern** restructure this logic to solve problems that reveal a critical need?

Applying the Singleton Principles

We will start by renaming the **ConfigLoader** class to reflect its evolving responsibilities better. It will become **ConfigManager** and will no longer simply load the **config.properties** file. It will now manage access, caching, and data consistency.

We will do some refactoring by isolating the file-loading logic using the **loadConfig** method.

```
public class ConfigManager {
   private void loadConfig() {
       try (InputStream input = getClass().getClassLoader().
getResourceAsStream("config.properties")) {
config.load(input);
       } catch (IOException e) {/*...*/}
   }
}
```

Private Constructor

The first step is to make the **ConfigManager** class constructor private. This prevents any direct instantiation of the class from the outside, ensuring that object creation is strictly controlled.

```
public class ConfigManager {
   private ConfigManager() {
loadConfig(); // File loading, called once
}
}
```

Static Instance

We declare a private static variable to hold the single instance of the class. This variable is initialized lazily, meaning it is created only when needed.

```
public class ConfigManager {
   private static ConfigManagerinstance;
}
```

Global Access Method

We provide a public static method, **getInstance()**, which returns the unique instance of the class. This method checks whether the instance already exists, and if not, it creates it.

```
public class ConfigManager {
   public static ConfigManagergetInstance() {
       if (instance == null) {
           instance = new ConfigManager();
       }
       return instance;
   }
}
```

Ensuring Thread Safety

Ensuring that the Singleton Pattern is thread-safe in a multithreaded environment is crucial. Several approaches can be used.

Complete Synchronization

The **getInstance()** method can be synchronized to prevent multiple threads from simultaneously accessing the critical section where the instance is created. However, this approach may lead to poor performance due to the cost of synchronization.

```
public class ConfigManager {
  private static ConfigManager instance;
  private ConfigManager() {
loadConfig();
   }
   public static synchronized ConfigManagergetInstance() {
       if (instance == null) {
           instance = new ConfigManager();
       }
       return instance;
   }
}
```

Double-Checked Locking

Double-checked locking is a technique that reduces synchronization by checking twice whether the instance is null. The first check is performed without synchronization, while the second check occurs inside a synchronized block. This approach improves performance but requires using the **volatile** keyword to ensure proper visibility of the instance across threads.

```
public class ConfigManager {
   private static volatile ConfigManagerinstance;
   private ConfigManager() {
loadConfig();
   }
   public static ConfigManagergetInstance() {
       if (instance == null) {
           synchronized (ConfigManager.class) {
               if (instance == null) {
instance = new ConfigManager();
               }
           }
       }
       return instance;
```

```
        }
    }
```

Static Initialization

Another approach is static initialization, where the instance is created at class loading time. This approach is thread-safe and does not require explicit synchronization.

```
    public class ConfigManager {
       private static final ConfigManagerINSTANCE = new ConfigManager();
       private ConfigManager() {
    loadConfig();
       }
       public static ConfigManagergetInstance() {
           return INSTANCE;
       }
    }
```

Using an Enumeration

Using an enumeration to implement a Singleton is generally considered best practice, as it ensures thread safety and guards against serialization and reflection issues. However, this approach can be resource-intensive, making it less ideal when performance is a priority or when inheritance is required.

Final Implementation

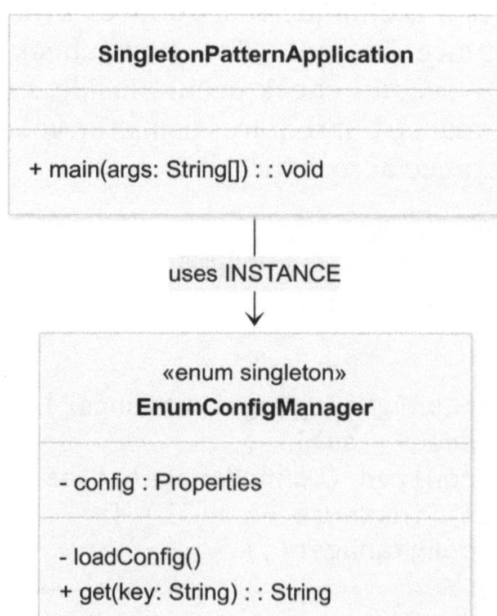

Figure 2.1: *Singleton Pattern - Enum*

Here is a complete implementation of the Singleton Pattern to provide a solution for our case study, using the enumeration approach:

```
public enumEnumConfigManager {
INSTANCE;
   private final Properties config = new Properties();
// Loaded only once, when enum is loaded
EnumConfigManager() {
loadConfig();
   }
   private void loadConfig() {
       try (InputStream input = getClass().getClassLoader().
getResourceAsStream("config.properties")) {
config.load(input);
       } catch (IOException e) {/*...*/}
   }
   public String get(String key) {
       return config.getProperty(key);
   }
}
```

Using the Singleton Implementation

```
public class SingletonPatternApplication {
   public static void main( String[] args ) {
       String apiKey = EnumConfigManager.INSTANCE.get("youtube.
key");
       String quality = EnumConfigManager.INSTANCE.get("video.
quality");
System.out.printf("API Key: %s\nVideo Quality: %s%n", apiKey,
quality);
   }
}
```

By applying the Singleton Pattern, we have resolved the initial issues of multiple configuration instances, parameter inconsistencies, and management complexity. The configuration of the video streaming platform is now centralized, secure, and easy to manage, ensuring a smooth user experience and simplified maintenance.

While the Singleton pattern is excellent for controlling a single resource, how can we handle the dynamic creation of objects with multiple variants without duplicating code? The **Factory Method Pattern** offers a structured approach to handling this.

Factory Method Pattern

The Factory Method Pattern enables a class to delegate the instantiation of objects to its subclasses. In other words, it enables a parent class to defer instantiation to its child classes. This pattern addresses a key need:

- **Flexibility:** Create objects without relying on their concrete classes.
- **Scalability:** Add new types without modifying existing code.

Let us consider the example of a real-world scenario where the need for flexibility in object creation leads to critical limitations.

Case Study

Imagine a SaaS application that allows users to store and manage their files in the cloud. Initially, the application supports only a single storage provider, such as AWS S3. However, it must now support multiple cloud storage providers, including Google Cloud Storage and Azure Blob Storage, to meet the growing demand.

The initial challenges include:

- **Tight Coupling:** The code is tightly coupled to AWS S3, making it difficult to add new storage providers.
- **Code Duplication:** Adding new providers would require duplicating a significant portion of the existing code, complicating maintenance.
- **Limited Flexibility:** Users cannot choose their preferred storage provider, limiting the application's flexibility.

To address these issues, we will apply the Factory Method Pattern. This design pattern allows objects to be created without specifying the exact class of the object to be instantiated, thereby promoting flexibility and code reusability.

Note: *In this case study, we will focus on the implementation of useful classes in order to apply the concept of the design model.*

Applying the Factory Method Pattern

This is the diagram class for our case study that utilizes the Factory Method Pattern.

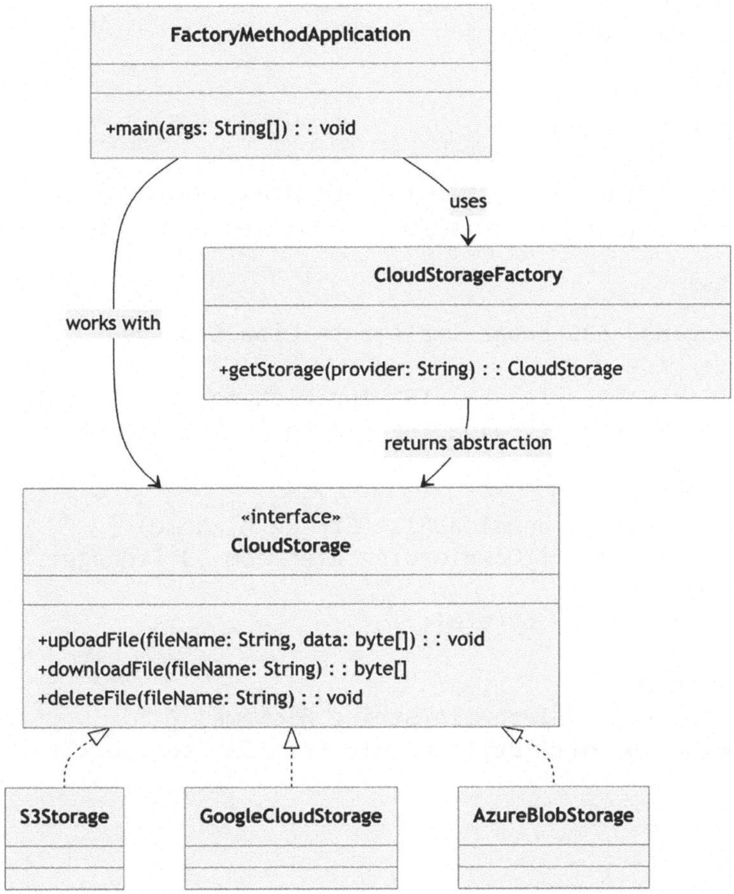

Figure 2.2: *Factory Method Pattern - Cloud Storage*

Before exploring the implementation in detail, it is essential to grasp how the Factory Method Pattern can reshape our development approach. We can decouple the application code from concrete implementations by defining a standard interface for all storage providers and using a factory class to create specific instances. This not only makes it easier to add new storage providers but also enhances the code's maintainability and extensibility.

Common Interface

The first step is to define a standard interface **`CloudStorage`**, for all storage providers. This interface declares the methods that each provider must implement, such as **`uploadFile`**, **`downloadFile`**, and **`deleteFile`**.

```
public interface CloudStorage {
   void uploadFile(String fileName, byte[] data);
```

```
byte[] downloadFile(String fileName);
   void deleteFile(String fileName);
}
```

Concrete Classes

Next, we will implement this interface for each storage provider. Each concrete class contains the code required to interact with the corresponding provider.

S3 Storage Class

```
public class S3Storage implements CloudStorage {
   @Override
   public void uploadFile(String fileName, byte[] data) {
System.out.printf("Uploading file to S3 Storage: %s%n", fileName);
   }
   @Override
   public byte[] downloadFile(String fileName) {
System.out.printf("Downloading file from S3 Storage: %s%n",
fileName);
       return new byte[0];
   }
   @Override
   public void deleteFile(String fileName) {
System.out.printf("Deleting file from S3 Storage: %s%n", fileName);
   }
}
```

Google Storage Class

```
public class GoogleCloudStorage implements CloudStorage {
   @Override
   public void uploadFile(String fileName, byte[] data) {
System.out.printf("Uploading file to Google Cloud Storage: %s%n",
fileName);
   }
   @Override
   public byte[] downloadFile(String fileName) {
System.out.printf("Downloading file from Google Cloud Storage:
%s%n", fileName);
       return new byte[0];
   }
   @Override
   public void deleteFile(String fileName) {
System.out.printf("Deleting file from Google Cloud Storage: %s%n",
fileName);
   }
}
```

Azure Blob Storage

```
public class AzureBlobStorage implements CloudStorage {
   @Override
   public void uploadFile(String fileName, byte[] data) {
System.out.printf("Uploading file to Azure Blob Storage: %s%n",
fileName);
   }
   @Override
   public byte[] downloadFile(String fileName) {
System.out.printf("Downloading file from Azure Blob Storage:
%s%n", fileName);
       return new byte[0];
   }
   @Override
   public void deleteFile(String fileName) {
System.out.printf("Deleting file from Azure Blob Storage: %s%n",
fileName);
   }
}
```

Factory Method

We create a factory class that contains a factory method for creating instances of the concrete classes. This method takes the desired type of storage provider as a parameter and returns an example of the corresponding class.

```
public class CloudStorageFactory {
   public static CloudStoragegetStorage(String provider) {
       return switch (provider.toLowerCase()) {
           case "s3" -> new S3Storage();
           case "google" -> new GoogleCloudStorage();
           case "azure" -> new AzureBlobStorage();
           default -> throw new IllegalArgumentException
("Unsupported storage provider: %s".formatted(provider));
       };
   }
}
```

Using the Factory Method Pattern

To use the Factory Method Pattern, simply call the **getStorage** method of the **CloudStorageFactory** class, specifying the desired storage provider.

```
public class FactoryMethodApplication {
   public static void main( String[] args ) {
```

```
// Using the Factory Method pattern to create instances of Cloud-
Storage
        // without exposing the instantiation logic to the client
code.
        // This allows for easy extension and modification of the
storage types

CloudStorage storage = CloudStorageFactory.getStorage("s3");
// Assuming S3Storage is a class that implements CloudStorage
storage.uploadFile("sample.txt", "Hello, S3!".getBytes());

CloudStoragegoogleStorage = CloudStorageFactory.getStorage
("google");
// Assuming GoogleCloudStorage is a class that implements Cloud-
Storage
googleStorage.uploadFile("example.txt", "Hello, Google!".get-
Bytes());

CloudStorageazureBlobStorage = CloudStorageFactory.getStor-
age("azure");
// Assuming AzureBlobStorage is a class that implements Cloud-
Storage
azureBlobStorage.uploadFile("example.txt", "Hello, Azure!".get-
Bytes());
    }
}
```

The Factory Method Pattern brings several significant advantages to our SaaS application example. First, it promotes **loose coupling** by decoupling the code from the specific implementations of storage providers, which greatly simplifies adding new providers. Additionally, it enhances **reusability** by centralizing shared logic within the CloudStorage interface, thereby reducing code duplication. Finally, it increases **flexibility** by allowing users to select their preferred storage provider.

By integrating the Factory Method Pattern, we overcame the initial challenges of tight coupling, code duplication, and limited flexibility. Our example can now support multiple cloud storage providers in an extensible and maintainable way, providing a robust and scalable solution.

While the Factory Method excels at creating isolated objects, how can we manage more complex sets, such as an entire ecosystem of IoT sensors, humidity, temperature, and pH tailored to different agricultural needs, vineyards, greenhouses, and open fields? This is where the `AbstractFactoryMethod` becomes relevant. It ensures that all sensors from the same brand operate together consistently and optimally.

Abstract Factory Method Pattern

The Abstract Factory Pattern enables the creation of families of related objects without relying on their concrete classes. It addresses two key needs: **consistency**, by ensuring that objects within the same family are compatible, and **interchangeability**, by making it easy to switch entirely from one family of objects to another.

Case Study

Imagine an intelligent agricultural system that uses IoT sensors that continuously track environmental parameters like humidity, temperature, and soil pH. These sensors come from different manufacturers like Ecoflux, Terrasynth, and Agropulse, each using proprietary communication protocols (CropCast, SoiLink, AgriMesh) and incompatible data formats (binary JSON, custom CSV, structured XML).

The initial challenges include:

- **Diversity of Protocols**: Each manufacturer uses a different communication protocol, complicating sensor integration and management.
- **Incompatible Data Formats**: Sensor data comes in various formats, requiring specific parsers.
- **Tight Coupling**: The code is tightly coupled to specific sensor implementations, making adding or modifying new sensors difficult.

We will apply the Abstract Factory Pattern to address these issues, which promotes flexibility and code reusability.

Note: *In this case study, we will focus on the implementation of useful classes in order to apply the concept of the design model. The manufacturers and their protocols are fictitious and used for demonstration purposes.*

Applying the Abstract Factory Method Pattern

This is the diagram class for our case study that utilizes the Abstract Factory Method Pattern.

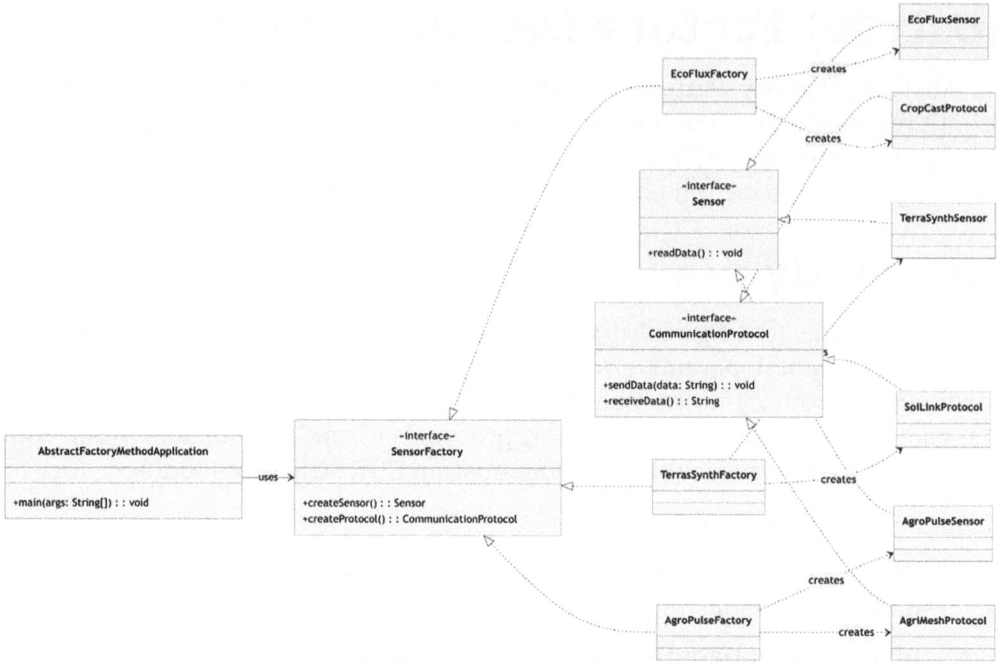

Figure 2.3: *Abstract Factory Pattern - Smart System*

Before exploring the implementation in detail, it is essential to understand how the Abstract Factory pattern can reshape our approach to development. By applying this pattern, we will structure the innovative agriculture system to efficiently manage the diversity of IoT sensors and communication protocols. We will define standard interfaces for sensors and protocols and then create concrete classes for each manufacturer, thus decoupling the code from specific implementations. Abstract Factories will enable the creation of related families of objects.

Common Interfaces

The first step is to define common interfaces for sensors and communication protocols. These interfaces declare the methods that each sensor and protocol must implement.

```
public interface Sensor {
     void readData();
}

public interface CommunicationProtocol {
   void sendData(String data);
   String receiveData();
}
```

Concrete Classes for Sensors

Next, we implement these interfaces for each type of sensor. Each concrete class contains the specific code required to interact with its corresponding sensor.

```
public class EcoFluxSensor implements Sensor{
   @Override
   public void readData() {
// Simulate reading data from the EcoFlux sensor
System.out.println("Reading data from EcoFlux sensor...");
   }
}

public class TerraSynthSensor implements Sensor {
   @Override
   public void readData() {
// Simulate reading data from the TerraSynth sensor
System.out.println("Reading data from TerraSynth sensor...");
   }
}

public class AgroPulseSensor implements Sensor {
   @Override
   public void readData() {
// Simulate reading data from the AgroPulse sensor
System.out.println("Reading data from AgroPulse sensor...");
   }
}
```

Concrete Classes for Communication Protocols

Similarly, we implement the interfaces for each communication protocol.

```
public class CropCastProtocol implements CommunicationProtocol {
   @Override
   public void sendData(String data) {
// Simulate sending data using the CropCast protocol
System.out.printf("Sending data using CropCast protocol: %s%n",
data);
   }

   @Override
   public String receiveData() {
// Simulate receiving data using the CropCast protocol
String receivedData = "Received data from CropCast protocol";
System.out.println(receivedData);
```

```
        return receivedData;
    }
}

public class SoilLinkProtocol implements CommunicationProtocol {
    @Override
    public void sendData(String data) {
// Simulate sending data using the SoiLink protocol
System.out.printf("Sending data using SoiLink protocol: %s%n",
data);
    }

    @Override
    public String receiveData() {
// Simulate receiving data using the SoiLink protocol
String receivedData = "Received data from SoiLink protocol";
System.out.println(receivedData);
        return receivedData;
    }
}

public class AgriMeshProtocol implements CommunicationProtocol {
    @Override
    public void sendData(String data) {
// Simulate sending data using the AgriMesh protocol
System.out.printf("Sending data using AgriMesh protocol: %s%n",
data);
    }

    @Override
    public String receiveData() {
// Simulate receiving data using the AgriMesh protocol
String receivedData = "Received data from AgriMesh protocol";
System.out.println(receivedData);
        return receivedData;
    }
}
```

Abstract Factory

We create an interface for the Abstract Factory that declares methods for creating instances of sensors and communication protocols.

```
public interface SensorFactory {
    Sensor createSensor();
CommunicationProtocolcreateProtocol();
}
```

Concrete Factories

Next, we implement this interface for each family of sensors and protocols.

```
public class EcoFluxFactory implements SensorFactory {
   @Override
   public Sensor createSensor() {
       return new EcoFluxSensor(); // EcoFlux uses EcoFlux sensor
}

   @Override
   public CommunicationProtocolcreateProtocol() {
       return new CropCastProtocol(); // EcoFlux uses CropCast
protocol
}
}

public class TerrasSynthFactory implements SensorFactory {
   @Override
   public Sensor createSensor() {
       return new TerraSynthSensor(); // TerraSynth uses Ter-
rasSynth sensor
}

   @Override
   public CommunicationProtocolcreateProtocol() {
       return new SoiLinkProtocol(); // TerrasSynth uses SoiLink
protocol
}
}

public class AgroPulseFactory implements SensorFactory {
   @Override
   public Sensor createSensor() {
       return new AgroPulseSensor(); // AgroPulse uses AgroPulse
sensor
}

   @Override
   public CommunicationProtocolcreateProtocol() {
       return new AgriMeshProtocol(); // AgroPulse uses AgriMesh
protocol
}
}
```

Using the Abstract Factory Pattern

To use the Abstract Factory Pattern in our smart agriculture system, one simply selects the factory corresponding to the sensor manufacturer and creates the necessary instances.

```
public class AbstractFactoryMethodApplication {
   public static void main( String[] args ) {
SensorFactoryecoFluxFactory = new EcoFluxFactory();
       Sensor ecoFluxSensor = ecoFluxFactory.createSensor();
CommunicationProtocolecoFluxProtocol = ecoFluxFactory.create
Protocol();

ecoFluxSensor.readData();
ecoFluxProtocol.sendData("Data from EcoFlux sensor");

SensorFactoryagroPulseFactory = new AgroPulseFactory();
       Sensor agroPulseSensor = agroPulseFactory.createSensor();
CommunicationProtocolagroPulseProtocol = agroPulseFactory.create-
Protocol();

agroPulseSensor.readData();
agroPulseProtocol.sendData("Data from AgroPulse sensor");
   }
}
```

Output Console:

```
Reading data from EcoFlux sensor...
Sending data using CropCast protocol: Data from EcoFlux sensor
Reading data from AgroPulse sensor...
Sending data using AgriMesh protocol: Data from AgroPulse sensor
```

By applying the Abstract Factory Pattern, we have addressed the initial issues of protocol diversity, incompatible data formats, and tight coupling. The intelligent agricultural system can now support various sensors and communication protocols in an extensible and maintainable manner.

Using an Abstract Class in the Abstract Factory Pattern

An abstract class is preferred when concrete factories share a common logic or internal state. It allows these elements to be centralized, avoiding code duplication and providing a structured foundation for subclasses. For example, a generic initialization method or parameter validation can be defined once in the abstract class and reused by all derived factories.

Tips: *Use an interface for factories that do not share code or state, especially since Java 8, where interfaces can include default methods. Prefer an abstract class if you need to centralize shared logic.*

While the Abstract Factory standardizes object creation, how can we structure complex processes without duplicating code? The **Builder Pattern** offers an elegant solution to this question.

Builder Pattern

Assembling complex objects in software development often involves multiple configuration steps and interdependent components. When constructors become overloaded with long parameter lists or object creation requires clarity and flexibility, the **Builder Pattern** provides a clean and structured alternative. Rather than constructing objects in a single, monolithic step, the Builder Pattern enables progressive and controlled assembly through a step-by-step process.

This creational pattern separates the **construction logic** from the **final representation of the object**, offering a fluent interface to configure each part independently.

The Builder Pattern is especially useful when an object requires many optional attributes or when the same construction process should produce different representations. It promotes code readability, maintainability, and reusability while simplifying complex management.

Case Study

Imagine a platform for creating conversational agent *chatbots* tailored to various sectors such as *healthcare*, *finance*, and *education*. Each AI agent shares common characteristics, such as name, domain, and language, but can also be extended with specialized modules like *sentiment analysis* and *voice recognition*.

The Challenge:

- How can we enable users to easily create customized AI agents without managing many complex constructors?
- How can we ensure each agent is built with the appropriate required and optional parameters?

Note: *In this case study, we will focus on the implementation of classes to apply the design model concept.*

Applying the Builder Pattern

This is the diagram class for our case study that utilizes the Builder Pattern.

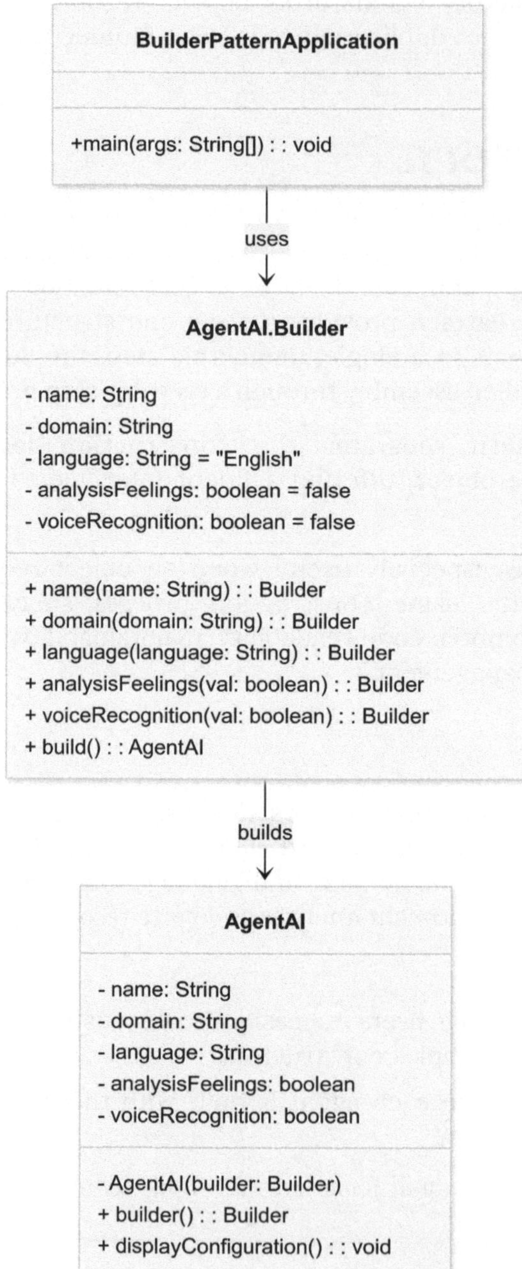

Figure 2.4: *Builder Pattern – AgentAI*

The implementation of the **AgentAI** class demonstrates a rigorous and safe application of the Builder Pattern. The object is constructed through a static inner Builder class, which enables the configuration of both required and optional parameters using a fluent and chainable syntax. Once the configuration is complete, the builder's build() method creates the final instance of **AgentAI** by passing the collected values to a private constructor.

Within this constructor, a critical step is introduced: the **validation of mandatory parameters** using assertions **Assert.assertNotNull(...)**. This ensures that fields such as **name** and **domain** are not null, thereby preventing silent runtime errors. This validation step strengthens the reliability of the constructed object and aligns the implementation with defensive programming best practices. Combining the Builder Pattern with these safeguards makes it possible to create flexible, consistent, and robust **AgentAI** instances.

```
public class AgentAI {
// Obligatory parameters
private final String name;
   private final String domain;
// Paramètresoptionnels
private final String language;
   private final booleananalysisFeelings;
   private final booleanvoiceRecognition;
   private AgentAI(Builder builder) {
Assert.assertNotNull(builder.name, "Name cannot be null");
Assert.assertNotNull(builder.domain, "Domain cannot be null");
       this.name = builder.name;
this.domain = builder.domain;
this.language = builder.language;
this.analysisFeelings = builder.analysisFeelings;
this.voiceRecognition = builder.voiceRecognition;
   }
   public static Builder build() {
       return new Builder();
   }
   public void displayConfiguration() {
System.out.printf("Agent AI: %s, Domaine: %s, Language: %s,
Sentiment analysis: %s, Voice recognition: %s%n", this.name,
this.domaine, this.language, this.analysisFeelings, this.voice-
Recognition);
   }
   public static class Builder {
// Obligatory parameters
private String name;
       private String domain;
```

```
// Optional parameters - initialized to default values
private String language = "English";
        private booleananalysisFeelings = false;
        private booleanvoiceRecognition = false;

        private Builder() {}
        public Builder name(String name) {
            this.name = name;
            return this;
        }
        public Builder domain(String domain) {
this.domain = domain;
            return this;
        }
        public Builder language(String language) {
this.language = language;
            return this;
        }
        public Builder analysisFeelings(booleananalysisFeelings) {
this.analysisFeelings = analysisFeelings;
            return this;
        }
        public Builder voiceRecognition(booleanvoiceRecognition) {
this.voiceRecognition = voiceRecognition;
            return this;
        }
        public AgentAIbuild() {
            return new AgentAI(this);
        }
    }
}
```

Using the Builder Implementation

```
public class BuilderPatternApplication {
   public static void main( String[] args ) {
// Create instances of AgentAI using the builder pattern
AgentAIagentFinance = AgentAI.builder()
                 .name("FinBot")
.domain("Finance")
.language("French")
.analysisFeelings(true)
.build();

// Create an instance of AgentAI with default values
AgentAIagentAgriculture = AgentAI.builder()
```

```
                .name("AgriBot")
.domain("Agriculture")
.voiceRecognition(true)
.build();

// Display the configurations
agentFinance.displayConfiguration();
agentAgriculture.displayConfiguration();
   }
}
```

Output Console:

```
Agent AI: FinBot, Domain: Finance, Language: French, Sentiment
analysis: true, Voice recognition: false
Agent AI: AgriBot, Domain: Agriculture, Language: English,
Sentiment analysis: false, Voice recognition: true
```

After exploring how to build complex objects using the Builder Pattern, we will examine how the Prototype Pattern enables efficient cloning of the existing objects to create new, customized instances.

Prototype Pattern

Creating multiple objects that are similar or even identical in software development with slight variations is not uncommon. When direct instantiation becomes costly, repetitive, or challenging, the **Prototype Pattern** offers an elegant and efficient solution. This creational pattern allows new objects to be generated by cloning the existing prototypes rather than building them from scratch. It asks: "*Why rebuild something we already have if we can duplicate and adapt it?*"

This pattern is particularly useful when objects are complex to instantiate or when multiple similar variants of the same object are needed. It helps save time, reduce memory usage, and avoid code duplication.

Fundamental Concepts

This diagram illustrates a principle of implementing the Prototype Pattern.

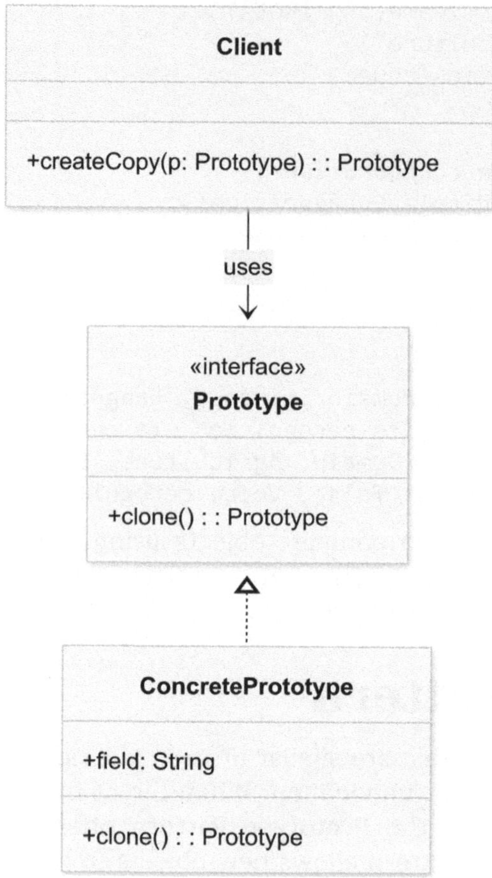

Figure 2.5: *Prototype Pattern - Fundamental Concepts*

The operation is based on three simple ideas:

Element	**Description**
Prototype	An interface or abstract class with a **`clone()`** method.
ConcretePrototype	Concrete class implementing **`clone()`** to copy its instances.
Client	Code that requests cloning without knowing the exact class.

Table 2.1: *Prototype Fundamental Concepts*

Case Study

Imagine a platform that offers virtual assistants or AI agents tailored to various sectors, such as healthcare, finance, education, and customer service. Each assistant is built upon a common structure, including a language model, a knowledge base, and conversational behavior, but requires specific configurations depending on the domain.

The initial challenges include:

- **Deployment Time:** Creating each AI assistant is time-consuming and slows down deployment.
- **Configuration Reuse:** Existing configurations are not reused efficiently, leading to duplicated effort.
- **User Customization:** Users cannot easily create personalized assistants without technical intervention.

To address these issues, we will apply the Prototype Pattern. This design pattern enables the creation of new objects by cloning existing prototypes, reduces deployment time, promotes the reuse of configurations, and allows users to customize easily.

Note: *In this case study, we will focus on the implementation of useful classes in order to apply the concept of the design model. The manufacturers and their protocols are fictitious and used for demonstration purposes.*

Applying the Prototype Pattern

Let us recall that the business requirement is to design a **Finance AI assistant** equipped with an economic knowledge base, a formal tone, and strict compliance rules, and then duplicate it to create a **Banking Assistant** by replacing only the underlying documentation. Each clone must remain autonomous while preserving the behavior of the original model, which is precisely what the prototype pattern enables.

Step 1: Defining the Prototype Interface

We will use the **`PrototypeAgentAI`** interface to define the cloning contract for all AI agents. It exposes a **`clone()`** method that ensures each implementation can be duplicated consistently. This mechanism makes creating new instances from an existing template easy while maintaining consistent behavior across agents, regardless of their specialization.

```
public interface PrototypeAgentIA<T> {
   T clone(); // Returns a clone of the object
}
```

Step 2: Defining the Prototype Concrete Class

For the concrete implementation of the prototype, we will define the **`AssistantAI`** class, which implements the **`PrototypeAgentAI`** interface by providing a concrete *clone()* method. This method goes beyond simply copying basic attributes; it can also handle more complex scenarios, such as duplicating nested objects or managing internal dependencies. Each specific variant of an assistant, such as *Finance* or *Banking*, can thus clone its behavior while adapting its data, ensuring instance independence while preserving the logic defined in the original prototype.

```
public class AssistantAI implements PrototypeAgentAI<AssistantAI> {
   private String domain;
   private String tone;
   private String knowledgeBase;

   public AssistantAI(String domain, String tone, String
knowledgeBase) {
this.domain = domain;
this.tone = tone;
this.knowledgeBase = knowledgeBase;
   }

/* Getters and Setters */

@Override
   public AssistantAIclone() {
       return new AssistantAI(this.domain, this.tone,
this.knowledgeBase);
   }
}
```

Step 3: Defining the Prototype Registry

The Prototype Registry is a centralized repository where preconfigured AI assistant prototypes, such as Finance, Banking, or other business domains, are stored. It allows quick access to an existing model via an identification key and supports on-demand cloning through the **`clone()`** method. This approach simplifies the creation of customized instances without requiring knowledge of their construction details while ensuring consistency and reusability of assistant behavior throughout the system.

```
public class RegistryAssistantAI {
// Map to store the assistants
private Map<String, AssistantAI> prototypes = new HashMap<>();

// Registers the assistant
public void enregister(String nom, AssistantAI assistant) {
prototypes.put(nom, assistant);
   }

// Returns a clone of the assistant
public AssistantAIcloner(String nom) {
AssistantAI prototype = prototypes.get(nom);
```

```
            return (prototype != null) ?prototype.clone() : null;
        }
    }
```

Prototype Pattern in Action

We have added a **displayConfig()** method to display the configuration of the AI assistant.

```
public class PrototypePatternApplication {
    public static void main( String[] args ) {
// Creating a registry for the AssistantAI prototypes
RegistryAssistantAI registry = new RegistryAssistantAI();

// Basic prototype for the healthcare sector
AssistantAIassistantHealthcare = new AssistantAI(
                "Healthcare", "Empathetic", "Medical corpus v3");
registry.enregister("healthcare", assistantHealthcare);

// Prototype for finance
AssistantAIassistantFinance = new AssistantAI(
                "Finance", "Formal", "Financial glossary v2");
registry.enregister("finance", assistantFinance);

// Creating a clone for a bank assistant
AssistantAIassistantBanque = registry.cloner("finance");
assistantBanque.displayConfiguration();

// Creating a clone for the insurance assistant
AssistantAIassistantInsurance = registry.cloner("healthcare");
assistantInsurance.displayConfiguration();
    }
}
```

Output Console:

```
Domain : Finance | Tone : Formal | Knowledge Base : Financial
glossary v2
Domain : Healthcare | Tone : Empathetic | Knowledge Base :
Medical corpus v3
```

By applying the Prototype Pattern, we addressed several challenges: the repetitive creation of preconfigured AI agents, the manual duplication of complex structures, and the rigid extension of assistants. The system can now dynamically generate intelligent agents, each specialized by domain, quickly, modularly, and independently. Every cloned assistant inherits the configuration of the reference prototype while remaining fully customizable. This makes the platform scalable, maintainable, and ready to integrate new business use cases without requiring a codebase overhaul.

Comparing Shallow Copy and Deep Copy

In this context, if an AI assistant contains a mutable structure such as *a list of modules or* AI *capabilities*, a deep copy becomes necessary to ensure that internal states are not inadvertently shared between instances.

```
@Override
public AssistantAIclone() {
AssistantAIcopie = new AssistantAI(this.domain, this.tone, this.
knowledgeBase);
copie.capabilities = new ArrayList<>();
   for (CapabilityAIp :this.capabilities) {
copie.capabilities.add(p.clone());
   }
   return copie;
}
```

Note: *Avoid deep cloning when it is unnecessary, for example, when internal structures are immutable or read-only, such as static prompts or shared cached corpora.*

Using the Java Cloneable Interface

In Java, the Cloneable interface enables the protected **`Object.clone()`** method to perform a shallow copy of an object. It is a marker interface, meaning it does not declare any methods but indicates to the JVM that an object is eligible for cloning via **`super.clone()`**.

We will make our **`AssistantAI`** class cloneable by implementing the Cloneable interface.

```
public class AssistantAI implements Cloneable {
   private String domain;
   private String tone;
   private String knowledgeBase;

   public AssistantAI(String domain, String tone, String knowl-
edgeBase) {
this.domain = domain;
this.tone = tone;
this.knowledgeBase = knowledgeBase;
   }

   public String getDomain() {
       return this.domain;
   }

   public void setDomain(String domain) {
```

```
this.domain = domain;
   }

   public String getTone() {
       return this.tone;
   }

   public void setTone(String tone) {
this.tone = tone;
   }

   public String getKnowledgeBase() {
       return this.knowledgeBase;
   }

   public void setKnowledgeBase(String knowledgeBase) {
this.knowledgeBase = knowledgeBase;
   }

   @Override
   public AssistantAIclone() {
       try {
           return (AssistantAI) super.clone(); // Shallow copy
} catch (CloneNotSupportedException e) {
           throw new AssertionError("Cloning not supported", e);
       }
   }

}
```

Note: *The **`clone()`** method must be explicitly made public, as the **`Object.clone()`** method is protected by default.*

While the Java Cloneable interface may seem appealing due to its simplicity, it presents several pitfalls: **partial cloning**, **tight coupling** to **`Object.clone()`**, and **unclear cloning logic**. In a professional context such as our case study, it is preferable to define an explicit cloning interface, such as **`PrototypeAgentAI<T>`**, and to handle cloning in a deterministic and controlled manner.

Comparative Analysis

This table summarizes the strengths and limitations of each patterns to help guide informed decision-making while respecting the technical constraints specific to each.

Pattern	Use Case	Pitfalls to Avoid
Singleton	Single instance management	• Hidden dependencies. • Testing difficulty (global state). • Overuse.
Factory Method	Subclass-driven object creation	• Proliferation of subclasses. • Rigidity when hierarchies change.
Abstract Factory	Families of related objects	• Increased complexity with new products. • Coupling between Families.
Builder	Complex object construction	• Verbose for simple objects. • Risk of over-engineering.
Prototype	Cloning to avoid initialization cost	• Shallow versus Deep Cloning. • Handling Circular Dependencies.

Table 2.2: *Pattern Comparative Analysis*

Conclusion

In this chapter, we have explored creational design patterns through various case studies and their implementations in Java. We further observed how these patterns empower developers to create objects in a controlled and scalable manner. Additionally, we saw how choosing the correct pattern can enhance the performance of our applications.

The next chapter now shall explore structural patterns, which aim to organize classes and objects into larger formations while maintaining a flexible and efficient interface. Here, we will discuss in detail the Java implementations of the *Adapter*, *Decorator*, *Facade*, *Proxy*, *Flyweight*, *Bridge*, and *Composite* patterns.

Points to Remember

- Creational Design Patterns allow controlling object instantiation, thereby improving code flexibility, maintainability, and consistency.
- The Prototype Pattern is a clever technique for cloning preconfigured objects, minimizing the need to instantiate them repeatedly.
- An effective creational design avoids direct dependencies on concrete classes, promoting extensibility and flexibility in the code.

Multiple Choice Questions

1. In the Prototype Pattern, how is a new object created?
   a. Calling a constructor with all parameters.
   b. Defining a new interface.
   c. Using a factory method.
   d. Copying an existing prototype.
2. Which of these patterns is best suited to gradually creating a configured object with many parameters?
   a. Factory Method
   b. Singleton
   c. Builder
   d. Prototype
3. Which is the main feature provided by the Abstract Factory pattern?
   a. Duplicate a prototype.
   b. Build the same product step by step.
   c. Return a subclass through a static method.
   d. Produce related objects through a family of factories.

Answers

1. d
2. c
3. d

Questions

1. What is the conceptual difference between Factory Method and Builder Pattern?
2. Why is the separation between construction and representation significant in dynamic systems?

3. How can you combine Builder and Prototype to speed up object creation while maintaining a fluid API?
4. What trade-offs can be considered between the Abstract Factory and the Factory Method patterns when managing multiple product families with few variations?

Key Terms

- **Prototype:** An object used as a model to create others via cloning.
- **Shallow Copy:** Cloning an object without duplicating the objects it references.
- **Product**: The final object is built using a design pattern.
- **Deep Copy**: Recursive copying where each referenced object is cloned independently.
- **Builders:** A guiding object that assembles the components of a complex product step by step.

CHAPTER 3
Structural Design Patterns

Introduction

Structural Design Patterns provide structured solutions for organizing classes and objects within a software system, balancing architectural flexibility and efficiency. They focus on composing entities to form larger and more complex structures while optimizing the relationships between those entities.

This chapter will cover several essential Structural Design Patterns, including ***Adapter***, ***Bridge***, ***Composite***, ***Decorator***, ***Facade***, ***Flyweight***, and ***Proxy***. Each pattern will be explored in detail, with clear definitions, practical examples, and practical use cases to illustrate its application in real-world scenarios. We will examine how each pattern addresses specific software design challenges and enhances applications' maintainability, flexibility, and performance.

By reading this chapter, you will understand each pattern deeply, its practical implementation, and also its impact on robust and scalable software design. You will be gradually equipped to apply these patterns in your projects, thereby improving the quality and efficiency of your code.

Structure

In this chapter, we will cover:

- Adapter Pattern
- Bridge Pattern
- Composite Pattern
- Decorator Pattern
- Facade Pattern

- Flyweight Pattern
- Proxy Pattern

Adapter Pattern

The Adapter Pattern is a structural design solution that transforms a class's interface into one that clients expect. It bridges between otherwise incompatible interfaces, allowing classes to collaborate without requiring changes to their source code.

The Adapter addresses a critical need to enable interoperability between software components and incompatible interfaces. Without it, integrating new libraries or reusing existing components in a different context can lead to several challenges:

- **Increased Complexity**: Due to the need to rewrite or modify the existing components.
- **Code Duplication**: Resulting from creating new classes solely to bridge interface differences.
- **Difficult Maintenance**: This is caused by managing multiple versions of similar components.

Let us consider a real-world scenario where the absence of an Adapter leads to critical malfunctions.

Case Study

Imagine an image processing application that relies on a legacy model to perform basic operations such as resizing and filtering. This legacy model is well-established and has been used for years. However, it has now become necessary to integrate a new AI library to add advanced object detection and image recognition features.

The initial challenges include:

- **Interface Incompatibility**: The legacy model uses a different interface from the new AI library, making direct integration difficult.
- **Modifying Legacy Code**: Changing the legacy code to work with the new AI library could introduce bugs and require extensive testing.
- **Code Duplication**: Creating a new version of the legacy model to integrate with the AI library would lead to code duplication and increased complexity.

To address these issues, we will apply the Adapter Pattern. This design pattern allows the interface of the legacy model to be converted into one compatible with the new AI library, enabling both to work together without modifying their source code.

Note: *In this case study, we will focus on implementing useful classes to apply the design model concept.*

Applying the Adapter Pattern

To better understand how the Adapter pattern resolves the incompatibility between the legacy model and the new AI library, let us first examine the class diagram, which illustrates the structure and relationships among the system's components.

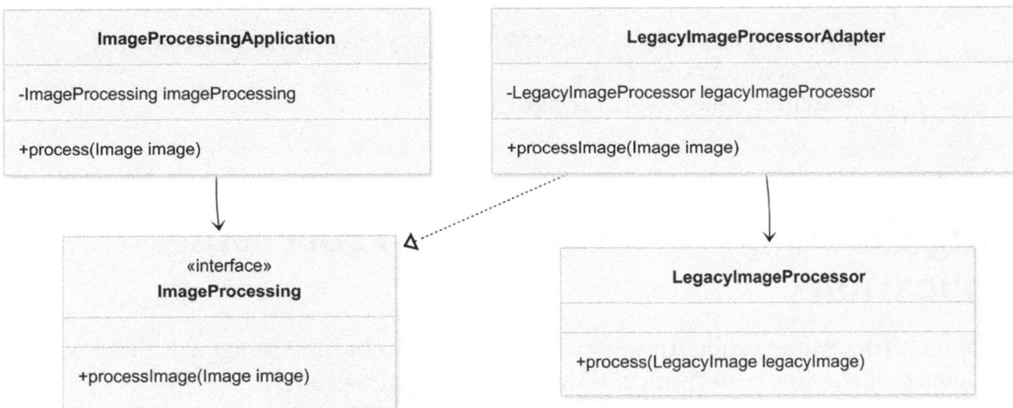

Figure 3.1: *Adapter Pattern - Legacy Model*

Let us move on to the detailed implementation of the Adapter pattern to resolve the incompatibility issue.

Create the Target Interface

The target interface is the one expected by the new AI library. In this case, it is the **ImageProcessing** interface with a **processImage(Image image)** method.

```
public interface ImageProcessing {
   void processImage(Image image);
}
```

Implementing the Adapter

The Adapter is a class that implements the target interface and uses the legacy model internally. It converts method calls from the target interface into method calls on the legacy model.

```
public class LegacyImageProcessorAdapter implements Image
Processing {
   private final LegacyImageProcessor legacyImageProcessor;
   public LegacyImageProcessorAdapter(LegacyImageProcessor
legacyImageProcessor) {
        this.legacyImageProcessor = legacyImageProcessor;
   }
   @Override
```

```
    public void processImage(Image image) {
        // Convert the image to the format expected by the legacy
model
        LegacyImage legacyImage = convertToLegacyImage(image);
        // Using the legacy model for image processing
        legacyImageProcessor.process(legacyImage);
    }
    private LegacyImage convertToLegacyImage(Image image) {
        // Conversion logic
        return new LegacyImage(image);
    }
}
```

Using the Adapter in the Image Processing Application

The image processing application uses the Adapter to handle images. It does not need to be aware of the implementation details of the legacy model.

```
public class ImageProcessingApplication {
    private final ImageProcessing imageProcessing;
    public ImageProcessingApplication(ImageProcessing image
Processing) {
        this.imageProcessing = imageProcessing;
    }
    public void process(Image image) {
        imageProcessing.processImage(image);
    }
}
```

To complete our example, here is a **Main** class demonstrating how to use the Adapter to integrate the legacy image processing model with the new AI library. This class shows how to initialize the objects and invoke the necessary methods to process an image.

```
public class Main {
    public static void main( String[] args ) {
        // Create an instance of the legacy model
        LegacyImageProcessor legacyImageProcessor = new Legacy
ImageProcessor();
        // Create the Adapter by passing the legacy model
        ImageProcessing imageProcessing = new LegacyImage
ProcessorAdapter(legacyImageProcessor);
        // Create an instance of the image processing application
with the Adapter
        ImageProcessingApplication imageProcessingApplication =
new ImageProcessingApplication(imageProcessing);
```

```
            // Create an image for processing
            Image image = new Image("example.jpg");
            // Image processing using the application
            imageProcessingApplication.process(image);
        }
    }
```

Output Console:

```
    Legacy image processing: example.jpg
```

The use of the Adapter Pattern made it possible to integrate a legacy image processing model with a new AI library without modifying the existing code. This approach made the application more flexible and easier to maintain while enabling modern AI libraries.

In the following pattern, we will explore the **Bridge Pattern**, which separates an abstraction from its implementation, offering greater flexibility in the design of complex systems.

Bridge Pattern

The Bridge pattern is a design solution that separates the abstraction from its implementation, allowing both to vary independently. This pattern is handy to avoid permanent coupling between an abstraction and its implementation, making the system more flexible and easier to extend.

The Bridge pattern meets a critical need to enable the independent evolution of abstractions and implementations.

Let us consider a real-life scenario in which the absence of a Bridge leads to critical malfunctions.

Case Study

Imagine an image processing application that needs to support multiple image formats, such as JPEG, PNG, and BMP, and multiple processing algorithms, such as *blur*, *contrast*, and *edge detection*. Initially, the application is designed to work with a single image format and processing algorithm. However, to meet the growing demand for flexibility and performance, the application must now support multiple image formats and processing algorithms.

The initial challenges include:

- **Tight Coupling**: The code is tightly coupled to a specific image format and processing algorithm, making adding new formats and algorithms difficult.
- **Code Duplication**: Adding new formats and algorithms would require

duplicating a significant portion of the existing code, complicating maintenance.

- **Limited Flexibility**: Users cannot choose their preferred image format or processing algorithm, which limits the flexibility of the application in handling complex scenarios.

To solve these problems, we will apply the Bridge pattern. This design pattern separates image formats *abstraction* from processing algorithms *implementation*, allowing both to vary independently.

Note: *In this case study, we will focus on implementing useful classes to apply the design model concept.*

Applying the Bridge Pattern

To better understand how the Bridge pattern solves the problem of coupling image formats and processing algorithms, let us first examine the class diagram, which illustrates the structure and relationships between the various system components.

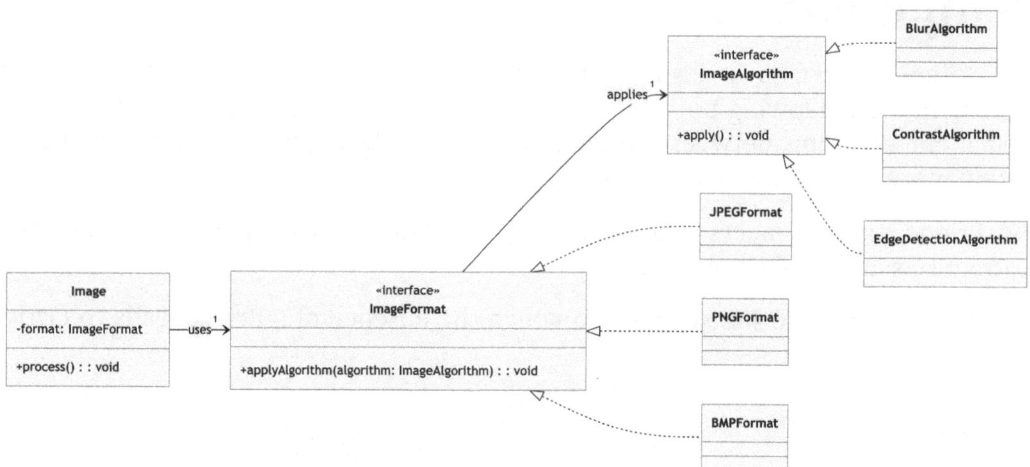

Figure 3.2: *Bridge Pattern - Image Processing*

Let us move on to the detailed implementation of the Bridge pattern to solve the coupling problem.

Create the Interface for Image Formats

The **`ImageFormat`** interface defines the method for applying a processing algorithm.

```
public interface ImageFormat {
   void applyAlgorithm(ImageAlgorithm algorithm);
}
```

Implement the Image Formats

The **JPEGFormat**, **PNGFormat**, and **BMPFormat** classes implement the **ImageFormat** interface and define how to apply a processing algorithm.

```
public class BMPFormat implements ImageFormat {
   @Override
   public void applyAlgorithm(ImageAlgorithm algorithm) {
       System.out.println("Applying algorithm to BMP image");
       algorithm.apply();
   }
}
public class PNGFormat implements ImageFormat {
   @Override
   public void applyAlgorithm(ImageAlgorithm algorithm) {
       System.out.println("Applying algorithm to PNG image");
       algorithm.apply();
   }
}
public class JPEGFormat implements ImageFormat {
   @Override
   public void applyAlgorithm(ImageAlgorithm algorithm) {
       System.out.println("Applying algorithm to JPEG image");
       algorithm.apply();
   }
}
```

Create the Interface for the Processing Algorithms

The **ImageAlgorithm** interface defines the method for applying a processing algorithm.

```
public interface ImageAlgorithm {
   void apply();
}
```

Implement the Processing Algorithms

The **BlurAlgorithm**, **ContrastAlgorithm**, and **EdgeDetectionAlgorithm** classes implement the **ImageAlgorithm** interface and define how to apply the processing algorithm.

```
public class BlurAlgorithm implements ImageAlgorithm{
   @Override
   public void apply() {
       System.out.println("Applying blur algorithm to the image.");
   }
```

```
}
public class ContrastAlgorithm implements ImageAlgorithm {
   @Override
   public void apply() {
       System.out.println("Applying contrast algorithm to the
image.");
   }
}
public class EdgeDetectionAlgorithm implements ImageAlgorithm {
   @Override
   public void apply() {
       System.out.println("Applying edge detection algorithm to
the image.");
   }
}
```

Create the Image Class to Represent an Image

The **Image** class uses an image format and a processing algorithm to process the image.

```
public class Image {
   private ImageFormat format;

   public Image(ImageFormat format) {
       this.format = format;
   }

   public void process(ImageAlgorithm algorithm) {
       format.applyAlgorithm(algorithm);
   }
}
```

To complete our example, here is a **Main** class demonstrating how to use the Bridge pattern to process images with different formats and processing algorithms.

```
public class Main {
   public static void main( String[] args ) {
       // Create instances of image formats
       ImageFormat jpegFormat = new JPEGFormat();
       ImageFormat pngFormat = new PNGFormat();
       ImageFormat bmpFormat = new BMPFormat();

       // Create instances of image algorithms
       ImageAlgorithm blurAlgorithm = new BlurAlgorithm();
       ImageAlgorithm contrastAlgorithm = new ContrastAlgo-
rithm();
       ImageAlgorithm edgeDetectionAlgorithm = new EdgeDetection-
Algorithm();
```

```
            // Create images with different formats and apply algorithms
            Image jpegImage = new Image(jpegFormat);
            jpegImage.process(blurAlgorithm);

            Image pngImage = new Image(pngFormat);
            pngImage.process(contrastAlgorithm);

            Image bmpImage = new Image(bmpFormat);
            bmpImage.process(edgeDetectionAlgorithm);
        }
    }
```

Output Console:

```
Applying algorithm to JPEG image
Applying blur algorithm to the image.
Applying algorithm to PNG image
Applying contrast algorithm to the image.
Applying algorithm to BMP image
Applying edge detection algorithm to the image.
```

Using the Bridge pattern, image formats and processing algorithms can be separated, making the application more flexible and easier to maintain. This allows new image formats and processing algorithms to be added without modifying existing code, avoiding code duplication and reducing maintenance complexity.

In the following pattern, we will explore the **Composite Pattern**, which enables the composition of objects into tree structures to represent part-whole hierarchies.

Composite Pattern

The **Composite Pattern** is a design solution that combines objects into tree structures to represent part-whole hierarchies. This pattern allows clients to treat individual objects and compositions of objects uniformly.

The Composite Pattern addresses a critical need: enabling consistent handling of individual objects and object groupings.

Let us consider a real-world scenario in which the absence of a composite structure leads to critical malfunctions.

Case Study

Imagine an AI system that needs to manage data processing pipelines. Individual processing steps are represented as separate objects, while composite pipelines are composed of objects that can include individual steps and other composite pipelines.

The system is initially designed to operate with standalone processing steps, but it must now support composite pipelines.

The initial challenges include:

- **Hierarchy Management**: The code is designed to handle individual processing steps, making it challenging to introduce composite pipelines and manage hierarchical structures.
- **Code Duplication**: Adding composite pipelines would require duplicating a significant portion of the existing code, complicating maintenance.
- **Limited Flexibility**: Users cannot create composite pipelines, which restricts the flexibility of the system.

To address these issues, we will apply the Composite Pattern. This design pattern allows objects to be composed into tree-like structures to represent part-whole hierarchies, enabling individual processing steps and composite pipelines to be treated uniformly.

Note: *In this case study, we will focus on implementing useful classes to apply the design model concept.*

Applying the Composite Pattern

To better understand how the Composite pattern solves the problem of managing hierarchies, let us first examine the class diagram, which illustrates the structure and relationships between the system's components.

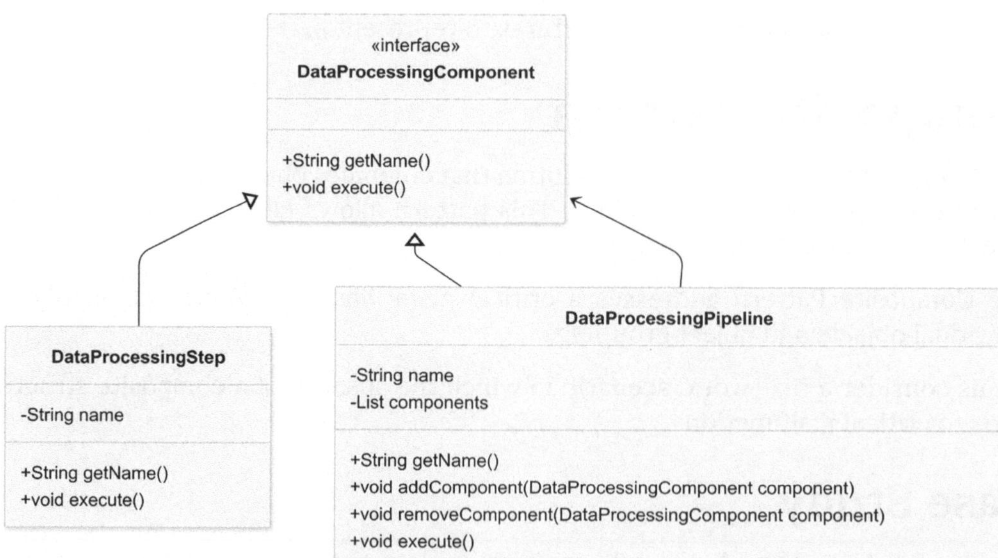

Figure 3.3: *Composite Pattern - Data Processing*

Let us move on to the detailed implementation of the Composite pattern to solve the hierarchy management problem.

Creating the Interface for Data Processing Components

The **DataProcessingComponent** interface defines the methods for retrieving names and executing data processing components.

```
public interface DataProcessingComponent {
   String getName();
   void execute();
}
```

Implementing the DataProcessingStep Class

The **DataProcessingStep** class implements the **DataProcessingComponent** interface to represent a data processing step and defines how to retrieve its name and execute it.

```
public class DataProcessingStep implements DataProcessing
Component {
   private String name;

   public DataProcessingStep(String name) {
       this.name = name;
   }

   @Override
   public String getName() {
       return this.name;
   }

   @Override
   public void execute() {
       System.out.printf("Executing step: %s%n", this.name);
   }
}
```

Implement the DataProcessingPipeline Class to Represent a Data Processing Pipeline

The **DataProcessingPipeline** class implements the **DataProcessingComponent** interface and defines how to retrieve the name, add and remove components, and execute a data processing pipeline.

```
public class DataProcessingPipeline implements DataProcessingComponent {
   private String name;
   private List<DataProcessingComponent> components;

   public DataProcessingPipeline(String name) {
       this.name = name;
       this.components = new ArrayList<>();
   }

   public void addComponent(DataProcessingComponent component) {
       components.add(component);
   }
   public void removeComponent(DataProcessingComponent component) {
       components.remove(component);
   }

   @Override
   public String getName() {
       return this.name;
   }

   @Override
   public void execute() {
       System.out.printf("Executing pipeline: %s%n", this.name);
       for (DataProcessingComponent component : components) {
           component.execute();
       }
   }
}
```

To complete our example, here is a **Main** class demonstrating how to use the Composite pattern to manage data processing steps and composite pipelines.

```
public class Main {
   public static void main( String[] args ) {
       // Create instances of data processing components
       DataProcessingComponent step1 = new DataProcessingStep
("Normalization");
       DataProcessingComponent step2 = new DataProcessingStep
("Feature Transformation");
       DataProcessingComponent step3 = new DataProcessingStep
("Dimensionality Reduction");

       // Create data processing pipeline instances
       DataProcessingPipeline pipeline1 = new DataProcessingPipe-
line("Pipeline1");
       DataProcessingPipeline pipeline2 = new DataProcessingPipe-
line("Pipeline2");
```

```
        // Add data processing steps and pipelines to pipelines
        pipeline1.addComponent(step1);
        pipeline1.addComponent(step2);
        pipeline2.addComponent(step3);
        pipeline1.addComponent(pipeline2);

        // Run the data processing pipeline
        pipeline1.execute();
    }
}
```

Output Console:

```
Executing pipeline: Pipeline1
Executing step: Normalization
Executing step: Feature Transformation
Executing pipeline: Pipeline2
Executing step: Dimensionality Reduction
```

The Composite Pattern enables objects to be organized into tree structures representing part-whole hierarchies, enhancing system flexibility and simplifying maintenance. It also allows individual data processing steps and composite pipelines to be treated uniformly, simplifying hierarchy management.

In the following pattern, we will explore the **Decorator Pattern**, which enables responsibilities to be dynamically attached to an object, offering a flexible alternative to subclassing for extending functionality.

Decorator Pattern

The Decorator pattern is a design solution for dynamically attaching additional responsibilities to an object. This pattern offers a flexible alternative to the subclass for extending functionality.

The Decorator pattern meets a critical need to enable flexible extension of an object's functionality without modifying its source code.

Let us consider a real-world scenario where the absence of a Decorator leads to critical system malfunctions.

Case Study

Imagine a scenario where an AI system is required to apply various filters and transformations to images. These filters and transformations are additional features that must be used dynamically. Initially, the system was designed to work with basic images, but it now needs to support the dynamic application of visual effects and modifications.

Several challenges arise:

- **Feature Extensibility**: The existing code is structured to handle basic images, making incorporating dynamic filters and transformations difficult.
- **Code Duplication**: Adding these features would require duplicating significant portions of the existing codebase, increasing maintenance complexity.
- **Limited Flexibility**: Users cannot apply filters and transformations at runtime, restricting the adaptability of the system.

To address these issues, we will apply the **Decorator Pattern**. This design pattern allows responsibilities to be dynamically attached to an object, enabling adding filters and transformations to images without modifying the existing code. It provides a flexible and scalable way to extend functionality while preserving the system's original architecture.

Note: *In this case study, we will focus on implementing useful classes to apply the design model concept.*

Applying the Decorator Pattern

To better understand how the Decorator Pattern addresses the challenge of extending functionality, let us first examine the class diagram, which illustrates the structure and relationships between the various system components.

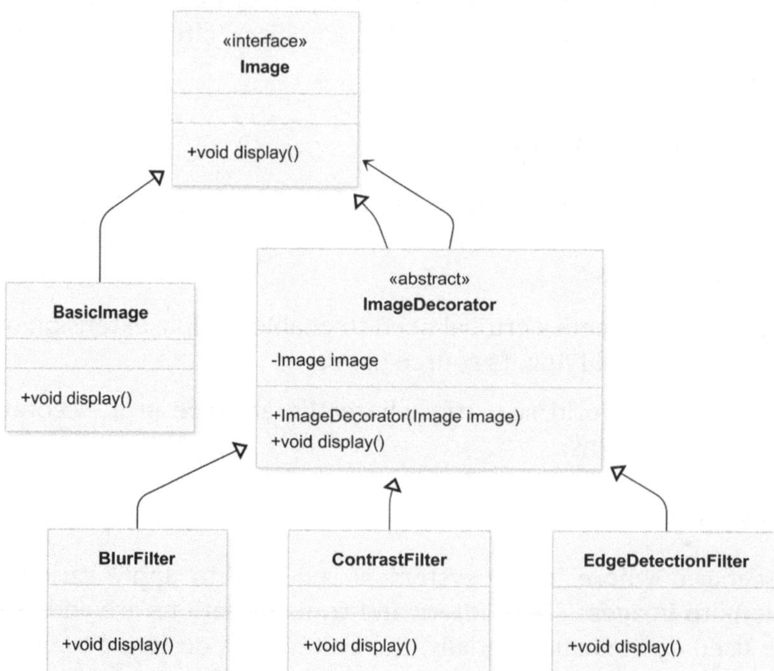

Figure 3.4: *Decorator Pattern - Dynamic Filters and Transformations*

Create the Interface for Images

The Image interface defines the method for displaying an image.

```
public interface Image {
   void display();
}
```

Implement the `BasicImage` Class to Represent a Base Image

The **`BasicImage`** class implements the Image interface and defines how to display a basic image.

```
public class BasicImage implements Image {
   @Override
   public void display() {
       System.out.println("Displaying basic image");
   }
}
```

Create the Abstract `ImageDecorator` Class to Represent an Image Decorator

The abstract class **`ImageDecorator`** implements the Image interface and defines how to display a decorated image.

```
public abstract class ImageDecorator implements Image {
   protected Image image;

   public ImageDecorator(Image image) {
       this.image = image;
   }

   @Override
   public void display() {
       this.image.display();
   }
}
```

Implement Concrete Decorator Classes to Represent Filters and Transformations

The **`BlurFilter`**, **`ContrastFilter`**, and **`EdgeDetectionFilter`** classes extend the

ImageDecorator class and define how to display an image with a specific filter or transformation.

```
public class BlurFilter extends ImageDecorator {

   public BlurFilter(Image image) {
       super(image);
   }

   @Override
   public void display() {
       super.display();
       System.out.println("Applying blur filter");
   }
}
public class ContrastFilter extends ImageDecorator {

   public ContrastFilter(Image image) {
       super(image);
   }

   @Override
   public void display() {
       super.display();
       System.out.println("Applying contrast filter");
   }
}
public class EdgeDetectionFilter extends ImageDecorator {

   public EdgeDetectionFilter(Image image) {
       super(image);
   }

   @Override
   public void display() {
       super.display();
       System.out.println("Applying edge detection filter");
   }
}
```

To complete our example, here is a **Main** class demonstrating how to dynamically use the Decorator Pattern to apply filters and transformations to an image.

```
public class Main {
   public static void main( String[] args ) {
       // Create a base image instance
       Image basicImage = new BasicImage();
```

```
        // Apply filters and transformations dynamically
        Image blurredImage = new BlurFilter(basicImage);
        Image contrastedImage = new ContrastFilter(blurredImage);
        Image edgeDetectedImage = new EdgeDetectionFilter
(contrastedImage);

        // Display image with filters and transformations applied
        edgeDetectedImage.display();
    }
}
```

Output Console:

```
Displaying basic image
Applying blur filter
Applying contrast filter
Applying edge detection filter
```

Using the Decorator Pattern allowed us to dynamically attach additional responsibilities to an object, making the system more flexible and easier to maintain. It enables filters and transformations to be added to images without modifying the existing code while avoiding code duplication and reducing maintenance complexity.

In the following pattern, we will explore the **Facade Pattern**, which offers a simplified and unified interface to a collection of interfaces within a subsystem, thereby streamlining its usage and reducing complexity for the client.

Facade Pattern

The Facade Pattern provides a unified interface for multiple interfaces within a subsystem. This pattern simplifies the subsystem's use by providing a consistent interface, thereby masking the complexity of interactions between its various components.

The Facade pattern addresses a critical need, simplifying the use of complex subsystems.

Let us consider a real-world scenario in which the absence of a Facade leads to critical malfunctions.

Case Study

Imagine an AI system that must interact with several complex subsystems to load, process, and save images. These subsystems include an image loader, an image processor, and an image saver. Initially, the system is designed to interact directly with each of these subsystems, which makes the code complex and difficult to maintain.

The initial challenges include:

- **Complex Interaction Logic**: The code is built to communicate directly with the subsystems, making it difficult to manage complex interactions.
- **Code Duplication**: Adding new features would require duplicating significant portions of existing code, complicating maintenance.
- **Difficult Maintenance**: Users must understand and handle multiple complex interfaces, limiting the flexibility of the system.

To address these issues, we will apply the **Facade pattern**. This design pattern provides a unified interface to a set of interfaces within a subsystem, thereby simplifying the use of that subsystem.

Note: *In this case study, we will focus on implementing useful classes to apply the design model concept.*

Applying the Facade Pattern

To better understand how the Facade pattern helps resolve the complexity of interactions, let us first examine the class diagram, which illustrates the structure and relationships among the various system components.

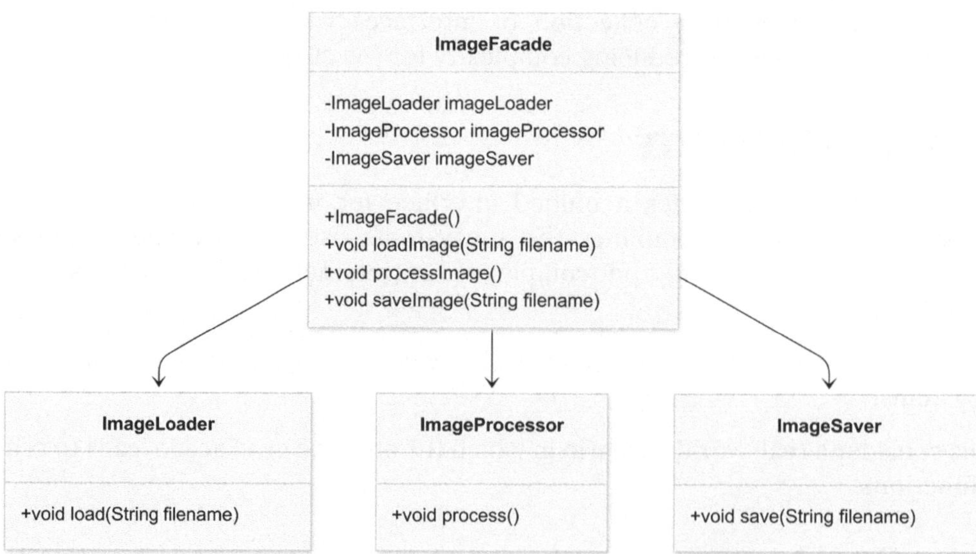

***Figure* 3.5:** *Facade Pattern - AI Subsystem*

Now, let us move on to the detailed implementation of the Facade pattern to address the complexity of interactions.

Creating the Classes for the Subsystems

The **ImageLoader**, **ImageProcessor**, and **ImageSaver** classes represent the subsystems responsible for loading, processing, and saving images.

```
public class ImageLoader {
   public void load(String filename) {
       System.out.printf("Loading image: %s%n", filename);
   }
}
public class ImageProcessor {
   public void process() {
       System.out.println("Processing image");
   }
}
public class ImageSaver {
   public void save(String filename) {
       System.out.printf("Saving image: %s%n", filename);
   }
}
```

Creating the ImageFacade Class to Provide a Unified Interface

The **ImageFacade** class offers a unified interface for interacting with the image loading, processing, and saving subsystems.

```
public class ImageFacade {
   private final ImageLoader imageLoader;
   private final ImageProcessor imageProcessor;
   private final ImageSaver imageSaver;

   public ImageFacade() {
       this.imageLoader = new ImageLoader();
       this.imageProcessor = new ImageProcessor();
       this.imageSaver = new ImageSaver();
   }

   public void loadImage(String filename) {
       this.imageLoader.load(filename);
   }

   public void processImage() {
       this.imageProcessor.process();
   }
```

```
    public void saveImage(String filename) {
        this.imageSaver.save(filename);
    }
}
```

To complete our example, here is a **Main** class demonstrating how to use the Facade pattern to simplify interactions with the image processing subsystems.

```
public class Main {
    public static void main( String[] args ) {
        // Create an instance of the facade
        ImageFacade imageFacade = new ImageFacade();

        // Using the front panel to load, process and save images
        imageFacade.loadImage("example.jpg");
        imageFacade.processImage();
        imageFacade.saveImage("processed_example.jpg");
    }
}
```

Output Console:

```
Loading image: example.jpg
Processing image
Saving image: processed_example.jpg
```

The use of the Facade Pattern provided a unified interface for a collection of interfaces within a subsystem., thereby simplifying the use of that subsystem. This approach hides the complexity of interactions between the different subsystem components, making the system more flexible and easier to maintain.

In the following pattern, we will explore how the **Flyweight Pattern** allows for sharing objects to efficiently support a large number of fine-grained objects.

Flyweight Pattern

The Flyweight pattern is a design solution that enables object sharing to support large numbers of fine-grained objects efficiently. This pattern is beneficial when managing a high volume of similar objects, as it reduces memory consumption by sharing common instances.

The Flyweight pattern addresses a critical need, enabling the efficient management of fine-grained objects.

Let us consider a real-world scenario in which the absence of a Flyweight leads to critical malfunctions.

Case Study

Imagine a system powered by artificial intelligence that must handle many similar images. These images share common data, such as metadata and color palettes. Initially, the system is designed to store redundant data for each image, which results in high memory consumption and degraded performance.

The initial challenges include:

- **High Memory Consumption**: The code is structured to store redundant data for each image, leading to excessive memory usage.
- **Reduced Performance**: Managing many similar images with duplicated data lowers the overall performance of the system.
- **Difficult Maintenance**: Users must deal with multiple similar objects containing redundant data, which limits the system's flexibility.

To address these issues, we will apply the **Flyweight Pattern**. This design pattern allows shared use of objects to efficiently support large numbers of fine-grained instances, thereby reducing memory usage and improving system performance.

Note: *In this case study, we will focus on implementing useful classes to apply the design model concept.*

Applying the Flyweight Pattern

To better understand how the Flyweight pattern addresses the problem of high memory consumption, let us first examine the class diagram that illustrates the structure and relationships between the different components of the system.

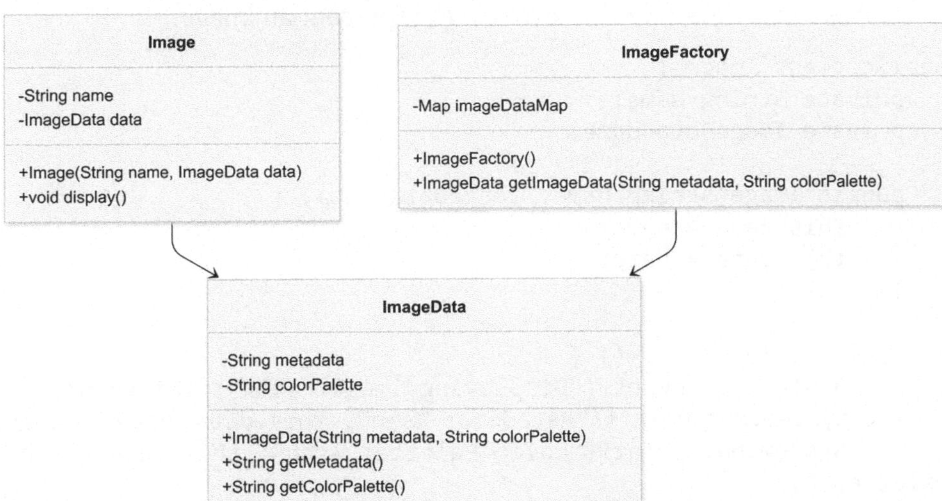

Figure 3.6*: Flyweight Pattern - Similar Images*

Now, let us move on to the detailed implementation of the Flyweight Pattern to address the problem of high memory consumption.

Create the `ImageData` Class to Represent Shared Data

The **`ImageData`** class represents the data shared between images, such as metadata and color palettes.

```
public class ImageData {
   private String metadata;
   private String colorPalette;

   public ImageData(String metadata, String colorPalette) {
       this.metadata = metadata;
       this.colorPalette = colorPalette;
   }

   public String getMetadata() {
       return this.metadata;
   }

   public String getColorPalette() {
       return this.colorPalette;
   }
}
```

Create the `Image` Class to Represent an Image

The **`Image`** class uses the shared **`ImageData`** to represent an image.

```
public class Image {
   private String name;
   private ImageData data;

   public Image(String name, ImageData data) {
       this.name = name;
       this.data = data;
   }

   public void display() {
       System.out.printf("Displaying image: %s%n", this.name);
       System.out.printf("Metadata: %s%n", this.data.getMetadata());
       System.out.printf("Color Palette: %s%n", this.data.getColor-
Palette());
   }
}
```

Create the `ImageFactory` Class to Manage Shared Data

The **`ImageFactory`** class manages the shared **`ImageData`** instances and provides a method to retrieve them.

```
public class ImageFactory {
   private Map<String, ImageData> imageDataMap;

   public ImageFactory() {
       this.imageDataMap = new HashMap<>();
   }

   public ImageData getImageData(String metadata, String color
Palette) {
       String key = metadata + colorPalette;
       if (!this.imageDataMap.containsKey(key)) {
           this.imageDataMap.put(key, new ImageData(metadata,
colorPalette));
       }
       return this.imageDataMap.get(key);
   }
}
```

To complete our example, here is a **`Main`** class that demonstrates how to use the Flyweight pattern to efficiently manage similar images.

```
public class Main {
   public static void main( String[] args ) {
       // Create an instance of the image factory
       ImageFactory imageFactory = new ImageFactory();

       // Get shared data for images
       ImageData data1 = imageFactory.getImageData("Metadata1",
"ColorPalette1");
       ImageData data2 = imageFactory.getImageData("Metadata2",
"ColorPalette2");

       // Create image instances with shared data
       Image image1 = new Image("Image1", data1);
       Image image2 = new Image("Image2", data1);
       Image image3 = new Image("Image3", data2);

       // Display images
       image1.display();
       image2.display();
       image3.display();
```

```
        }
    }
```

Output Console:

```
Displaying image: Image1
Metadata: Metadata1
Color Palette: ColorPalette1
Displaying image: Image2
Metadata: Metadata1
Color Palette: ColorPalette1
Displaying image: Image3
Metadata: Metadata2
Color Palette: ColorPalette2
```

The use of the Flyweight pattern allowed objects to be shared in order to efficiently support large numbers of fine-grained instances, thereby reducing memory consumption and improving system performance. It enables effective management of similar images through shared data, simplifying memory handling.

In the next pattern, we will explore the **Proxy pattern**, which serves as a substitute for another object to manage access to it.

Proxy Pattern

The Proxy Pattern is a design pattern that substitutes or represents another object to control access to it. This pattern is particularly useful when you want to add an additional layer of control for accessing an object, such as managing access, caching, or lazy loading. The Proxy Pattern addresses a critical need, allowing additional control over object access.

Consider a real-world scenario where the absence of a Proxy leads to critical malfunctions.

Case Study

Imagine an AI system that needs to load large images. The images are stored on a remote server, and loading them can be resource-intensive in terms of time and resources. Initially, the system was designed to load images directly, leading to inefficient loading and difficult access management.

Initial challenges include:

- **Inefficient Loading**: The code is designed to load images directly, leading to inefficient loading of large images.
- **Difficult Access Management**: Managing direct access to large images makes it difficult to control access and manage resources.

- **Difficult Maintenance**: Users must directly manage large images, limiting the flexibility of the system.

To solve these problems, we will apply the Proxy Pattern. This design pattern provides a substitute for large images, thereby controlling their loading and improving system performance.

Note: *In this case study, we will focus on implementing useful classes to apply the design model concept.*

Applying the Proxy Pattern

To better understand how the Proxy Pattern can solve the problem of inefficient loading, let us first examine the class diagram, which illustrates the structure and relationships between the system's different components.

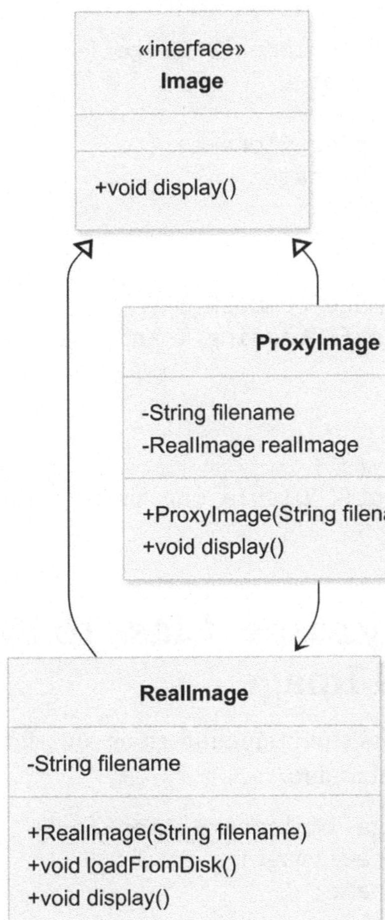

Figure 3.7: *Proxy Pattern - Loading of Large Images*

Now, let us move on to the detailed implementation of the Proxy Pattern to solve the problem of inefficient loading.

Create the Interface for Images

The **Image** interface defines the method to display an image.

```
public interface Image {
   void display();
}
```

Implement the RealImage Class to Represent a Real Image

The **RealImage** class implements the Image interface and defines how to load and display a real image.

```
public class RealImage implements Image {
   private String filename;

   public RealImage(String filename) {
       this.filename = filename;
       loadImageFromDisk();
   }

   private void loadImageFromDisk() {
       System.out.printf("Loading %s%n", filename);
   }

   @Override
   public void display() {
       System.out.printf("Displaying %s%n", filename);
   }
}
```

Implement the ProxyImage Class to Represent a Substitute for a Real Image

The **ProxyImage** class implements the Image interface and defines how to display an image using a substitute for a real image.

```
public class ProxyImage implements Image {
   private RealImage realImage;
   private String filename;
```

```
    public ProxyImage(String filename) {
        this.filename = filename;
    }

    @Override
    public void display() {
        if (realImage == null) {
            realImage = new RealImage(filename);
        }
        realImage.display();
    }
}
```

To complete our example, here is a **Main** class that demonstrates how to use the Proxy Pattern to control the loading of large images.

```
public class Main {
    public static void main( String[] args ) {
        // Create an instance of the proxy image
        Image image1 = new ProxyImage("large_image1.jpg");
        Image image2 = new ProxyImage("large_image2.jpg");

        // Display the images
        image1.display();
        image2.display();
    }
}
```

Output Console:

```
Loading large_image1.jpg
Displaying large_image1.jpg
Loading large_image2.jpg
Displaying large_image2.jpg
```

Using the Proxy Pattern allowed providing a substitute for large images, thereby controlling their loading and improving system performance. This allows efficiently managing large images with lazy loading, simplifying resource management.

Conclusion

In this chapter, we explored several Structural Design Patterns, including *Adapter*, *Bridge*, *Composite*, *Decorator*, *Facade*, *Flyweight*, and *Proxy*. Every pattern was illustrated with specific examples and implementation, demonstrating how they can be applied to resolve particular software design issues. These patterns offer proven solutions for organizing classes and objects in a software system, making the system more flexible, easier to maintain, and scalable.

In the next chapter, we will explore **Behavioral Design Patterns**, which focus on the interactions between objects and the distribution of responsibilities. These patterns offer solutions for managing complex behaviors and interactions between objects, making the system more robust and easier to extend.

Points to Remember

- **Adapter:** Utilize the Adapter pattern to convert a class's interface into one that clients expect, enabling incompatible classes to collaborate effectively.
- **Bridge:** Use the Bridge to separate abstraction from its implementation, allowing both to vary independently.
- **Composite:** Use the Composite to compose objects into tree structures to represent part-whole hierarchies.
- **Decorator:** Utilize the Decorator pattern to dynamically add responsibilities to an object, providing a flexible alternative to subclassing for enhancing functionality.
- **Facade:** Utilize the Facade pattern to create a single interface for a set of interfaces within a subsystem, streamlining the interactions with the subsystem.
- **Flyweight:** Use the Flyweight to use sharing to support large quantities of fine-grained objects efficiently.
- **Proxy:** Utilize the Proxy to serve as a surrogate or placeholder for another object and manage access to it.

Multiple Choice Questions

1. Which pattern is useful for attaching additional responsibilities to an object dynamically?

    a. Adapter

    b. Bridge

    c. Composite

    d. Decorator

2. In the Facade Pattern, which of the following is the main purpose of the facade class?

    a. To create a new instance of a class.

    b. To provide a unified interface to a set of interfaces in a subsystem.

   c. To convert the interface of a class into another interface.
   d. To compose objects into tree structures.

3. In the Proxy Pattern, which is the primary purpose of the proxy object?
   a. To create a new instance of a class.
   b. To provide a surrogate or placeholder for another object to control access to it.
   c. To convert the interface of a class into another interface.
   d. To compose objects into tree structures.

Answers

1. d
2. b
3. b

Questions

1. How can the Adapter Pattern be used to integrate third-party libraries into an existing system?
2. How can the Composite Pattern simplify the management of hierarchies in a file management system?
3. What are typical use cases for the Decorator Pattern in software development?
4. What are the advantages of using the Flyweight Pattern to manage large quantities of fine-grained objects?
5. How can the Proxy pattern be used to control access to objects in a software system?

Key Terms

- **Adapter**: A pattern that converts a class interface into another interface expected by clients.
- **Bridge**: A pattern that allows separating abstraction from its implementation, allowing both to vary independently.
- **Composite**: A pattern that allows composing objects into tree structures to represent part-whole hierarchies.

- **Decorator**: A pattern that allows attaching additional responsibilities to an object dynamically, offering a flexible alternative to subclassing for extending functionality.
- **Facade**: A pattern that offers a consistent interface to various interfaces in a subsystem, making it easier to use.
- **Flyweight**: A pattern that uses sharing to support large quantities of fine-grained objects efficiently.
- **Proxy**: A design pattern that acts as a placeholder for another object, managing access to it.

CHAPTER 4
Behavioral Design Patterns

Introduction

Behavioral Design Patterns are proven solutions to common software design challenges. They focus on the interactions between objects and the responsibilities assigned to them. The primary goal of these patterns is to make systems more flexible, maintainable, and scalable.

This chapter explores a variety of essential Behavioral Design Patterns, including ***Chain of Responsibility***, ***Command***, ***Interpreter***, **Iterator**, **Mediator**, ***Memento***, ***Observer***, **State**, ***Strategy***, ***Template Method***, and **Visitor**. Each pattern will be explored in detail, with clear definitions, practical examples, and practical use cases to illustrate its application in real-world scenarios.

By exploring this chapter, you will gain insights into determining the suitable context for each pattern, grasp the benefits and constraints of each method, and implement these patterns in your projects to improve code quality and maintainability.

Structure

In this chapter, we will cover the following topics:

- Chain of Responsibility Pattern
- Command Pattern
- Interpreter Pattern
- Iterator Pattern
- Mediator Pattern
- Memento Pattern
- Observer Pattern
- State Pattern

- Strategy Pattern
- Template Method Pattern
- Visitor Pattern

Chain of Responsibility Pattern

The Chain of Responsibility Pattern is a behavioral design solution that manages complex requests by dynamically passing them along a chain of specialized objects until an appropriate handler is found. This approach decouples request senders from receivers, enhancing flexibility and simplifying component interactions.

The Chain of Responsibility addresses critical needs in handling dynamic, complex requests where direct coupling between request initiators and processors could hinder scalability and maintainability. Without it, systems handling diverse user requests may encounter several challenges:

- **Rigid Architectures**: Tight coupling between components leads to inflexible systems that are difficult to modify or extend.
- **Reduced Maintainability**: Handling diverse logic in a single entity complicates updates and debugging.
- **Increased Complexity**: Managing requests across multiple functionalities without a clear delegation structure often leads to redundant or complex code.

Case Study

Imagine a Generative AI platform designed to handle various user requests, such as text generation, image creation, and sentiment analysis. Initially, the platform processed all requests through a monolithic service, causing maintenance and scalability challenges as user interactions diversified.

The initial challenges include:

- **Complex Request Handling**: Each new request type required significant alterations to the existing system.
- **Direct Coupling**: Adding new functionalities increased dependencies within the main service, complicating further updates.
- **Difficult Extensibility:** Extending the platform to support new generative features became cumbersome and prone to errors.

To address these issues, the Chain of Responsibility Pattern is applied. This design pattern creates a clear separation between request senders and handlers, dynamically forwarding requests through a defined chain of specialized modules without altering their source code.

Note: *In this case study, we will focus on implementing useful classes to apply the design model concept.*

Applying the Chain of Responsibility Pattern

The following is a step-by-step implementation of the Chain of Responsibility Pattern in our generative AI scenario:

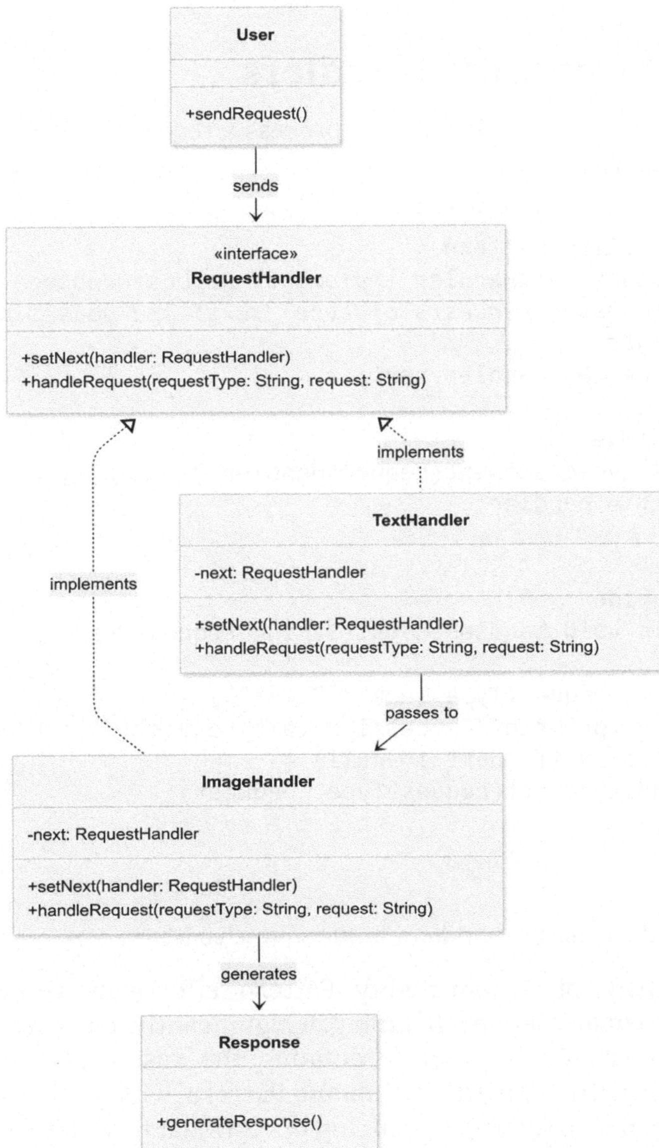

Figure 4.1: *Chain of Responsibility - Handle Various User Requests*

Define the Handler Interface

This interface establishes methods for setting the next handler in the chain and handling requests.

```
public interface RequestHandler {
   void setNext(RequestHandler handler);
   void handleRequest(String requestType, String request);
}
```

Implement Concrete Handlers

Concrete handlers determine if they can process a request or forward it to the next handler in the chain.

```
// This class handles text requests in the chain of
responsibility pattern.
public class TextHandler implements RequestHandler {
// It processes requests of type "text" and passes others to the
next handler.
private RequestHandler next;

   @Override
   public void setNext(RequestHandler handler) {
this.next = handler;
   }

   @Override
   public void handleRequest(String requestType, String request)
{
       if (requestType.equals("text")) {
System.out.println("Processing text request: " + request);
       } else if (next != null) {
next.handleRequest(requestType, request);
       }
   }
}
```

Note: *The rest of the concrete handlers in the source code.*

Applying the Chain of Responsibility Pattern effectively resolves the issues associated with dynamic request handling. It significantly improves maintainability, flexibility, and scalability by clearly defining the responsibilities for handling requests. Next, we will explore the **Command Pattern**, which encapsulates requests into executable objects, further enhancing operational flexibility and control.

Command Pattern

The Command Pattern is a behavioral design approach that transforms a request or action into an object, effectively decoupling the entity that issues the command from the one that executes it.

This enables the ability to:

- Store, Chain, or Undo operations.
- Manage delayed or scheduled actions.
- Centralize the logic of operations within dedicated classes.

It is particularly useful in contexts where user actions need to be recorded, *Undo* or *Redo* functionality is required, or complex tasks must be dynamically orchestrated.

Case Study

Imagine an application that enables users to define AI generation tasks such as writing summaries, generating charts, or sending synthesized reports at scheduled times. Initially, each action was handled directly through procedural code, resulting in growing complexity as the number of trigger types and user scenarios expanded.

The initial challenges include:

- **Tight Coupling**: User interfaces were directly linked to the business logic, resulting in a rigid system that was difficult to evolve and maintain.
- **Limited Flexibility**: Actions could not be easily scheduled, canceled, or reused in different contexts.
- **Lack of Traceability**: There was no standardized way to log or replay sequences of AI actions for auditing or debugging purposes.

To address these issues, we apply the **Command Pattern**. This pattern encapsulates each AI action as an object, allowing for flexible scheduling, centralized execution, and support for features such as *undo* and *redo*, logging, and deferred execution. It cleanly decouples the command initiator from the logic that executes the command, paving the way for a more modular and scalable architecture.

Note: *In this case study, we will focus on implementing useful classes to apply the design model concept.*

Applying the Command Pattern

We will encapsulate each action, *generating a summary*, *creating an image*, and *sending a report* into a single command. A `CommandExecutor` will execute these *commands* and can be stored in a queue or a stack.

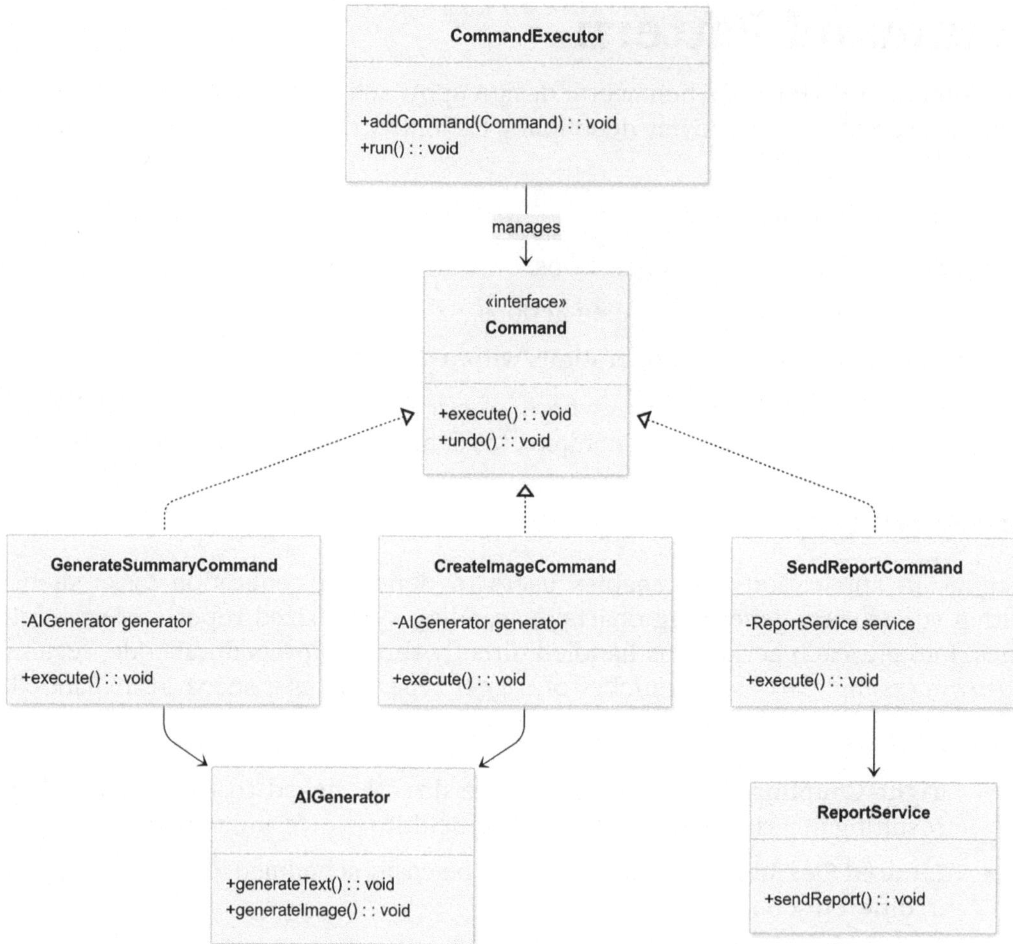

Figure 4.2: *Command Pattern - Orchestration of Deferred Generative Commands*

Create the Command Interface

It defines an **`execute()`** method that all commands must implement.

```
public interface Command {
   void execute();
   void undo(); // Optional, for commands that can be undone
}
```

Create Concrete Command Classes

The **`GenerateSummaryCommand`**, **`CreateImageCommand`**, and **`SendReportCommand`** classes implement the **`Command`** interface and define how to execute or undo their respective actions, while encapsulating the logic independently from the caller.

```
public class GenerateSummaryCommand implements Command {
   private final AIGenerator generator;
   private final String topic;

   public GenerateSummaryCommand(AIGenerator generator, String
topic) {
this.generator = generator;
this.topic = topic;
   }

   @Override
   public void execute() {
generator.generateText("Summary on : " + topic);
   }

   @Override
   public void undo() {
System.out.println("[UNDO] Deleting the summary generated on : "
+ topic);
   }
}
```

Note: *The rest of the concrete command in the source code.*

Create a Command Executor

It receives commands and executes them immediately or later.

```
public class CommandExecutor {
// CommandExecutor is responsible for executing commands and
managing their history
   // It allows commands to be executed, undone, and replayed
private final Stack<Command> history = new Stack<>();

// Execute a command and store it in the history
public void executeCommand(Command command) {
command.execute();
history.push(command);
   }

// Undo the last command executed
public void undoLastCommand() {
      if (!history.isEmpty()) {
           Command last = history.pop();
last.undo();
      } else {
System.out.println("No orders to cancel.");
```

```
        }
    }

    // Replays all commands in the history.
    public void replayAll() {
    System.out.println("--- Replay all commands ---");
        for (Command cmd : history) {
    cmd.execute();
        }
    }
}
```

The Command Pattern provides an elegant solution to the challenges of modularity, flexibility, and traceability in complex systems. By encapsulating actions into independent command objects, this pattern separates user intentions from actual execution, making the code more transparent, extensible, and reusable. Next, we will explore the **Interpreter Pattern**, which addresses the challenges of understanding and executing specialized languages.

Interpreter Pattern

The Interpreter Pattern is a behavioral design approach that defines a grammatical representation of a language and provides an interpreter to process and execute instructions expressed in that language.

This pattern enables a system to:

- Parse and evaluate structured or domain-specific expressions.
- Provide flexibility for defining rules, instructions, or logic in a human-readable or scriptable form.
- Decouple expression evaluation logic from the core application behavior.

It is particularly valuable when applications require a mini-language to describe operations, behaviors, or configurations, especially when these instructions must be interpreted dynamically at runtime.

Case Study

Imagine a generative AI platform designed to support user-defined rules and prompt logic in a structured expression format. Users want to define conditional instructions like:

```
IF topic IS "education" AND sentiment IS "positive" THEN GENERATE
"motivational quote"
```

The initial challenges include:

- **Complex Rule Management**: Each new rule type required new branches in code, increasing technical debt.

- **Rigid Architecture**: Adding new grammar elements or keywords such as **`OR`**, **`NOT`**, or **`CONTAINS`** necessitated invasive changes.
- **Limited Extensibility**: There was no unified way to compose or reuse rule logic across different modules or prompt workflows.

To address these issues, we apply the **Interpreter Pattern**. This pattern enables the platform to define a simple grammar, such as **`IF`**, **`AND`**, **`IS`**, *and* **`THEN`**, and process user-defined expressions as objects. Each part of the rule, such as the topic *education*, becomes an expression object that knows how to interpret itself in a given context.

Note: *In this case study, we will focus on implementing useful classes to apply the design model concept.*

Applying the Interpreter Pattern

We are going to build a structured instruction mini-language for generative AI with the following components:

- **Terminal Expression**: These are keywords such as *education*, *positive*, and *motivational quotes*.
- **Non-Terminal Expression**: One can understand them as combinations similar to **`AND`**, **`IF`**, **`THEN`**.
- **Context**: This includes the execution environment, current topic, tone, and so on.
- **Expression**: It is a standard interface for all instructions.

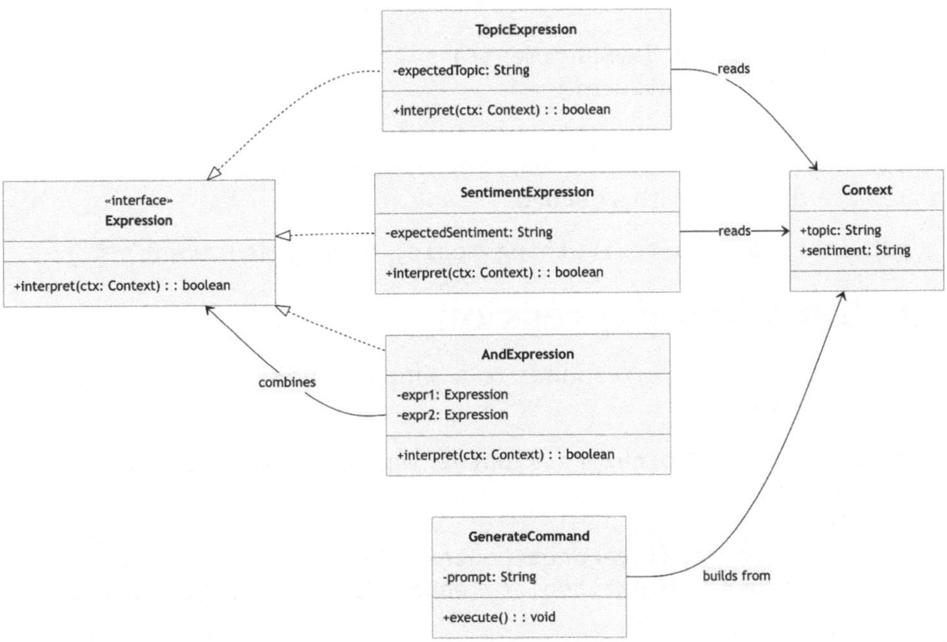

Figure 4.3: *Interpreter Pattern Build – A Mini-Structured Instruction Language*

Create the Expression Interface

It defines the common **interpret()** method for all expressions, whether they are simple or combined.

```
public interface Expression {
booleaninterpret(Context context); // For conditions
}
```

Create Context Class

The **Context** class represents the information provided by the user or the system, against which the rules are evaluated.

```
public class Context {
   private final String topic;
   private final String sentiment;

   public Context(String topic, String sentiment) {
this.topic = topic;
this.sentiment = sentiment;
   }

   public String getTopic() {
       return topic;
   }

   public String getSentiment() {
       return sentiment;
   }
}
```

We can replace this class with a **record**.

```
public record Context(String topic, String sentiment) { }
```

Create Terminal Expression

Each terminal expression corresponds to a simple condition: topic is education or sentiment is positive.

```
public record TopicExpression(String expectedTopic) implements
Expression {
   @Override
   public booleaninterpret(Context context) {
       return context.topic().equalsIgnoreCase(expectedTopic);
   }
}
```

```
public record SentimentExpression(String expectedSentiment)
implements Expression {
   @Override
   public booleaninterpret(Context context) {
       return context.sentiment().equalsIgnoreCase(expectedSenti-
ment);
   }
}
```

Create Composite Expressions: AND

Here, we combine two simple conditions to form a more complex rule.

```
public record AndExpression(Expression expr1, Expression expr2)
implements Expression {
   @Override
   public booleaninterpret(Context context) {
       return expr1.interpret(context) && expr2.interpret
(context);
   }
}
```

Create an Action: Executed if the Condition is true

We simulate a conditional generation action when the rules are satisfied.

```
public record GenerateCommand(String prompt) {
   public void execute() {
System.out.println("AI generated content: " + prompt);
   }
}
```

The Interpreter Pattern provides a powerful abstraction for systems that require processing structured commands, rules, or logic, particularly in AI contexts where dynamic behavior and human-readable rule configuration are crucial. Next, we explore the **Iterator Pattern**, which enables us to navigate multiple outputs generated by an AI system while keeping its internal structure hidden and consistent.

Iterator Pattern

The Iterator Pattern is a behavioral design solution that provides a standardized way to access elements in a collection sequentially without exposing the underlying representation or structure of that collection.

This pattern enables:

- Uniform traversal of heterogeneous or complex data structures.
- Decoupling of data access logic from collection implementation.
- Support for multiple simultaneous iterations or filtering strategies.

It is beneficial when working with generated content collections, such as multiple outputs from an AI model that need to be navigated, filtered, or previewed without knowing how the data is internally stored.

Case Study

Imagine a Generative AI system that produces multiple alternative outputs for a single request, such as 10 different marketing slogans, five image variations, or several alternative chatbot responses.

Initially, these results were handled in arrays or lists, which were manually iterated in the user interface. However, as feature complexity increased, including pagination, filtering, rating, and feedback, the system became increasingly difficult to manage and prone to errors.

The initial challenges include:

- **Exposed Internal Structure**: User Interface components accessed List or Array directly, tightly coupling logic to storage.
- **Duplicated Logic**: Traversal and filtering behavior were rewritten in various places.
- **Poor Scalability**: Adding support for custom iteration, such as next only positive responses became unmanageable.

To address these issues, we apply the **Iterator Pattern**, which encapsulates iteration behavior in a dedicated object. Consumers can navigate the collection without knowing its structure, and custom iterators can be introduced to support different traversal modes, such as random, paginated, and filtered.

Note: *In this case study, we will focus on implementing useful classes to apply the design model concept.*

Applying the Iterator Pattern

We will design an iterator to traverse generated AI responses text or image metadata, allowing:

- Sequential navigation `next()`, `hasNext()`
- Encapsulation of internal structure

- Extensibility for filtered views

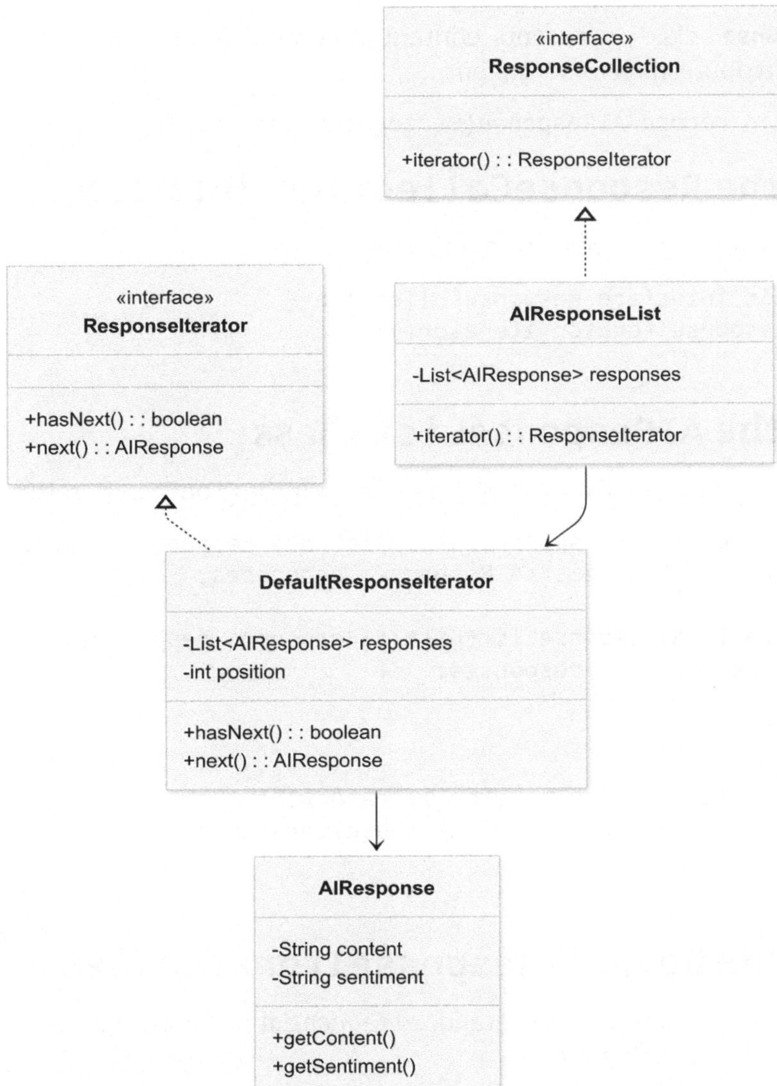

Figure 4.4: *Iterator Pattern - Traverse Generated Responses*

Create the Iterator Interface

We will define a standardized interface for sequential navigation.

```
public interface ResponseIterator {
booleanhasNext();
AIResponsenext();
}
```

Create the AIResponse Class

The **AIResponse** class represents content generated by the AI, accompanied by a contextual attribute such as sentiment.

```
public record AIResponse(String content, String sentiment) { }
```

Create the ResponseCollection Interface

We will define an iterable collection interface.

```
public interface ResponseCollection {
   ResponseIterator iterator();
}
```

Create the AIResponseList Class

This class encapsulates a list of AI objects while exposing only an iterator.

```
public class AIResponseList implements ResponseCollection {
   private final List<AIResponse> responses;

   public AIResponseList(List<AIResponse> responses) {
this.responses = responses;
   }

   @Override
   public ResponseIterator iterator() {
       return new DefaultResponseIterator(responses);
   }
}
```

Create the DefaultResponseIterator Class

This is an implementation of the standard *sequential* iteration that does not expose the structure of the collection.

```
public class DefaultResponseIterator implements ResponseIterator
{
   private final List<AIResponse> responses;
   private int position = 0;

   public DefaultResponseIterator(List<AIResponse> responses) {
this.responses = responses;
   }
   @Override
   public booleanhasNext() {
       return position <responses.size();
```

```
        }

        @Override
        public AIResponsenext() {
            return responses.get(position++);
        }
    }
```

The Iterator Pattern provides a clean abstraction for traversing generated content, making systems more modular and robust.

In our case, the pattern enabled us to decouple the logic that consumes AI responses from the details of how those responses are stored. We also paved the way for future enhancements, such as filtered iteration, reverse iteration, or lazy loading of generated content.

Next, we explore the **Mediator Pattern**, which helps us centralize communication between multiple components.

Mediator Pattern

The Mediator Pattern is a behavioral design pattern that centralizes communication between components by introducing a mediator object. Rather than components interacting directly with one another, they interact with the mediator, which coordinates and routes messages or actions between them.

This pattern is ideal for:

- Reducing tight coupling between interdependent objects.
- Simplifying complex communication flows in distributed or event-based systems.
- Improving scalability and maintainability by isolating logic into a single coordination layer.

Case Study

Imagine a Generative AI platform where multiple components work together to fulfill a single user request:

- The **Text Generator** writes a product description.
- The **Image Generator** creates an illustration.
- The **Report Compiler** formats the results and sends a document.

Initially, these modules communicated directly with each other, resulting in:

- Tightly coupled components that were hard to change individually.

- Scattered logic, with orchestration spread across services.
- Complex debugging occurs as component dependencies multiply.

To solve this, we apply the **Mediator Pattern**. We introduce a central coordinator responsible for triggering and connecting the components in the correct sequence, depending on the request context.

Note: *In this case study, we will focus on implementing useful classes to apply the design model concept.*

Applying the Mediator Pattern

We will implement:

- A *Mediator interface and a concrete* **`AIWorkflowMediator`** *class.*
- Components (colleagues) that collaborate via the mediator: **`TextModule`**, **`ImageModule`**, **`ReportModule`**.
- A simulation of a complete AI workflow from request to delivery.

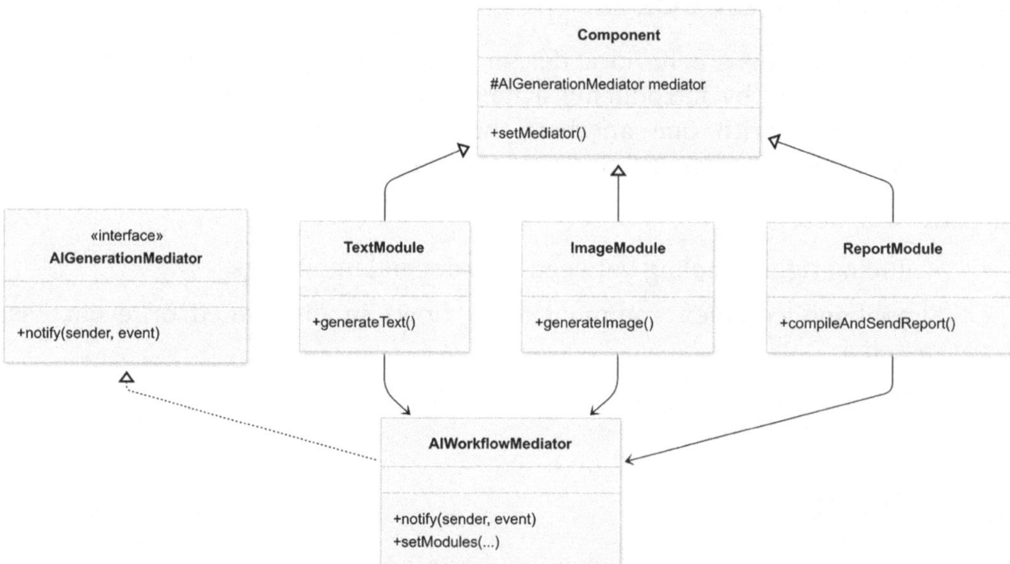

***Figure* 4.5:** *Mediator Pattern - An AI platform with Multiple Components*

Create the Mediator Interface

It defines a communication protocol between the mediator and the components.

```
public interface AIGenerationMediator {
   void notify(Component sender, String event);
}
```

Create the Component Abstract Class

The base class for all AI modules, containing a reference to the mediator:

```
public abstract class Component {
   protected AIGenerationMediator mediator;

public Component(AIGenerationMediator mediator) {
this.mediator = mediator;
   }

   public void setMediator(AIGenerationMediator mediator) {
this.mediator = mediator;
   }
}
```

Create Collaborating Components

The base class for all AI modules, containing a reference to the mediator:

```
public class ImageModule extends Component {

   public ImageModule(AIGenerationMediator mediator) {
       super(mediator);
   }

   public void generateImage() {
System.out.println("Image generated: [Illustration of an AI
robot]");
mediator.notify(this, "imageGenerated");
   }
}
```

Note: *The rest of the components in the source code.*

Implementation of Mediator

The mediator orchestrates actions in response to events sent by the components.

```
public class AIWorkflowMediatorimplements  AIGenerationMediator {

   private TextModuletextModule;
   private ImageModuleimageModule;
   private ReportModulereportModule;

   public void setModules(TextModule text, ImageModule image,
ReportModule report) {
```

```
this.textModule = text;
this.imageModule = image;
this.reportModule = report;
   }

   @Override
   public void notify(Component sender, String event) {
       if (sender == textModule&&event.equals("textGenerated")) {
imageModule.generateImage();
       } else if (sender == imageModule&&event.equals("imageGen-
erated")) {
reportModule.compileAndSendReport();
       }
   }
}
```

The Mediator Pattern provides an elegant solution to the challenges of coordination, coupling, and scalability in complex systems. By centralizing interactions between components into a dedicated mediator, this pattern simplifies communication flows, reduces direct dependencies, and makes the overall architecture more modular and maintainable.

Next, we will explore the **Memento Pattern**, which addresses the challenges of saving and restoring the internal state of objects.

Memento Pattern

The Memento Pattern is a behavioral design pattern that captures and preserves the internal state of an object, thus, allowing it to be restored later without violating encapsulation. The saved state called a *memento*, can be restored at any point, thereby enabling undo, rollback, or versioning features.

This pattern is particularly useful when:

- The state of an object changes frequently but needs to be reversible.
- We want to implement features such as *undo*, *checkpoint*, or *recovery*.
- We must store and restore context in a secure and controlled way.

Case Study

Imagine a Generative AI writing assistant that helps users write product descriptions, summaries, or creative content in multiple iterations. Users often want to:

- Undo the last change,
- Restore a previous version,
- Compare various draft versions.

Initial challenges:

- **No Version Control**: Each generation overwrites the previous result.
- **State Entanglement**: The content state and system configuration are tightly coupled.
- **Undo Not Supported**: Users could not revert to earlier versions, once new content was generated.

To address these issues, we apply the **Memento Pattern**. Each time the user makes a meaningful change, such as editing a paragraph or regenerating text, the current state is captured in a memento. The system can then *roll back* to any previous version, enabling a full undo/redo stack or revision history.

Note: *In this case study, we will focus on implementing useful classes to apply the design model concept.*

Applying the Memento Pattern

We will define an Originator **`EditorSession`** whose state can change and be saved, a Memento **`EditorSnapshot`** that stores state securely, and a Caretaker **`HistoryManager`** that manages the stack of saved states.

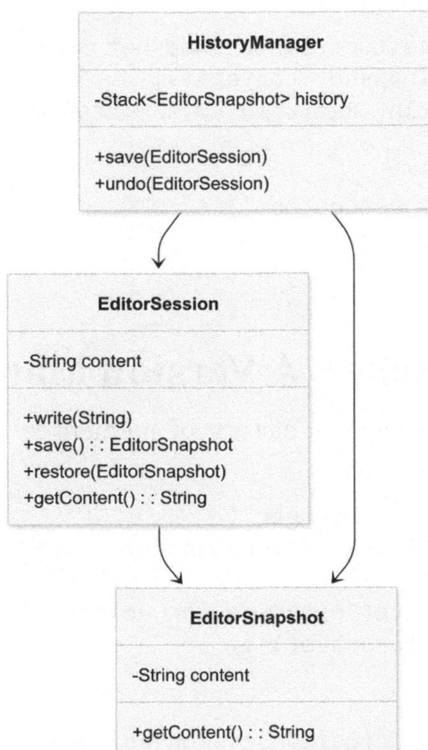

Figure 4.6: *Memento Pattern - An AI Writing Assistant*

Create the Memento Snapshot

`EditorSnapshot` record represents a "frozen" version of the generated or edited textual content.

```
public record EditorSnapshot(String content) { }
```

Create the Originator: A Stateful Object

This class modifies its state based on the current text and can save or restore it.

```
public class EditorSession {
   private String content;

   public void write(String newText) {
       content = newText;
System.out.println("Current content: " + content);
   }

   public EditorSnapshotsave() {
       return new EditorSnapshot(content);
   }

   public void restore(EditorSnapshot snapshot) {
this.content = snapshot.content();
System.out.println("Restored to: " + content);
   }

   public String getContent() {
       return content;
   }
}
```

Create the Caretaker: A Version Manager

The version manager maintains a history of mementos and allows actions to be undone.

```
public class HistoryManager {
   private final Stack<EditorSnapshot> history = new Stack<>();

   public void save(EditorSession editor) {
history.push(editor.save());
   }

   public void undo(EditorSession editor) {
       if (!history.isEmpty()) {
```

```
EditorSnapshot snapshot = history.pop();
editor.restore(snapshot);
      } else {
System.out.println("No history to undo.");
      }
   }
}
```

The Memento Pattern provides a clean and reliable mechanism for tracking and restoring object states in systems that evolve dynamically. By encapsulating the saved state, it avoids breaking encapsulation while enabling undo, versioning, and state recovery.

Next, we will explore the **Observer Pattern**, which enables real-time synchronization between components, making it perfect for live feedback or adaptive user interfaces.

Observer Pattern

The Observer Pattern is a behavioral design pattern that enables a one-to-many dependency between objects such that when one object, the subject, changes state, all its observers are automatically notified and updated.

This pattern is ideal for:

- Real-time data synchronization between components.
- Creating reactive architectures where changes propagate automatically.
- Supporting event-driven designs such as UI updates, notifications, or AI model feedback.

Case Study

Imagine a collaborative Generative AI writing tool where multiple components need to stay synchronized:

- The **AI Generator** updates the content.
- A **Sentiment Analyzer** evaluates tone changes.
- A **User Interface Preview** refreshes live output.
- A **Logging Service** tracks all auditing changes.

Initial challenges:

- **Manual Updates**: Each component had to be manually triggered whenever content changed.
- **Tight Coupling**: Components were aware of each other, breaking modularity.

- **Inconsistent State**: Some modules processed stale data if not updated in a timely manner.

To solve this, we apply the **Observer Pattern**, allowing all interested components to subscribe to the state of the editor and receive automatic, decoupled notifications when the content changes.

Note: *In this case study, we will focus on implementing useful classes to apply the design model concept.*

Applying the Observer Pattern

We design a collaborative writing module using the Observer Pattern, implementing a Subject `EditorSession` that holds the text and notifies observers. This includes an Observer interface with concrete classes such as `SentimentAnalyzer`, `LivePreview`, and `ChangeLogger`, as well as a flow where changes to content automatically trigger updates across observers.

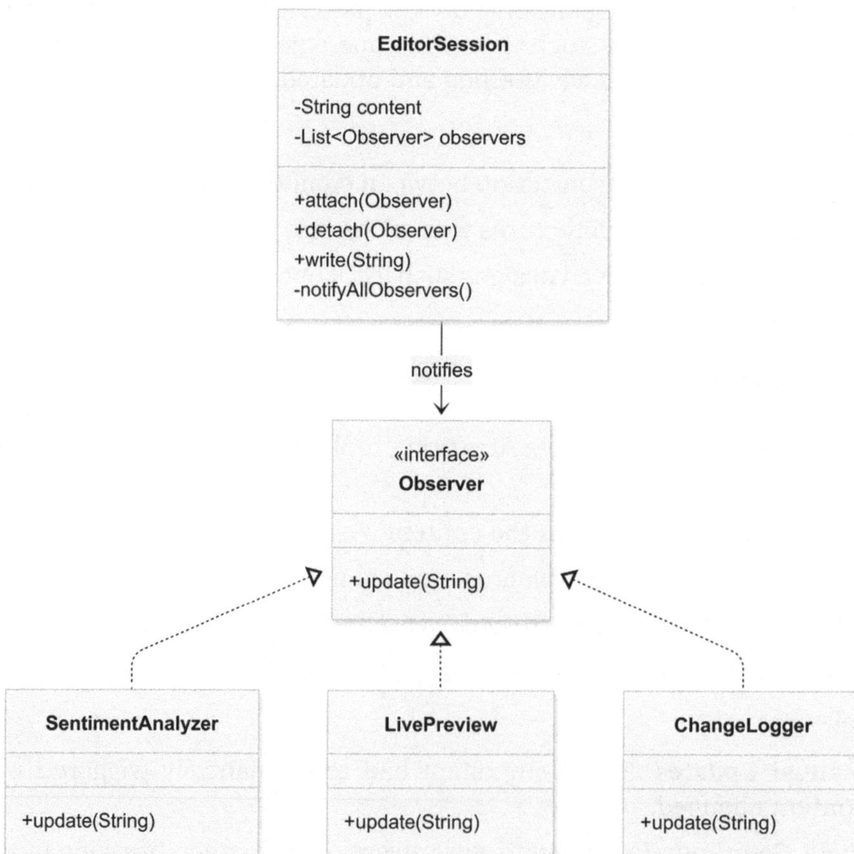

Figure 4.7: *Observer Pattern - Real-Time Generative AI Editor*

Define the Observer Interface

A simple yet powerful interface: each observer defines what it does when notified.

```
public interface Observer {
   void update(String newContent);
}
```

Create the Subject: An Editor Class

This class manages the textual content; whenever writing occurs, all observers are automatically notified.

```
public class EditorSession {
   private String content = "";
   private final List<Observer> observers = new ArrayList<>();

   public void attach(Observer observer) {
observers.add(observer);
   }

   public void detach(Observer observer) {
observers.remove(observer);
   }

   public void write(String newContent) {
this.content = newContent;
System.out.println("New content written: " + content);
notifyAllObservers();
   }

   private void notifyAllObservers() {
       for (Observer observer : observers) {
observer.update(content);
       }
   }
}
```

Implement Concrete Observers

Each of these observers plays a specific role, independent of the **EditorSession**.

```
public class SentimentAnalyzer implements Observer {
   @Override
   public void update(String newContent) {
       String sentiment = newContent.toLowerCase().contains
("success") ? "positive" : "neutral";
```

```
System.out.println("Sentiment analysis: " + sentiment);
    }
}
```

Note: *The rest of the concrete implement in the source code.*

The Observer Pattern provides an elegant and efficient solution for building reactive systems where components need to stay synchronized automatically. By decoupling the subject from its observers, it enables modular and scalable designs, eliminating the need for manual updates across dependent components.

Next, we will explore the **State Pattern**, which addresses the challenge of dynamically changing the behavior of an object based on its internal state.

State Pattern

The State Pattern is a behavioral design pattern that enables an object to dynamically change its behavior when its internal state changes. Instead of using conditionals to manage state-based behavior, the pattern delegates state-specific logic to separate classes.

This pattern enables:

- A clean separation of concerns between states and transitions.
- Simplified logic when managing multiple behavioral modes.
- Scalability for systems where behavior evolves based on internal or external stimuli.

Case Study

Imagine a Generative AI assistant used in customer service chat. It behaves differently depending on the emotional state or interaction context of the user:

- In a *neutral* mode, it gives standard informative responses.
- In *frustrated* mode, it becomes more empathetic and apologetic.
- In *happy* mode, it adds engaging or promotional tones.

Initial challenges:

- **Spaghetti Logic**: Behavior controlled via multiple if/else or switch statements.
- **Unscalable Design**: Adding a new mode required modifying a monolithic method, which is not scalable.
- **Low Cohesion**: All behaviors are combined in a single class, making it difficult to test or evolve.

We address this by applying the **State Pattern**, where each emotional state is represented as a separate class, encapsulating specific response logic. The chatbot can then change state at runtime, altering its behavior cleanly and contextually.

Note: *In this case study, we will focus on implementing useful classes to apply the design model concept.*

Applying the State Pattern

We implement a stateful chatbot whose tone changes dynamically based on detected user sentiment by building a **`Context`** class, **`Chatbot`**, which holds the current state. This class includes a **`ChatState`** interface with concrete state classes, such as **`NeutralState`**, **`FrustratedState`**, and **`HappyState`**, enabling dynamic switching of behavior based on internal conditions.

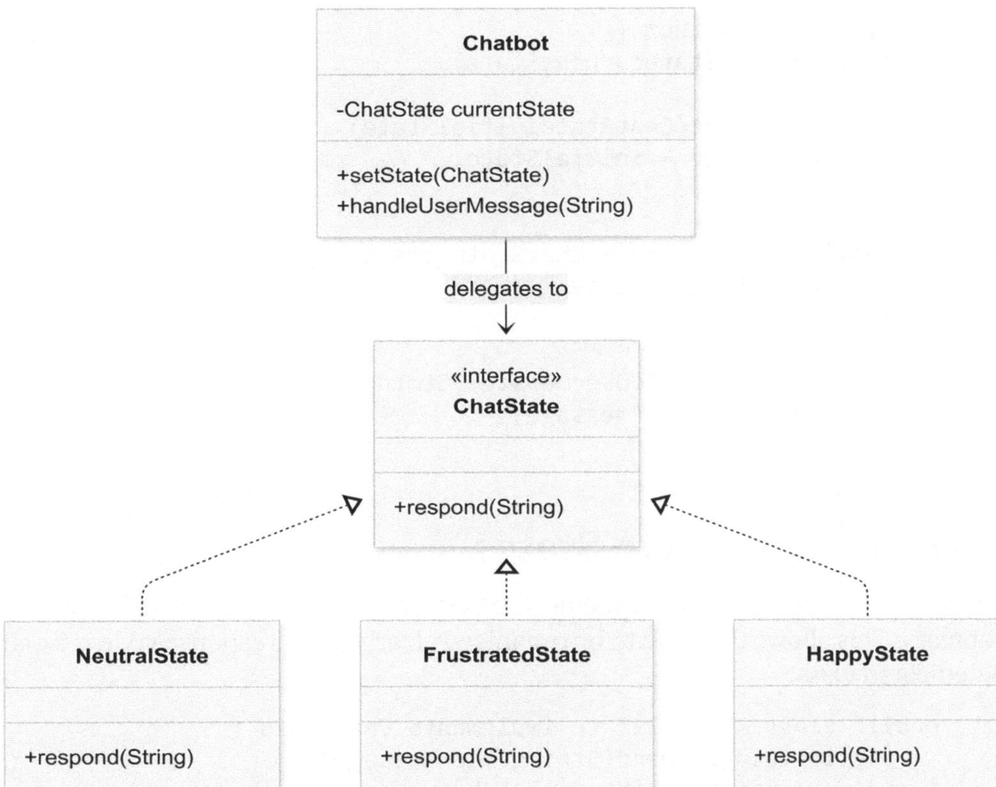

Figure 4.8: *State Pattern - An Adaptive AI Chatbot*

Define the ChatState Interface

An abstraction that ensures each state implements a consistent response strategy.

```
public interface ChatState {
   void respond(String userMessage);
}
```

Create the ChatBot Class

The **Chatbot** class does not directly decide how to respond; it fully delegates this responsibility to an object representing its current state. To change its behavior, you inject a new state, allowing its responses to be dynamically modified without altering the internal logic of the **Chatbot**.

```
public class Chatbot {
   private ChatStatecurrentState;

   public Chatbot(ChatStateinitialState) {
this.currentState = initialState;
   }

   public void setState(ChatState state) {
this.currentState = state;
   }

   public void handleUserMessage(String message) {
currentState.respond(message);
   }
}
```

Implement Concrete States

Each state class represents a specific behavior of the chatbot, with its tone and vocabulary. This allows the code to be organized clearly: each response style is isolated in a dedicated class.

```
public class NeutralState implements ChatState {
   public void respond(String userMessage) {
System.out.println("[Neutral] Thank you for your question. Let me
look that up for you.");
   }
}
```

Note: *The rest of the concrete implementation is in the source code.*

The State Pattern provides an elegant solution to the challenges of dynamic behavior and mode switching in intelligent systems. By encapsulating state-specific logic in dedicated classes it eliminates conditional complexity and improves scalability.

Next, we will explore the **Strategy Pattern**, which focuses on choosing and swapping algorithms dynamically to select the best generative approach depending on the context.

Strategy Pattern

The Strategy Pattern is a behavioral design pattern that enables the dynamic selection and interchange of algorithms at runtime. Instead of embedding algorithm logic inside a class, the pattern delegates it to interchangeable strategy objects, promoting flexibility and reusability.

This pattern is ideal when:

- Multiple algorithms can be used to perform the same task.
- The best approach depends on the context, input, configuration, and user preferences.
- You want to avoid conditional branching or hardcoding logic.

Case Study

Imagine a content generation platform that offers multiple AI models to produce text:

- GPT Model for a rich, creative generation.
- Claude Model for accurate summarization.
- Gemini Model for fast responses with minimal resources.

The system should dynamically choose the right strategy based on user preferences, generation context, creative, factual, fast, or runtime configuration.

Initial challenges:

- **Rigid Implementation**: Generation logic is tightly coupled with a single AI model.
- **Low Adaptability**: Switching algorithms required modifying core logic.
- **Limited Testing**: Strategy comparison was not modular or configurable.

To solve this, we apply the **Strategy Pattern**. Each generation algorithm is encapsulated in a class implementing a standard interface. The client can dynamically choose or switch between strategies at runtime, cleanly and without changing the core logic.

Note: *In this case study, we will focus on implementing useful classes to apply the design model concept.*

Applying the Strategy Pattern

We build a flexible text generation system using the Strategy Pattern by implementing a **`GenerationStrategy`** interface for all strategies, including concrete strategies such as **`GPTStrategy`**, **`ClaudeStrategy`**, and **`GeminiStrategy`**, as well as a **`ContentGenerator`** context class that delegates generation to the selected strategy.

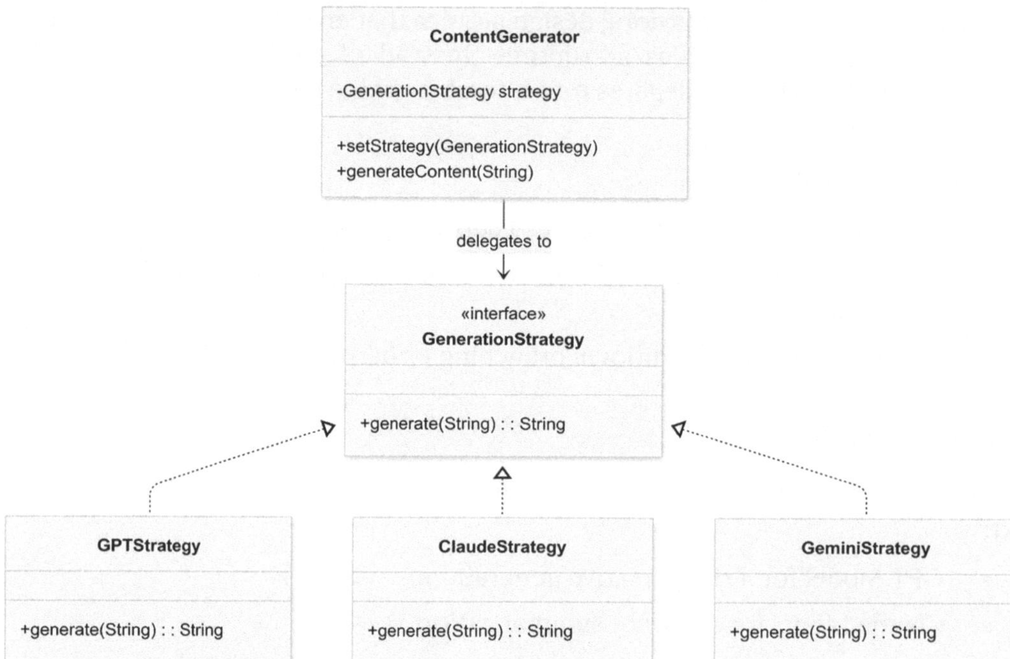

Figure 4.9: *Strategy Pattern - Dynamic AI Text Generator*

Define the `GenerationStrategy` Interface

The **`GenerationStrategy`** interface serves as a standard contract that all generation models must adhere to. Through this single interface, models can be easily swapped without modifying the rest of the code, ensuring maximum flexibility and facilitating the evolution or adaptation of the application.

```
public interface GenerationStrategy {
   String generate(String prompt);
}
```

Implement Concrete Strategies

Each class implements a specific behavior while adhering to the same interface contract.

```
public class GPTStrategy implements GenerationStrategy {
   public String generate(String prompt) {
       return "[GPT] Generated creative content for: " + prompt;
   }
}
```

Note: *The rest of the concrete strategy is in the source code.*

Create the `ContentGenerator` Class

This component delegates generation to the chosen strategy while remaining agnostic to the actual implementation.

```
public class ContentGenerator {
   private GenerationStrategy strategy;

   public ContentGenerator(GenerationStrategy strategy) {
this.strategy = strategy;
   }

   public void setStrategy(GenerationStrategy strategy) {
this.strategy = strategy;
   }

   public void generateContent(String prompt) {
       String result = strategy.generate(prompt);
System.out.println(result);
   }
}
```

The Strategy Pattern offers a powerful and elegant way to manage algorithm selection in systems that must adapt dynamically. By encapsulating each strategy in its class, the pattern promotes modularity, testability, and runtime flexibility.

Next, we will explore the **Template Method Pattern**, which standardizes the structure of an algorithm while allowing key steps to be customized.

Template Method Pattern

The Template Method Pattern is a behavioral design pattern that outlines the structure of an algorithm within a base class, allowing subclasses to override specific steps without altering the structure of the algorithm.

This pattern is ideal when:

- We have multiple variations of a process that share the same overall structure.
- We want to enforce consistency while allowing for controlled customization.
- We need to avoid duplicating common logic across similar operations.

Case Study

Imagine a generative AI platform that supports the automated creation of reports. Every report follows the same overall structure:

- Introduction
- Main content generation varies depending on the report type
- Conclusion

However, depending on the type of report marketing, technical or educational, the primary generation step differs significantly in tone, model choice, and structure.

Initial challenges:

- **Duplicated Logic**: Shared steps such as introduction and conclusion were copied across classes.
- **Inconsistent Workflows**: The lack of an enforced structure resulted in varying formats.
- **Challenging Onboarding**: New report types required for writing boilerplate logic repeatedly.

To address these, we apply the **Template Method Pattern**. The overall workflow is defined once in an abstract class, and each type of report overrides only the content generation logic.

This ensures consistency across reports, improves maintainability, and supports flexible customization.

Note: *In this case study, we will focus on implementing useful classes to apply the design model concept.*

Applying the Template Method Pattern

We will design a report generator that enforces a three-step structure: intro, content, conclusion, with only the primary content step customizable.

We will build:

- An abstract base class `ReportGenerator` with a `generateReport()` template method.
- Concrete subclasses for each report type: `MarketingReport`, `TechnicalReport`, `EducationalReport`.

- A client class that triggers the report creation.

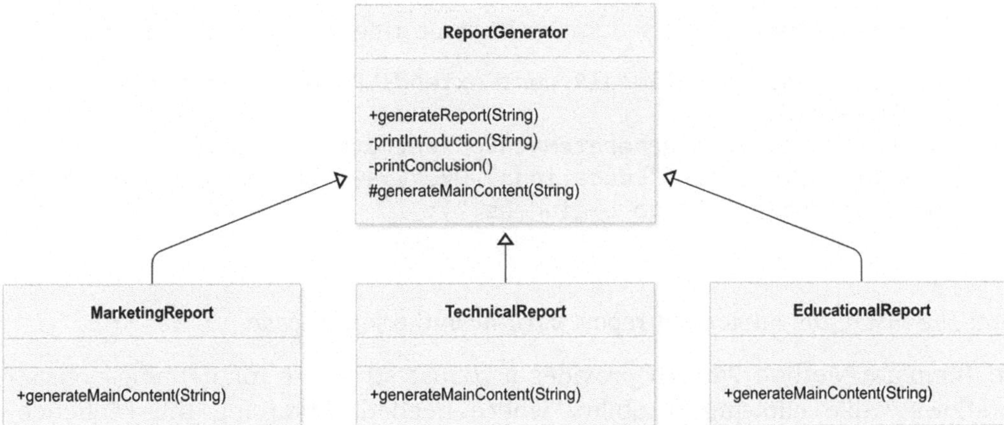

Figure 4.10: *Template Method Pattern - Structured AI Report Generation*

Create the Abstract `ReportGenerator` Class

The **`ReportGenerator`** class defines a **`generateReport()`** method that sets the structure, with the introduction and conclusion steps standardized, while the core content is left to the subclasses.

```
public abstract class ReportGenerator {

// Template method
public final void generateReport(String topic) {
printIntroduction(topic);
generateMainContent(topic);   // Abstract - varies by subclass
printConclusion();
   }

   private void printIntroduction(String topic) {
System.out.println("Introduction: This report covers the topic of
" + topic + ".");
   }

   protected abstract void generateMainContent(String topic);

   private void printConclusion() {
System.out.println("Conclusion: Report generated using AI
automation.");
   }
}
```

Implement Report Variants

Each class defines the variable section without altering the process skeleton.

```
public class EducationalReport extends ReportGenerator {
   @Override
   protected void generateMainContent(String topic) {
System.out.println("Educational Overview: Teaching fundamentals
of '" + topic + "' to beginners.");
   }
}
```

Note: *The rest of the implement report variant in the source code*

The Template Method Pattern provides a robust structure for defining consistent workflows while allowing flexibility where needed. Enforcing the sequence of operations and isolating variation points simplifies maintenance and guarantees predictable output.

Next, we will explore the **Visitor Pattern**, which separates algorithms from the objects on which they operate.

Visitor Pattern

The Visitor Pattern is a behavioral design pattern that allows you to separate algorithms from the objects they operate on, enabling the addition of new operations without modifying the objects themselves.

This pattern is ideal when:

- We want to apply multiple unrelated operations on complex object structures.
- We need to extend functionalities without changing the data models.

Case Study

Imagine an AI system that generates document content composed of various sections, each represented by a distinct class:

- **`TextSection`:** Plain generated content.
- **`ImageSection`:** Generated visual content.
- **`QuoteSection`:** Generated inspirational quotes.

Now, we want to:

- Export this content in different formats: HTML, Markdown, and PDF.
- Run analytics such as word counting and sentiment detection.

- Log or transform certain content types.

Initial challenges:

- **Scattered Logic**: Export, logging, and transformation were implemented inside each section class.
- **Poor Extensibility**: Adding a new operation meant modifying every class.
- **Violated SRP**: Each content type had too many responsibilities, including data and logic.

To solve this, we apply the **Visitor Pattern**. Each section class accepts visitors, exporters, and analyzers that encapsulate specific operations. This keeps the data model clean while allowing flexible and extensible behaviors to be applied externally.

Note: *In this case study, we will focus on implementing useful classes to apply the design model concept.*

Applying the Visitor Pattern

We built a visitor-based content processing system.

We will implement:

- A **`ContentVisitor`** interface and multiple concrete visitors, such as **`MarkdownExporter`**.
- A **`ContentElement`** interface is implemented by section types **`TextSection`**, **`QuoteSection`**, and **`ImageSection`**.
- A client class that passes visitors to the elements for processing.

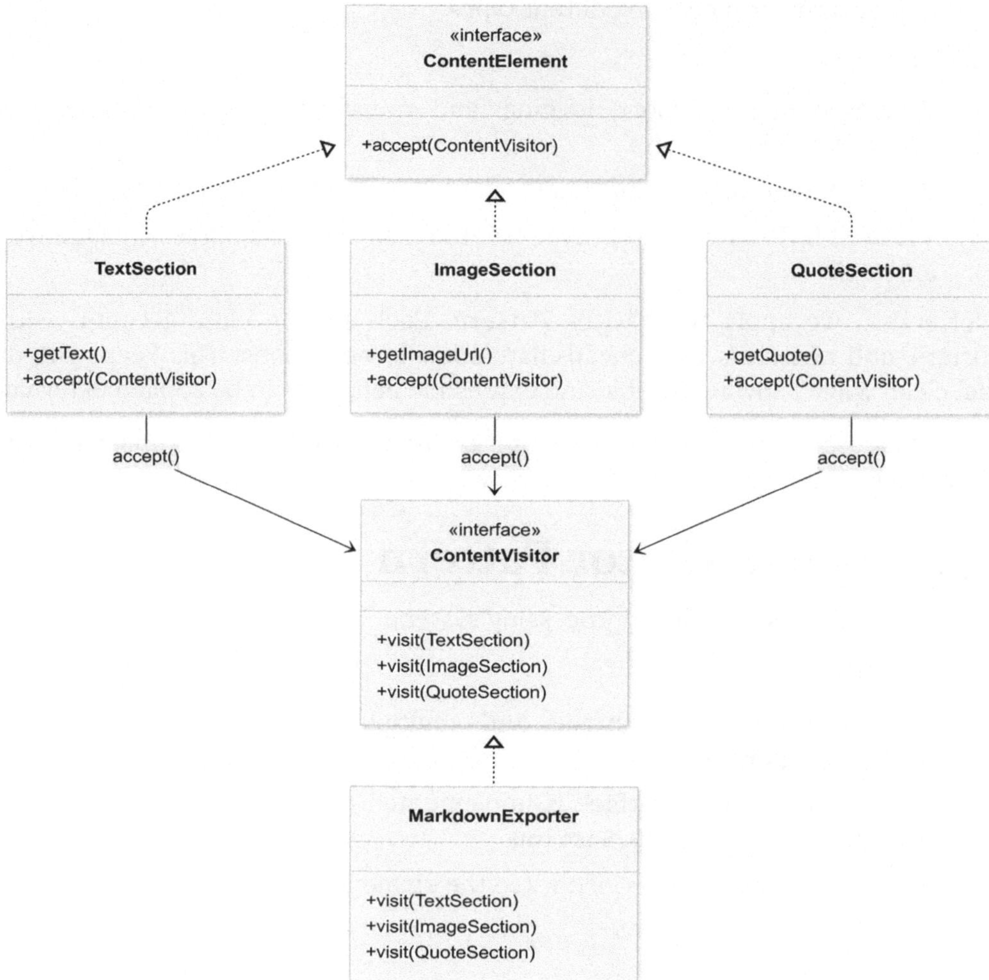

Figure 4.11: *Visitor Pattern - Processing AI-Generated Document Sections*

Create the `ContentVisitor` Interface

This interface defines a specific method for each type of visitable element. This ensures targeted and consistent processing.

```
public interface ContentVisitor {
   void visit(TextSection text);
   void visit(ImageSection image);
   void visit(QuoteSection quote);
}
```

Create the `ContentElement` Interface

All content elements implement this interface to enable external visitors to process them.

```
public interface ContentElement {
   void accept(ContentVisitor visitor);
}
```

Implement Content Elements

Each class is minimalist, responsible only for its data, and exposes an **`accept()`** method to delegate processing.

```
public record TextSection(String text) implements ContentElement {
   @Override
   public void accept(ContentVisitor visitor) {
visitor.visit(this);
   }
}
```

Note: *The rest of the content elements are in the source code.*

Create a Concrete Visitor: `MarkdownExporter`

This visitor transforms the content into Markdown format without changing the content classes.

```
public class MarkdownExporter implements ContentVisitor {
   @Override
   public void visit(TextSection text) {
System.out.println("-" + text.text());
   }

   @Override
   public void visit(ImageSection image) {
System.out.println("![image](" + image.imageUrl() + ")");
   }

   @Override
   public void visit(QuoteSection quote) {
System.out.println("> " + quote.quote());
   }
}
```

The Visitor Pattern offers a clean and powerful way to extend system behavior without modifying the existing data structures. It brings modularity, clarity, and proper separation of concerns in systems where content needs to be enriched, exported, or analyzed in multiple ways.

With this final pattern, you now possess a complete toolkit of Behavioral Design Patterns that can enhance the design of scalable, maintainable, and intelligent Java applications.

Conclusion

In this chapter, we have explored several essential Behavioral Design Patterns, including *Chain of Responsibility*, *Command*, *Interpreter*, *Iterator*, *Mediator*, *Memento*, *Observer*, *State*, *Strategy*, *Template Method*, and *Visitor*. Each pattern was discussed with practical use cases, clear motivations, and Java-based implementations relevant to modern applications.

These patterns provide robust solutions for managing the flow of logic, coordinating interactions, and assigning responsibilities between objects. By decoupling behaviors and improving modularity, they make software systems more adaptable, testable, and easier to evolve.

In the next chapter, we shall explore **Concurrency Design Patterns in Java**, which address the challenges of executing tasks in parallel, managing shared resources, and ensuring thread-safe operations. These patterns are essential for building performant and responsive applications in multi-threaded environments.

Points to Remember

- Behavioral Patterns enhance the modularity, flexibility, and testability of code.
- When well applied, they strengthen maintainability and facilitate the long-term evolution of systems.
- Each pattern has its strengths and limitations: it is necessary to choose them based on the context.

Multiple Choice Questions

1. Which pattern allows you to dynamically change the execution algorithm?
    a. Strategy
    b. State
    c. Memento
    d. Observer

2. Which pattern allows you to delegate the execution of an operation to an object encapsulating the request?
    a. Chain of Responsibility
    b. Strategy
    c. Command
    d. Mediator
3. Which pattern is best suited to applying multiple actions to a structure without modifying it?
    a. Interpreter
    b. Visitor
    c. Template Method
    d. Iterator

Answers

1. a
2. c
3. b

Questions

1. When would using the Strategy pattern be preferable to using the State pattern? Why or why not?
2. How can the Observer Pattern be combined with the Mediator Pattern to build a responsive but well-structured architecture?
3. If you were to design an adaptive AI learning platform, what behavior patterns would you use and why?

Key Terms

- **Context**: Object that holds the current state or execution data passed to strategies or states.
- **Strategy**: Object representing an interchangeable algorithm.
- **State**: Object encapsulating conditional behavior based on internal state.

- **Command**: Object encapsulating an action, executable independently.
- **Visitor**: Object that traverses a data structure to apply one or more operations without modifying it.
- **Memento**: Object that stores an internal state without exposing its structure.
- **Template Method**: Method that defines an algorithm structure with customizable steps.
- **Subject/Observer**: Pattern where the observed subject notifies observers of state changes.
- **Handler**: Element in a chain of responsibility that processes or forwards a request.
- **Iterator**: Object that allows sequential access to a collection without exposing its internal structure.

CHAPTER 5
Concurrency Design Patterns in Java

Introduction

Concurrency Design Patterns are established and reusable solutions to common challenges encountered when building multithreaded software systems. They provide structured approaches to managing tasks that execute in parallel, coordinating access to shared resources, and ensuring the integrity and responsiveness of applications in a concurrent environment. The primary goal of these patterns is to enhance the efficiency, thread safety, and scalability of Java systems.

This chapter explores a range of fundamental Concurrency Design Patterns, including ***Thread Pools***, ***Producer-Consumer***, ***Read-Write Locks***, ***Futures***, ***the fork/join pattern***, and the Java Concurrency Utilities. Each pattern will be analyzed through a precise technical definition, a real-world problem that motivates its usage, a step-by-step practical implementation in Java, and a visual representation to facilitate understanding.

By exploring this chapter, you will gain the skills to recognize common concurrency issues in Java, choose the right patterns to handle synchronization and performance challenges, implement them using core Java concurrency tools, and design multithreaded systems that are robust, maintainable, and efficient.

Structure

In this chapter, we will cover the following topics:

- Thread Pool Pattern
- Producer-Consumer Pattern
- Read-Write Lock Pattern
- Future Pattern

- Fork/Join Pattern
- Java Concurrency Utilities

Thread Pool Pattern

The Thread Pool Pattern is a structural concurrency design solution that enables efficient management of parallel task execution. It relies on a predefined and reusable set of threads, known as a *pool*. Tasks are submitted to this pool and executed asynchronously, without the need to create a new thread for each request.

This pattern addresses common concurrency issues such as:

- CPU overload due to excessive thread creation.
- Uncontrolled memory consumption.
- Lack of execution control.
- Increased complexity in synchronizing parallel tasks.

Case Study

Imagine an e-health platform that allows patients to schedule appointments, receive reminders, and synchronize their medical records with partner hospitals. The system must handle thousands of concurrent user requests, such as appointment bookings, SMS notifications, and PDF report generation.

Problems encountered without the Thread Pool:

- Uncontrolled thread creation, memory saturation.
- Slow and unstable system during peak times.
- Difficulty in maintaining and prioritizing processes.

Note: *In this case study, we will focus on implementing useful classes to apply the design model concept.*

Applying the Thread Pool Pattern

As shown in the diagram, the **`ExecutorService`** receives tasks submitted by the user, assigns them to available threads, or places them in an internal queue when all threads are busy.

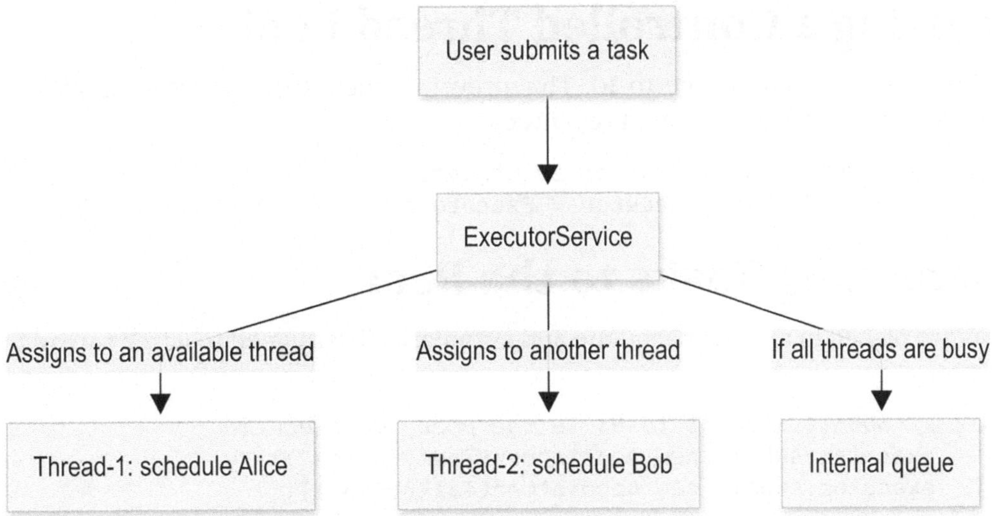

Figure 5.1: *Thread Pool - Execution Flow*

Defining the Task to Execute

Each task implements **Runnable**, which allows it to be easily submitted to the thread pool. The contents of the **run()** method contain the logic to be executed in parallel.

```
// Class representing a business task (appointment scheduling) to
be executed concurrently
public class AppointmentTask implements Runnable {
   private final String patientName;

   public AppointmentTask(String patientName) {
       this.patientName = patientName; // Patient name to person-
alize the task
   }

   @Override
   public void run() {
       // Simulating the appointment scheduling logic
       System.out.println("Scheduling appointment for " +
patientName +
                  " on thread: " + Thread.currentThread().
getName());
       // Here you might check availability, persist to DB, send
confirmation email...
   }
}
```

Creating a Controlled Thread Pool

The pool limits thread usage to 10. This prevents uncontrolled thread creation and ensures controlled use of system resources.

```
// Create a fixed pool of 10 threads
ExecutorService executor = Executors.newFixedThreadPool(10);
```

Submitting Tasks to the Pool

Tasks are placed in an internal queue and automatically assigned to a free thread from the pool.

```
// Submit several tasks to the pool for execution
executor.submit(new AppointmentTask("Alice"));
executor.submit(new AppointmentTask("Bob"));
```

Cleanly Shut down the Executor

It is crucial to call `shutdown()` to properly release resources. This signals the executor to stop accepting new tasks.

```
// Gracefully shut down the pool after task submission
executor.shutdown();
```

Output console:

```
Scheduling appointment for Bob on thread: pool-1-thread-2
Scheduling appointment for Alice on thread: pool-1-thread-1
```

The Thread Pool Pattern is essential for any Java application that executes many simultaneous tasks. It helps prevent overloads while simplifying concurrent task management.

In more advanced scenarios, tasks are often produced by generators such as user actions, schedulers, and need to be processed by dedicated consumers such as services, and workers. To manage this flow, we will explore the **Producer-Consumer Pattern**, which enables synchronized task exchange using shared queues.

Producer-Consumer Pattern

The Producer-Consumer Pattern is a concurrency design solution used to synchronize the exchange of data or tasks between two or more independent components:

- **Producers**, which generate data or tasks;
- **Consumers**, which process them.

A shared queue, bounded or unbounded, is used to decouple the rate of production from consumption. This pattern prevents contention, overload, and data loss and is often implemented with thread-safe data structures, such as *BlockingQueue*, in Java.

Case Study

Imagine a food delivery platform that connects hungry customers with nearby restaurants. Customers place orders through a mobile or web application, while backend services are responsible for validating, dispatching, and routing those orders to the kitchen in real-time. Initially, each order was processed immediately upon arrival, with the system relying on tightly coupled procedural logic.

The initial challenges include:

- **High CPU Usage and Contention:** Orders were handled synchronously, resulting in intense CPU activity and thread contention, particularly under high load.
- **Scalability Limitations**: During peak hours, the system struggled to process simultaneous orders, resulting in delays and even dropped requests.
- **Rigid Architecture**: The consumer logic was directly tied to the incoming request pipeline, making the system inflexible and rigid to extend.

To address these issues, we apply the **Producer-Consumer Pattern** using a thread-safe queue such as a BlockingQueue. This pattern introduces a decoupled architecture where producers order submissions, enqueue tasks, and consumers order processors to handle them asynchronously. It enables the system to absorb surges in demand gracefully, ensures that no orders are lost, and promotes better scalability and responsiveness, especially during high-traffic periods.

Note: *In this case study, we will focus on implementing useful classes to apply the design model concept.*

Applying the Producer-Consumer Pattern

We will implement a **thread-safe queue-based communication system** where producers enqueue new orders, and consumers dequeue and process them independently. We will use `LinkedBlockingQueue` of Java for thread safety and automatic blocking when the queue is full or empty.

The following figure presents the interaction diagram of the Producer-Consumer pattern, where a producer submits orders to a shared queue, and multiple consumers retrieve and process these orders concurrently.

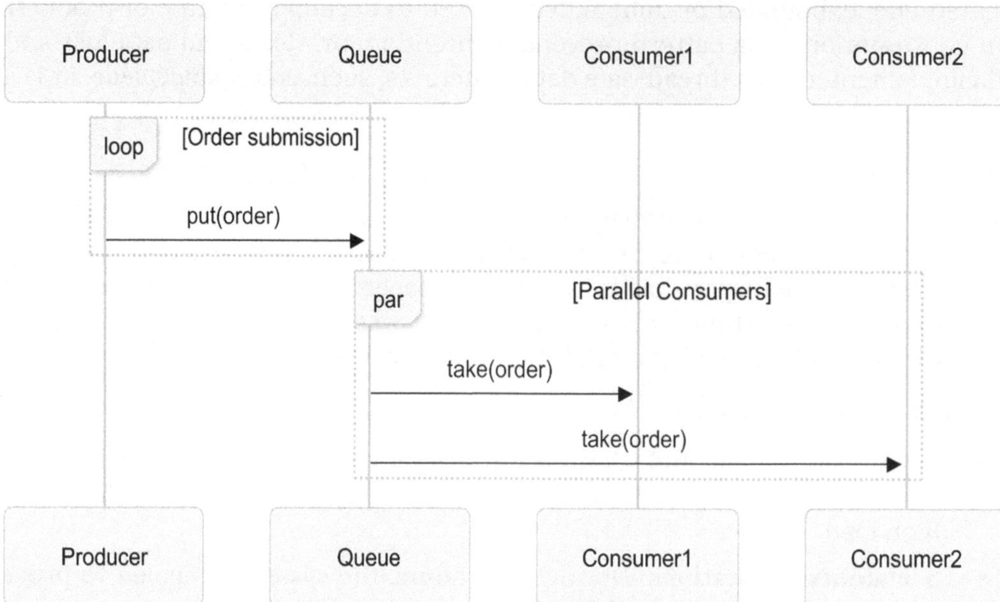

Figure 5.2: *Producer-Consumer Pattern - Interaction*

Defining the Order Entity

This class models the objects exchanged between producers and consumers. It encapsulates the data that will move through the queue.

```
// Represents a food delivery order from a customer.
// Simple value object that holds order metadata such as an order ID.
public record Order(String orderId) { }
```

Creating the Shared Order Queue

The **BlockingQueue** handles thread-safe communication and automatic blocking when full for producers or empty for consumers, eliminating busy waiting and race conditions.

```
// Shared queue that holds orders between producers and consumers.
// Using a bounded queue prevents memory overflow under high load.
BlockingQueue<Order> orderQueue = new LinkedBlockingQueue<>(50);
```

Implementing the Producer

The producer continuously creates new orders and adds them to the queue. Blocking behavior ensures that the system does not overwhelm consumers or exhaust resources.

```
// Simulates incoming orders from customers, one at a time.
public class OrderProducer implements Runnable {
   private final BlockingQueue<Order> queue;

   public OrderProducer(BlockingQueue<Order> queue) {
       this.queue = queue;
   }

   @Override
   public void run() {
       int i = 1;
       while (true) {
           try {
               // Create a new order with a unique ID
               Order order = new Order("Order-" + i++);

               // Put the order into the queue, blocks if the
queue is full
               queue.put(order);
               System.out.println("New order received: " + order.
orderId());

               // Simulate delay between customer orders
               Thread.sleep(500);
           } catch (InterruptedException e) {
               Thread.currentThread().interrupt(); // Respect
interruption policy
           }
       }
   }
}
```

Implementing the Consumer

The consumer thread pulls orders from the queue and processes them. Multiple consumers can run in parallel, improving throughput. Blocking ensures proper flow control.

```
// Simulates backend workers who process the orders in parallel.
public class OrderConsumer implements Runnable {
   private final BlockingQueue<Order> queue;

   public OrderConsumer(BlockingQueue<Order> queue) {
       this.queue = queue;
```

```
    }

    @Override
    public void run() {
        while (true) {
            try {
                // Retrieve an order from the queue, blocks if the
queue is empty
                Order order = queue.take();

                // Simulate processing the order
                System.out.println("Processing " + order.orderId()
+
                        " on thread " + Thread.currentThread().
getName());

                Thread.sleep(1000); // Simulate time taken for
processing
            } catch (InterruptedException e) {
                Thread.currentThread().interrupt();
            }
        }
    }
}
```

Launching Producers and Consumers

This is the system entry point. It wires up the producers and consumers with a shared queue, allowing them to interact concurrently. We can easily scale the number of consumers here.

```
public class Main {
    public static void main( String[] args ) {
        // Initialize the shared order queue
        BlockingQueue<Order> orderQueue = new LinkedBlocking
Queue<>(50);

        // Start one producer thread
        Thread producerThread = new Thread(new OrderProducer
(orderQueue));

        // Start two consumer threads for processing orders
        Thread consumerThread1 = new Thread(new OrderConsumer
(orderQueue));
        Thread consumerThread2 = new Thread(new OrderConsumer
(orderQueue));
```

```
            // Start all threads
            producerThread.start();
            consumerThread1.start();
            consumerThread2.start();
        }
    }
```

Output Console:

```
New order received: Order-1
Processing Order-1 on thread Thread-1
New order received: Order-2
Processing Order-2 on thread Thread-2
New order received: Order-3
Processing Order-3 on thread Thread-1
New order received: Order-4
Processing Order-4 on thread Thread-2
```

The Producer-Consumer Pattern provides a clean, scalable solution for asynchronous task handling between decoupled components. It is ideal for data pipelines, order management, logging systems, or any workflow involving continuous task exchange.

However, not all concurrency problems involve task flow. Sometimes, multiple threads access the same resource and must do so in a controlled and optimized way. When reading is frequent and writing is rare, locking everything leads to poor performance. This brings us to the **Read-Write Lock Pattern**, which allows for high concurrency with **differentiated access policies.**

Read-Write Lock Pattern

The Read-Write Lock Pattern is a concurrency design strategy used to optimize access to shared resources that are frequently read but infrequently modified. Instead of allowing only one thread at a time, like traditional mutual exclusion, this pattern distinguishes between readers and writers:

- Multiple threads can **read** the data simultaneously.
- Only one thread can **write** at a time, and it requires **exclusive access** with no readers or writers.

Java provides the **`ReadWriteLock`** **interface** and the **`ReentrantReadWriteLock`** implementation to help developers build performant and thread-safe systems. Java 8 introduced **`StampedLock`**, a lightweight locking mechanism that supports optimistic reads and atomic lock upgrading and downgrading, but it does not support reentrancy.

Case Study

Imagine a digital platform called **SmartLibrary**, designed to let users browse, search, and update information about books, such as titles, authors, availability, and ratings. To ensure fast access, the system keeps book metadata in memory.

The initial challenges include:

- **Heavy Read Traffic**: Thousands of users regularly perform read operations, such as searching by title or checking availability.
- Occasionally, a smaller group of administrators update book details or modify stock levels.
- **Inefficient Synchronization**: Using a standard synchronized lock caused contention, as read operations were unnecessarily serialized, resulting in degraded overall performance.

To address these issues, we apply the **Read-Write Lock Pattern**. This pattern allows multiple threads to read shared data concurrently while still ensuring that write operations have exclusive access. It optimizes concurrency by allowing high-throughput read operations without compromising consistency during updates.

Note: *In this case study, we will focus on implementing useful classes to apply the design model concept.*

Applying the Read-Write Lock Pattern

We will use a **`ReentrantReadWriteLock`** to protect access to a shared `Map<String, String>` that stores book metadata.

- Readers will acquire the **read lock** to safely view book data concurrently.
- Writers will acquire the **write lock** for exclusive updates.

The following figure illustrates the Read-Write Lock pattern, where multiple reader threads acquire shared read access to the book catalog, while a single writer thread obtains exclusive write access to update the underlying in-memory map.

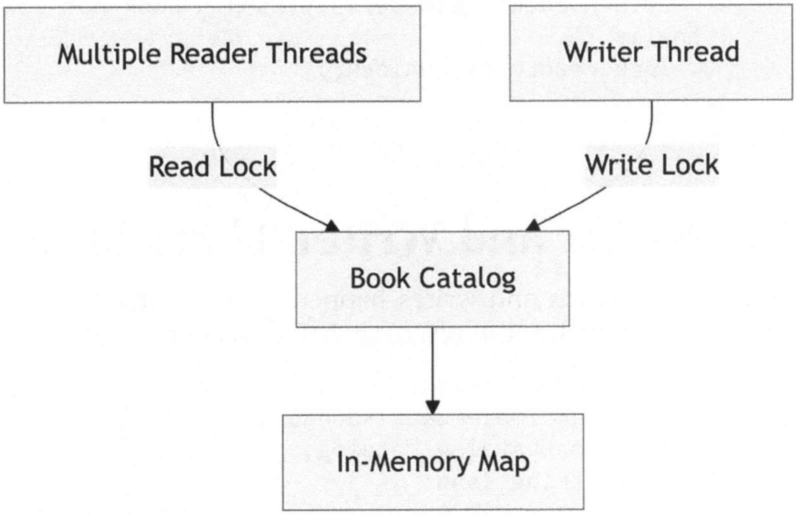

Figure 5.3: *Read-Write Lock Pattern - Read versus Write Flow*

Creating the Shared Data Structure and Lock

`ReentrantReadWriteLock` allows many concurrent reads but ensures write exclusivity. The try-finally structure guarantees proper unlocking.

```
// Simulates a shared book database (in-memory)
public class BookCatalog {
   private final Map<String, String> books = new HashMap<>();
   private final ReadWriteLock lock = new ReentrantRead-
WriteLock();

   // Adds or updates a book entry (write operation)
   public void addOrUpdateBook(String isbn, String title) {
       lock.writeLock().lock();
       try {
           books.put(isbn, title);
           System.out.println("Book updated: " + isbn + " -> " +
title);
       } finally {
           lock.writeLock().unlock();
       }
   }

   // Retrieves a book title by ISBN (read operation)
   public String getBook(String isbn) {
       lock.readLock().lock();
       try {
```

```
            return books.getOrDefault(isbn, "Book not found");
        } finally {
            lock.readLock().unlock();
        }
    }
}
```

Creating Reader and Writer Threads

In a real-world system, reads and writes happen concurrently and unpredictably. This example ensures clarity by adding a delay before readers begin.

```
// Simulates a reader thread: users browsing the library
public class Reader implements Runnable {
   private final BookCatalog catalog;
   private final String isbn;

   public Reader(BookCatalog catalog, String isbn) {
       this.catalog = catalog;
       this.isbn = isbn;
   }

   @Override
   public void run() {
       String book = catalog.getBook(isbn);
       System.out.println("Reading: " + isbn + " -> " + book +
               " on thread " + Thread.currentThread().getName());
   }
}
// Simulates a writer thread: an admin updating book metadata
public class Writer implements Runnable {
   private final BookCatalog catalog;
   private final String isbn;
   private final String title;

   public Writer(BookCatalog catalog, String isbn, String title)
{
       this.catalog = catalog;
       this.isbn = isbn;
       this.title = title;
   }

   @Override
   public void run() {
       catalog.addOrUpdateBook(isbn, title);
   }
}
```

Run the simulation

```
public class Main {
   public static void main( String[] args ) {
       BookCatalog catalog = new BookCatalog();

       // Create writer threads to update book data
       Thread writer1 = new Thread(new Writer(catalog,
"978-0132350884", "Clean Code"));
       Thread writer2 = new Thread(new Writer(catalog,
"978-0134494166", "Clean Architecture"));

       // Start writers
       writer1.start();
       writer2.start();

       // Delay allow to write complete before reads
       try { Thread.sleep(1000); } catch (InterruptedException
ignored) {}

       // Create reader threads
       for (int i = 0; i < 5; i++) {
           Thread reader = new Thread(new Reader(catalog,
"978-0132350884"));
           reader.start();
       }
   }
}
```

Output Console:

```
Book updated: 978-0132350884 -> Clean Code
Book updated: 978-0134494166 -> Clean Architecture
Reading: 978-0132350884 -> Clean Code on thread Thread-2
Reading: 978-0132350884 -> Clean Code on thread Thread-4
Reading: 978-0132350884 -> Clean Code on thread Thread-6
Reading: 978-0132350884 -> Clean Code on thread Thread-5
Reading: 978-0132350884 -> Clean Code on thread Thread-3
```

The Read-Write Lock Pattern is the go-to choice for systems with read-dominant workloads and shared resources. It strikes a smart balance between concurrency and consistency, improving performance without sacrificing correctness.

However, what if we want to schedule tasks for future execution, handle timeouts, or work with asynchronous results? That is where the **Future Pattern** comes in, enabling non-blocking operations with robust task control and result retrieval.

Future Pattern

The Future Pattern is a concurrency design strategy that enables the asynchronous execution of tasks, allowing the calling thread to continue processing while a background task is being completed. Instead of blocking until a result is available, the program receives a Future object as a placeholder and can later retrieve the result when needed.

In Java, this is commonly implemented using the `ExecutorService` and also through its `submit()` method, which returns a `Future<T>` object.

Note: *The* `CompletableFuture` *pattern extends Future by enabling non-blocking, composable asynchronous programming in Java. Through task chaining, combination, and built-in exception handling, developers are allowed to express complex asynchronous workflows without relying on blocking calls such as .get().*

Case Study

Imagine a travel booking platform that helps users find the best deals on flights and hotels. When a user searches for a trip, the system simultaneously:

- Queries multiple flight APIs;
- Queries various hotel booking engines;
- Aggregates and returns the best results to the user.

The initial challenges include:

- **Inconsistent Response Times**: External APIs respond anywhere between 500ms and 2 seconds, leading to unpredictable delays.
- **Slow User Experience**: A sequential approach to querying each service results in long page load times and frustrated users.
- **Resource Inefficiency**: Blocking calls keeps threads occupied unnecessarily, increasing server costs and limiting scalability.

To address these issues, we apply asynchronous programming with parallel execution. By sending flight and hotel search requests concurrently and using non-blocking techniques such as futures and reactive streams, the system significantly improves response times. This design minimizes thread usage, reduces latency, and enhances the overall user experience, especially under high-traffic conditions.

Note: *In this case study, we will focus on implementing useful classes to apply the design model concept.*

Applying the Future Pattern

The following sequence diagram illustrates this execution flow, showing how asynchronous flight and hotel search tasks are submitted, processed in parallel, and later combined, once both Future results become available.

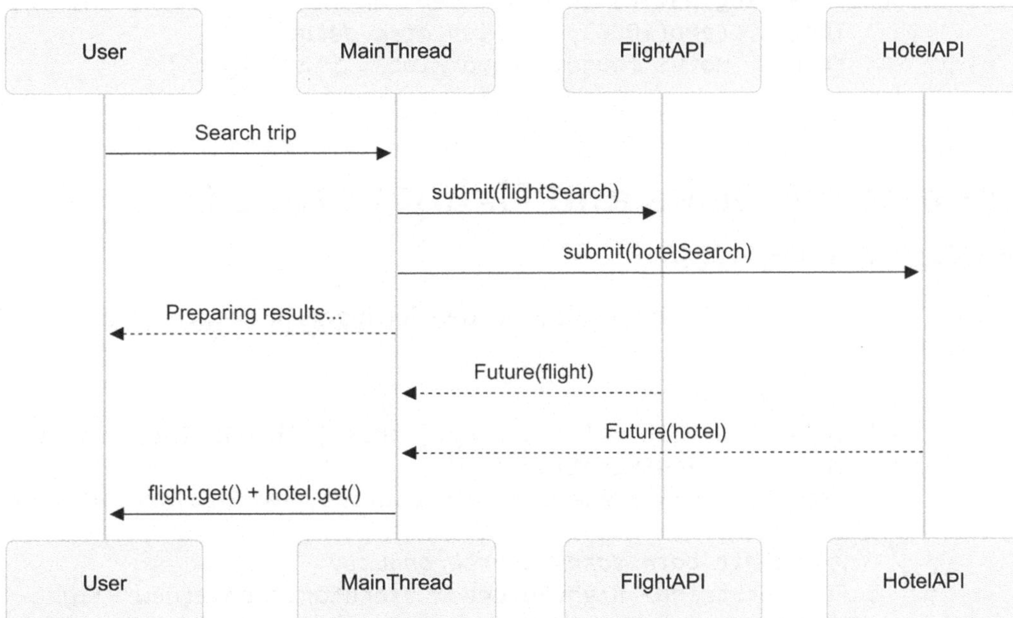

Figure 5.4: *Future Pattern - Asynchronous Task Execution*

We will:

- Use **`ExecutorService`** to submit asynchronous tasks for flight and hotel searches;
- Return **`Future<String>`** results from each task;
- Combine the results, once both are available.

Defining Tasks for Flight and Hotel Search

The **`Callable<T>`** interface allows us to return a result, unlike Runnable. The simulated delays mimic real-world network and API latency.

```
// Simulates a long-running flight search operation
public class FlightSearchTask implements Callable<String> {
   @Override
   public String call() throws Exception {
       Thread.sleep(1500); // Simulated delay
```

```
        return "Flight found: TravelNow Airlines, $199";
    }
}
// Simulates a hotel search operation
public class HotelSearchTask implements Callable<String> {
    @Override
    public String call() throws Exception {
        Thread.sleep(1000); // Simulated delay
        return "Hotel found: Grand Plaza, $120/night";
    }
}
```

Submitting Tasks and Using Future to Retrieve Results

The **.get()** blocks only when the result is needed, letting us perform valuable work in the meantime.

```
public class Main {
    public static void main( String[] args ) throws Interrupted
Exception, ExecutionException {
        ExecutorService executor = Executors.newFixedThreadPool(2);

        // Submit both tasks asynchronously
        Future<String> flightFuture = executor.submit(new Flight-
SearchTask());
        Future<String> hotelFuture = executor.submit(new Hotel-
SearchTask());

        System.out.println("Searching flights and hotels...");

        // Simulate doing other things while tasks execute
        Thread.sleep(300);
        System.out.println("Preparing summary...");

        // Retrieve the results (blocks if not yet complete)
        String flightResult = flightFuture.get();
        String hotelResult = hotelFuture.get();

        System.out.println("Results Ready:");
        System.out.println(flightResult);
        System.out.println(hotelResult);

        executor.shutdown();
    }
}
```

Output Console:

```
Searching flights and hotels...
Preparing summary...
Results Ready:
Flight found: TravelNow Airlines, $199
Hotel found: Grand Plaza, $120/night
```

The Future Pattern offers a simple yet powerful way to implement asynchronous computation in Java. It is ideal for tasks that require time, such as I/O or remote calls, but do not require immediate results. This pattern improves performance, system responsiveness, and user experience, especially in latency-sensitive services.

However, for divide-and-conquer workloads, where tasks need to be recursively broken down into subtasks and processed in parallel, the Future Pattern is insufficient. That is where the **Fork/Join Framework** comes in, enabling highly parallelized processing on multicore systems through intelligent work-stealing algorithms.

Fork/Join Pattern

The Fork/Join Pattern is a parallel programming model designed to efficiently divide large tasks into smaller subtasks, execute them concurrently, and combine their results. Java provides a Fork/Join Framework, an implementation of this pattern, introduced in Java 7, enhanced in Java 8, using work-stealing algorithms, allowing idle threads to take over unfinished subtasks from busy ones.

It is built for **CPU-intensive operations** that benefit from recursive decomposition.

Case Study

Imagine an NLP system designed to analyze sentiment across thousands of customer reviews. Each document must be scored individually, with reviews stored in large batches containing several thousand entries. The application is deployed on multicore servers and is expected to process data as quickly and efficiently as possible.

The initial challenges include:

- **Sequential Processing Bottleneck**: Scoring each document sequentially leads to unacceptably long execution times.
- **Complex Task Orchestration**: Although thread pools are used to manage concurrency, coordinating task execution and merging results becomes increasingly challenging to maintain.
- **Inefficient Workload Distribution**: There is no precise mechanism for recursively dividing tasks and aggregating results in a clean, scalable manner.

To address these issues, we apply the **Fork/Join Pattern**. This approach enables recursive task decomposition, where a large batch of documents can be split into smaller subsets processed in parallel. Each subset computes partial sentiment scores, which are then efficiently combined into a single aggregated result. This pattern leverages multicore processing to deliver both speed and simplicity in managing parallel workloads.

Note: *In this case study, we will focus on implementing useful classes to apply the design model concept.*

Applying the Fork/Join Pattern

The following diagram illustrates how the Fork/Join Pattern recursively splits a large document-scoring task into smaller subtasks, executes them in parallel, and aggregates their results.

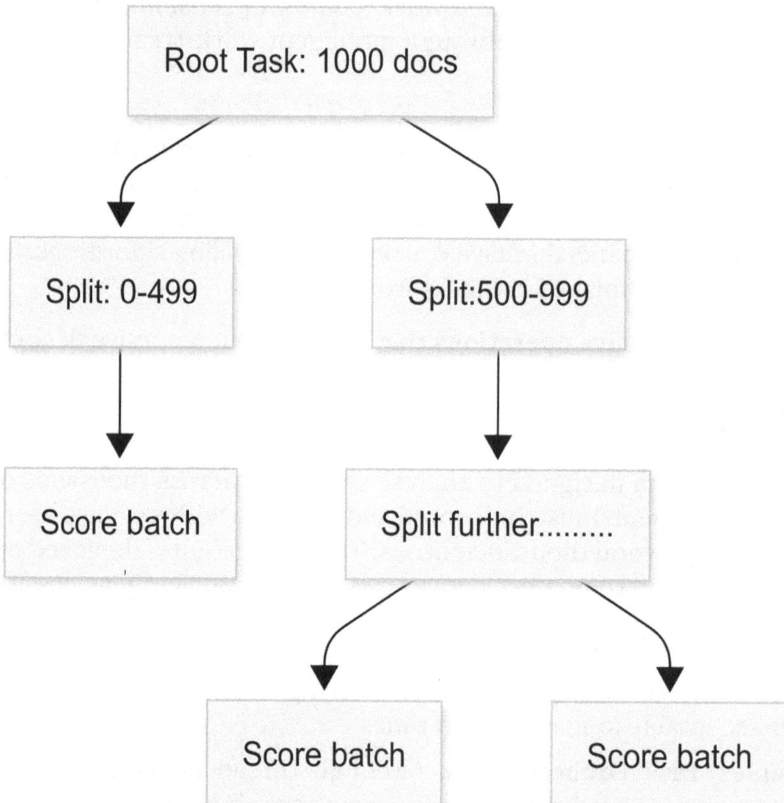

Figure 5.5: *Fork/Join Pattern - Parallel Document Sentiment Scoring*

We will use a Fork/Join Framework within **`java.util.concurrent`** package to:

- Define a **`RecursiveTask<Double>`** to score a batch of documents.
- Recursively **split the task** into subtasks.

- Use **ForkJoinPool** to execute the recursive logic concurrently.
- Aggregate the results of the subtasks.

Defining the Recursive Task

The **RecursiveTask<Double>** class represents a task that returns a value. We recursively split the input and aggregate the scores with **fork()** and **join()**.

```
// Simulated sentiment scorer task
public class SentimentScoringTask extends RecursiveTask<Double> {
   private static final int THRESHOLD = 100;
   private final List<String> documents;

   public SentimentScoringTask(List<String> documents) {
       this.documents = documents;
   }

   @Override
   protected Double compute() {
       // Base case: process directly if below threshold
       if (documents.size() <= THRESHOLD) {
           return scoreBatch(documents);
       }

       // Recursive case: split into two parts
       int mid = documents.size() / 2;
       SentimentScoringTask leftTask = new SentimentScoring-
Task(documents.subList(0, mid));
       SentimentScoringTask rightTask = new SentimentScoring-
Task(documents.subList(mid, documents.size()));

       // Fork one half, compute the other, then join
       leftTask.fork();
       double rightResult = rightTask.compute();
       double leftResult = leftTask.join();

       return leftResult + rightResult;
   }

   // Simulate scoring by assigning 1.0 per document (in reality:
NLP logic)
   private double scoreBatch(List<String> docs) {
       return docs.size(); // Fake score: one point per doc
   }
}
```

Running the Task Using ForkJoinPool

The **pool.invoke(rootTask)** starts execution of the recursive scoring. Threads are reused, and work is balanced automatically using work-stealing.

```
public class Main {
   public static void main( String[] args ) {
        // Simulate a list of 1,000 customer review documents
        List<String> reviews = new ArrayList<>();
        for (int i = 0; i < 1000; i++) {
            reviews.add("Review " + i);
        }

        // Create the main task
        SentimentScoringTask rootTask = new SentimentScoring-
Task(reviews);

        // Use the common ForkJoinPool or create a custom one
        ForkJoinPool pool = ForkJoinPool.commonPool();
        double totalScore = pool.invoke(rootTask);

        System.out.println("Total sentiment score: " + total-
Score);
   }
}
```

Output console:

```
Total sentiment score: 1000.0
```

The Fork/Join Pattern enables high-performance parallel computation for recursive, CPU-bound tasks. It is best suited for scenarios such as file processing, scientific computation, machine learning inference, or processing any independent dataset.

Now that we have explored concurrency design patterns in Java for task execution, resource coordination, and parallelization, we will conclude with an overview of **Java Concurrency Utilities**. These powerful out-of-the-box tools support and extend the patterns we have seen.

Java Concurrency Utilities

Java provides a rich set of concurrency utilities in the **java.util.concurrent** package to help developers write efficient, thread-safe applications. These utilities provide **high-level building blocks** for common coordination problems, designed to **reduce complexity, prevent concurrency bugs**, and **enhance scalability**.

The goal is to empower developers with ready-to-use concurrency constructs that simplify synchronization, task scheduling, and thread communication.

Case Study

Imagine a real-time news distribution engine, **NewsFlow,** designed to aggregate and broadcast breaking news stories from various sources. The system fetches stories in parallel, buffers them, and ensures a controlled delivery to the end-users. It must operate efficiently under tight time constraints and unpredictable input flows.

The system behaves as follows:

- Fetches breaking news stories from multiple sources in parallel.
- Waits for all sources to respond before delivering the compiled stories to users.
- Controls concurrent consumption, limiting the number of user agents that can access stories simultaneously.
- Buffers articles in queues prior to dispatch, smoothing out spikes in load.

This architecture mirrors common challenges found in data pipelines, event-driven platforms, and real-time streaming systems.

How can **NewsFlow** coordinate asynchronous tasks, manage access to shared resources, and efficiently buffer messages using built-in concurrency utilities?

Note: *In this case study, we will focus on implementing useful classes to apply the design model concept.*

Applying Java Concurrency Utilities

We will use:

- `CountDownLatch` to wait for multiple fetchers to complete.
- Semaphore to control access to limited user slots.
- BlockingQueue to buffer articles before dispatch.

The following figure illustrates a real-time news distribution engine leveraging Java concurrency utilities, where multiple sources synchronize data fetching using a `CountDownLatch`, and articles are subsequently dispatched to users through a queue managed by semaphores for controlled access.

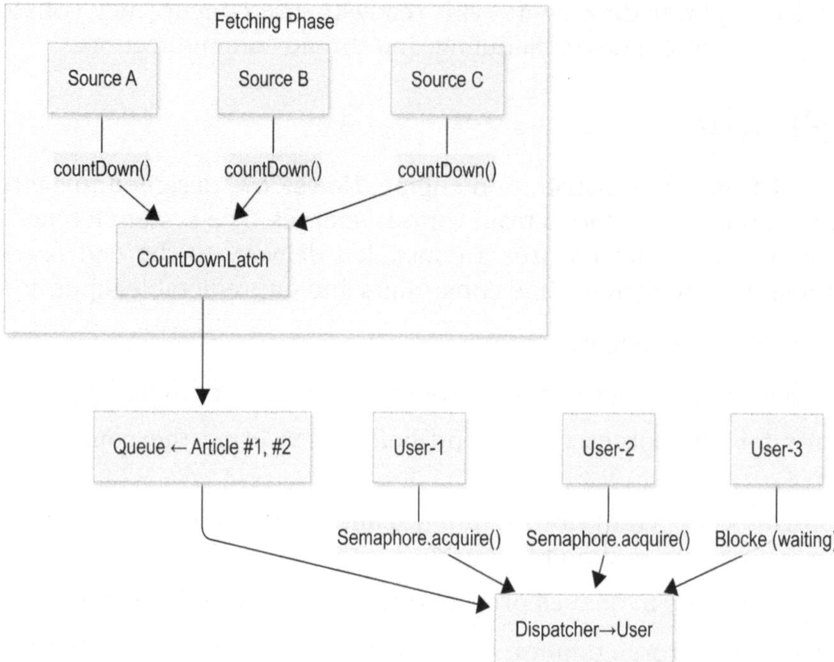

Figure 5.6: *Java Concurrency Utilities - Real-Time News Distribution Engine*

Defining the Article Fetcher with `CountDownLatch`

`CountDownLatch` waits for all fetchers before proceeding, which is useful when synchronizing a launch point after many async tasks.

```
public class ArticleFetcher implements Runnable {
   private final String source;
   private final CountDownLatch latch;

   public ArticleFetcher(String source, CountDownLatch latch) {
       this.source = source;
       this.latch = latch;
   }

   @Override
   public void run() {
       try {
           Thread.sleep((long) (Math.random() * 1000));
// Simulate variable latency
           System.out.println("Fetched article from: " + source);
       } catch (InterruptedException ignored) {
```

```
            } finally {
                latch.countDown(); // Signal completion
            }
        }
    }
```

Defining the Article Dispatcher with `BlockingQueue`

`BlockingQueue` decouples producer and consumer logic, offering a clean and thread-safe buffer.

```
public class ArticleDispatcher implements Runnable {
    private final BlockingQueue<String> queue;

    public ArticleDispatcher(BlockingQueue<String> queue) {
        this.queue = queue;
    }

    @Override
    public void run() {
        try {
            while (true) {
                String article = queue.take(); // Blocks if empty
                System.out.println("Dispatching: " + article);
                Thread.sleep(500);
            }
        } catch (InterruptedException ignored) {}
    }
}
```

Limiting Access to Consumers Using Semaphore

`Semaphore` is ideal for controlling access to finite resources, in this case, by limiting the number of active consumers.

```
public class UserConsumer implements Runnable {
    private final Semaphore slots;
    private final String user;

    public UserConsumer(Semaphore slots, String user) {
        this.slots = slots;
        this.user = user;
    }
```

```
    @Override
    public void run() {
        try {
            slots.acquire(); // Wait for permission
            System.out.println("* " + user + " is consuming
articles");
            Thread.sleep(1500); // Simulate reading
        } catch (InterruptedException ignored) {
        } finally {
            slots.release(); // Free slot
            System.out.println("- " + user + " done consuming");
        }
    }
}
```

Put it all together;

```
public class Main {
   public static void main( String[] args ) throws Interrupted
Exception {
        CountDownLatch latch = new CountDownLatch(3);
        BlockingQueue<String> articleQueue = new LinkedBlocking
Queue<>();
        Semaphore userSlots = new Semaphore(2); // Max 2 users at
once

        // Start fetchers
        new Thread(new ArticleFetcher("Source A", latch)).start();
        new Thread(new ArticleFetcher("Source B", latch)).start();
        new Thread(new ArticleFetcher("Source C", latch)).start();

        // Wait for all articles to be fetched
        latch.await();
        System.out.println("All sources fetched. Loading into
queue...");

        articleQueue.put("Article #1");
        articleQueue.put("Article #2");

        // Start dispatcher
        new Thread(new ArticleDispatcher(articleQueue)).start();

        // Simulate users consuming articles
        new Thread(new UserConsumer(userSlots, "User-1")).start();
        new Thread(new UserConsumer(userSlots, "User-2")).start();
```

```
            new Thread(new UserConsumer(userSlots, "User-3")).start();
        }
    }
```

Output Console:

```
Fetched article from: Source B
Fetched article from: Source C
Fetched article from: Source A
All sources fetched. Loading into queue...
Dispatching: Article #1
* User-1 is consuming articles
* User-2 is consuming articles
Dispatching: Article #2
* User-3 is consuming articles
- User-2 done consuming
- User-1 done consuming
- User-3 done consuming
```

The concurrency utilities of Java are powerful abstractions that simplify common concurrency patterns, such as task synchronization, coordination, resource throttling, and message buffering. When combined with patterns such as Thread Pool, Producer-Consumer, and Fork/Join, they greatly enhance the readability, stability, and scalability of concurrent systems.

Conclusion

In this chapter, we have learned how to build concurrent systems in Java with confidence, using a mix of design patterns and built-in concurrency tools. From simple thread reuse to complex asynchronous orchestration and data parallelism, each pattern serves a well-defined purpose and fits naturally into modern Java applications.

More than just concurrency, these patterns promote code clarity, system responsiveness, and scalable architecture, three pillars of professional software engineering.

With a solid foundation in **Concurrency Design Patterns**, we are now equipped to build responsive, thread-safe, and performant components. However, robust applications require more than isolated optimizations. They demand a **well-thought-out architecture.**

In the next chapter, we will take a step back from code-level concerns and zoom out to the structural blueprint of entire systems. We will explore Architectural Design Patterns, which define how software components are organized, interact, and evolve in large-scale Java applications.

Points to Remember

- Concurrency is about more than threads; it is about coordination, performance, and control.
- Each pattern solves a distinct concurrency problem: task management, resource sharing, async orchestration, or data parallelism.
- Java provides a comprehensive toolkit to implement and reinforce these patterns, including Executors, Locks, Futures, Queues, and Semaphores.
- Choosing the correct pattern depends on data flow, workload type, and performance constraints.
- Avoiding deadlocks, contention, and starvation requires both pattern understanding and runtime monitoring.

Multiple Choice Questions

1. Amongst which of these can be said as a role of **`CountDownLatch`**?
   a. Replaces locks in high-throughput applications.
   b. Coordinates multiple tasks to wait for a single event.
   c. Coordinates one or more tasks, waiting for multiple events.
   d. Ensures FIFO ordering in queues.
2. Which of the following is the main benefit of using a BlockingQueue in the Producer-Consumer pattern?
   a. It eliminates the need for threads.
   b. It prevents producers from ever blocking.
   c. It handles safe communication between threads automatically.
   d. It always uses a fixed thread pool.
3. What does the Fork/Join framework optimize for?
   a. Long-lived background tasks
   b. I/O operations
   c. Recursively parallelizable CPU-bound tasks
   d. UI responsiveness

4. Which of the following enables the chaining of asynchronous tasks without blocking the main thread?
   a. `Future`
   b. `CompletableFuture`
   c. `ThreadPool`
   d. `ForkJoinTask`

Answers

1. c
2. d
3. c
4. b

Questions

1. Which concurrency pattern would we use to design a stock trading engine that processes orders in real time? Why?
2. How could the **`CompletableFuture`** pattern improve responsiveness in a web service gateway that calls multiple APIs?
3. How can Java's concurrency utilities simplify thread orchestration in complex data ingestion pipelines?

Key Terms

- **Thread Pool**: A set of reusable threads for executing tasks asynchronously.
- **`BlockingQueue`**: A thread-safe queue that blocks on take/put when empty/full.
- **`ReadWriteLock`**: A lock that allows multiple readers or a single writer.
- **Future**: A placeholder for a result that will be available in the future.
- **`CompletableFuture`**: An enhanced Future that supports async chaining.
- **`ForkJoinPool`**: A framework for parallelizing recursive tasks.
- **`CountDownLatch`**: A latch that waits until a given number of events have occurred.
- **`Semaphore`**: A mechanism that limits the number of concurrent accesses to a resource.

CHAPTER 6
Architectural Design Patterns

Introduction

In software development, writing reliable functions and managing concurrent tasks are necessary skills, but they are not sufficient to ensure long-term system success. As projects grow, what truly determines their maintainability, scalability, and adaptability is how the system is architected.

Architectural Design Patterns provide strategic blueprints for organizing software systems at a macro level. They define how components interact, how responsibilities are distributed, and how applications are evolving, thereby offering proven structures that help avoid chaos as complexity increases.

These patterns are framework-agnostic and technology-neutral, making them essential tools for any developer or architect building Java systems, whether monolithic, modular, or distributed.

This chapter presents five vital architectural design patterns used to shape modern Java systems. Each pattern is grounded in a realistic case study, accompanied by architectural sketches, and concludes with practical guidance on implementation trade-offs.

Structure

In this chapter, we will cover the following topics:

- Model-View-Controller
- Layered Architecture
- Event-Driven Architecture
- Service-Oriented Architecture
- Microservices Architecture

Model-View-Controller

The Model-View-Controller, also known as MVC pattern is a foundational architectural pattern that separates the user interface logic from the business logic and the underlying data model. It divides a system into three interconnected components:

- **Model**: Manages the data and business rules of the application.
- **View**: Handles the visual representation and user interaction.
- **Controller**: Acts as an intermediary between the Model and the View, processing input and coordinating updates.

Case Study

Imagine an online education platform where students can view course materials and grades, submit assignments, and track their progress over time.

The original system had a monolithic interface where:

- All logic was in JSPs or HTML files.
- Business rules were mixed with rendering code.
- Any change to data or presentation logic introduced bugs in other parts of the system.

Design Problem: How can we cleanly separate UI, logic, and data so that developers can independently modify each part without breaking the others?

Note: *In this case study, we will focus on implementing useful classes to apply the design model concept.*

Applying the Model-View-Controller Pattern

We will refactor *the platform* to adopt an MVC structure, improving its modularity and testability. Each layer will have a clear responsibility:

- The **Model** handles student and course data.
- The **View** displays information in HTML or JavaFX.
- The **Controller** manages user actions, including submitting assignments and viewing grades.

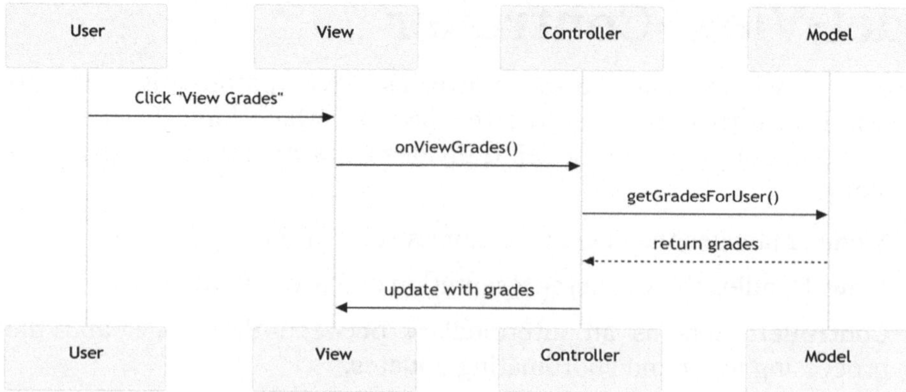

Figure 6.1: *Model-View-Controller -MCV Flow*

We are using Spring-like pseudo-implementation.

Define the Model

The Student model encapsulates core business logic and hides implementation details from the UI.

```
// Represents the domain logic
public class Student {
    private String name;
    private List<Grade> grades;
    // Domain logic: average calculation
    public double calculateGPA() {
        return grades.stream()
                     .mapToDouble(Grade::getScore)
                     .average()
                     .orElse(0.0);
    }
    // Getters / setters omitted for brevity
}
```

Create the Controller

The controller responds to HTTP requests, delegates to business logic, and returns structured data. It knows nothing about how the UI will render it.

```
// Processes requests and delegates to service/model
@RestController
@RequestMapping("/students/")
public class StudentController {

    @Autowired
```

```
        private StudentService service;

        @GetMapping("{id}/grades")
        public ResponseEntity<List<Grade>> getGrades(@PathVariable
    Long id) {
            List<Grade> grades = service.getGradesForStudent(id);
            return ResponseEntity.ok(grades);
        }
    }
```

Define the View

The view is responsible for presentation only. It receives data, such as via a template engine or front-end framework, and renders it. We are using **Thymeleaf** as Our View here.

```
<!-- Example of a Thymeleaf View -->
<h1>Student Grades</h1>
<ul>
    <li th:each="grade : ${grades}">
        [[${grade.course}]]: [[${grade.score}]]
    </li>
</ul>
```

Results and Benefits

After applying the MVC pattern, *the platform* improved on multiple levels:

Benefit	**Impact**
Separation of concerns	Changes to UI do not affect business logic and vice versa
Improved testability	Models and controllers can be tested independently
Cleaner codebase	Each layer is simpler and easier to maintain
Team parallelism	Frontend and backend teams can work independently

Table 6.1: *MVC Pattern Results and Benefits*

The Model-View-Controller Pattern is the gold standard for interactive Java applications, especially in web, desktop, and mobile environments. It fosters code clarity, modularity, and rapid development.

However, while MVC structures the application within a single component, larger systems often require clear boundaries between subsystem**s**, such as UI, business services, and persistence. This leads us to the **Layered Architecture**, where responsibilities are organized into vertical layers, a natural next step in enterprise system design.

Layered Architecture

The Layered Architecture Pattern organizes a system into horizontal layers, each with a distinct role and responsibility. These layers are stacked on top of each other, forming a clear path from the user interface to the data storage and back.

Typical layers include:

- **Presentation Layer**: It handles UI and user interaction.
- **Service Layer**: This contains business logic and application workflows.
- **Persistence Layer**: It manages database interactions.
- **Data Layer / Entities**: This represents domain objects and database mappings.

The goal is to promote separation of concerns, facilitate testability, and simplify maintenance by organizing responsibilities into well-defined tiers.

Case Study

Imagine a patient record management system designed to streamline hospital operations by centralizing medical data and user responsibilities. Doctors can view and update patient records, ensuring real-time access to critical information during consultations. Administrators assign roles, manage access levels, and generate compliance reports to support hospital governance and ensure adherence to regulations. Additionally, the system integrates with external insurance APIs to verify patient coverage and automate claims processing. Initially, all operations were handled through tightly coupled modules, making the system difficult to scale, maintain, and adapt to evolving hospital needs.

Originally, the application had mixed logic:

- UI components directly accessed the database,
- Business rules were duplicated in multiple controllers,
- Small changes led to wide-ranging regressions.

How can the system be structured into independent layers so that each responsibility is isolated, reusable, and easy to maintain?

Note: *In this case study, we will focus on implementing useful classes to apply the design model concept.*

Applying the Layered Architecture Pattern

We will define four layers:

- **Controller Layer:** Receives HTTP requests and delegates to services.

- **Service Layer:** Contains business logic such as validating patient status.
- **Repository Layer:** Interacts with the database.
- **Domain Layer:** Holds entities like *Patient*, *Record*, *Doctor.*

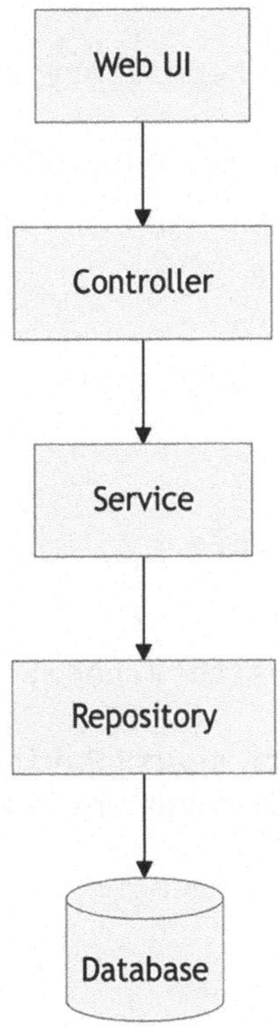

Figure 6.2: *Layered Architecture - Layered Flow*

We are using a spring-based structure.

Define the Domain Entity

The domain layer encapsulates the core business logic and rules of the system. It defines entities, value objects, and interfaces that represent the problem domain, remaining independent of technical concerns like data storage or user interfaces.

```
@Entity
public class Patient {
    @Id
    private Long id;
    private String name;
    private LocalDate birthDate;
    // Business rule could go here (e.g., age calculation)
}
```

Define the Repository Layer

The repository encapsulates data access and can be swapped or mocked independently of the rest.

```
@Repository
public interface PatientRepository extends JpaRepository<Patient,
Long> {
    List<Patient> findByNameContainingIgnoreCase(String name);
}
```

Service Layer

The service layer contains the core business logic, which is reusable across controllers and tests.

```
@Service
public class PatientService {

    @Autowired
    private PatientRepository repo;

    public List<Patient> searchPatients(String query) {
        return repo.findByNameContainingIgnoreCase(query);
    }
}
```

Controller Layer

The controller orchestrates input/output. No business logic leaks in here.

```
@RestController
@RequestMapping("/patients/")
public class PatientController {

    @Autowired
    private PatientService service;

    @GetMapping("search")
    public ResponseEntity<List<Patient>> search(@RequestParam
String name) {
        return ResponseEntity.ok(service.searchPatients(name));
    }
}
```

Results and Benefits

After refactoring to a layered architecture, the system gained.

Benefit	Impact
Clear boundaries	Easier onboarding and refactoring
Reusability	Services can be used across APIs, schedulers, and jobs
Testing	Each layer is independently testable such as, mock repo in-service tests
Scalability	System supports multi-team development and deployment

Table 6.2: *Layered Architecture Pattern Results and Benefits*

The Layered Architecture Pattern is one of the most widely used designs in enterprise Java. It brings order and structure to complex systems by enforcing logical separation of responsibilities.

However, this structure assumes direct calls between layers, which can become rigid or overly synchronous in distributed or real-time systems. To support loose coupling and reactive workflows, our next step is the **Event-Driven Architecture**, where components interact not through method calls but by publishing and consuming events asynchronously.

Event-Driven Architecture

Event-driven architecture is an architectural pattern where components communicate by producing and responding to events. Events are messages that describe a change in state or the occurrence of an action, such as a sensor threshold being exceeded or an order being shipped.

In Event-driven Architecture:

- **Producers** emit events when something significant occurs.
- **Consumers** react to these events asynchronously, often via a message broker.

The goal is to enable loose coupling, asynchronous communication, and scalability in distributed or real-time systems.

Case Study

Imagine an innovative agriculture monitoring system built to optimize farm productivity through real-time environmental monitoring. The platform collects data on soil, humidity, and temperature from thousands of IoT sensors deployed across various agricultural zones. When abnormal readings are detected, it automatically triggers irrigation systems or sends alerts to the appropriate personnel. Agronomists and farm managers utilize real-time dashboards to monitor conditions, address anomalies, and make informed, data-driven decisions. Initially, the system relied on synchronous data polling and manual intervention, which limited scalability and responsiveness.

The initial system was synchronous:

- Each sensor push triggered a direct call to a controller.
- Performance degraded with load spikes.
- Any failure in one module caused delays in others.

How can the system decouple its components, handle high-frequency sensor data, and scale horizontally without overloading the system?

Note: *In this case study, we will focus on implementing useful classes to apply the design model concept.*

Applying the Event-Driven Architectural Pattern

To implement this architecture, the soil sensor acts as a data producer, publishing `moistureLow` events to a Kafka topic. Kafka serves as a distributed messaging platform that decouples producers and consumers, ensuring scalability and fault tolerance.

On the consumer side:

- The **Irrigation Service** subscribes to the topic and, upon receiving a `moistureLow` event, triggers the irrigation system.
- The **Alert Notifier** listens to the same topic and sends alerts, such as SMS, email, and app notifications, to agronomists when conditions fall below thresholds.
- The **Dashboard Updater** processes the event to refresh visual indicators and real-time graphs displayed in the farm management interface.

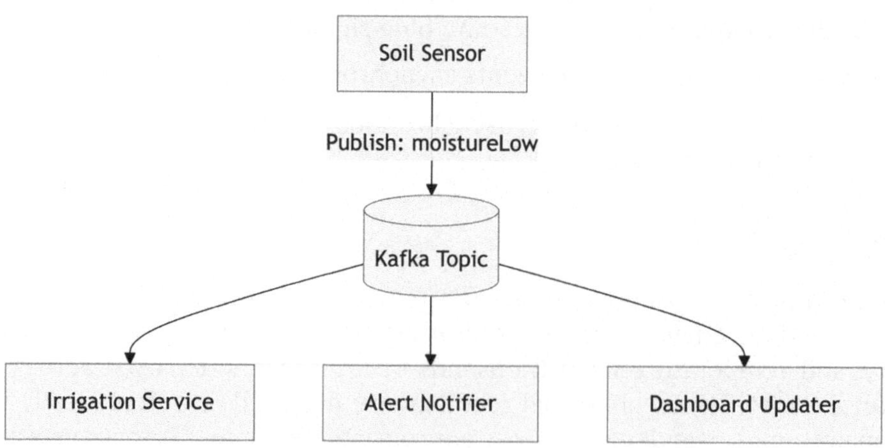

Figure 6.3: *Event-driven Architecture - EDA Flow*

Define the Event Model

ReentrantReadWriteLock allows many concurrent reads but ensures write exclusivity. The try-finally structure guarantees proper unlocking.

```
public class SensorEvent {
    private String sensorId;
    private String type; // e.g. "humidity"
    private double value;
    private Instant timestamp;

    // Getters and setters omitted
}
```

Produce Events to Kafka

The producer sends events to a Kafka topic. This decouples sensors from the logic that processes their data.

```
@Service
public class SensorProducer {

    @Autowired
    private KafkaTemplate<String, SensorEvent> kafkaTemplate;

    public void publish(SensorEvent event) {
        kafkaTemplate.send("sensor-data-topic", event.get
SensorId(), event);
    }
}
```

Produce Events to Kafka

The consumer reacts to events based on content. Multiple consumers can handle the same event independently.

```
@Service
public class SensorProducer {
    @Autowired
    private KafkaTemplate<String, SensorEvent> kafkaTemplate;

    public void publish(SensorEvent event) {
        kafkaTemplate.send("sensor-data-topic", event.get
SensorId(), event);
    }
}
```

Consume Events Asynchronously

The producer sends events to a Kafka topic. This decouples sensors from the logic that processes their data.

```
@Service
public class IrrigationConsumer {
    @KafkaListener(topics = "sensor-data-topic", groupId
= "agrisense")
    public void onSensorData(SensorEvent event) {
        if ("humidity".equals(event.getType()) && event.get
Value() < 20.0) {
            System.out.println("Triggering irrigation for sensor
" + event.getSensorId());
        }
    }
}
```

Results and Benefits

After refactoring to a layered architecture, the system gained.

Benefit	Impact
Loose coupling	Sensors, dashboards, and triggers operate independently
Scalability	New consumers added without impacting producers
Resilience	Failures in one module don't affect others
Real-time processing	Events handled as soon as they occur

Table 6.3: *Event-Driven Architecture Pattern Results and Benefits*

The Event-Driven Architecture Pattern enables systems like AgriSense to be reactive, modular, and scalable. It is particularly suited for IoT, streaming analytics, and systems requiring near real-time responsiveness.

However, while events excel at decoupling, they do not define service boundaries or contracts, which are critical when different systems need to collaborate in a predictable and interoperable way. To address that, we will now explore the **Service-Oriented Architecture** pattern, where services expose well-defined interfaces and operate across organizational and technological boundaries.

Service-Oriented Architecture

Service-Oriented Architecture (SOA) is an architectural style that structures an application as a collection of loosely coupled services, each of which exposes a contract-defined interface and communicates via standardized protocols, often XML/SOAP or REST/JSON.

SOA focuses on interoperability, reuse, and integration across systems that may be built in different technologies, managed by different teams, or even owned by different organizations.

The goal is to promote business-aligned modularity and inter-system collaboration by exposing application functionality as discoverable, contract-based services.

Note: *In this case study, we will focus on implementing useful classes to apply the design model concept.*

Case Study

Imagine a hospital interoperability platform designed to unify healthcare services across a national ecosystem. The platform connects public and private hospitals, enabling seamless data exchange between patient care providers. It integrates with insurance providers to facilitate real-time coverage validation and billing coordination. Laboratories and pharmacies are also linked, allowing prescriptions, test results, and diagnostics to flow effortlessly across the network. Initially, the system relied on isolated data silos and manual integrations, leading to delays, inconsistencies, and a lack of real-time visibility across stakeholders.

Before SOA:

- Each organization used a different technology stack,
- Integrations were custom-built, brittle, and duplicated,
- Updating one partner system meant modifying multiple interfaces manually.

How can the system enable interoperability between independent systems, without sacrificing modularity or requiring full rewrites?

Note: *In this case study, we will focus on implementing useful classes to apply the design model concept.*

Applying the Service-Oriented Architecture Pattern

We will structure `HealthBridge` as follows:

- A network of **coarse-grained services** such as `PatientService`, `InsuranceService`,
- Each service exposes a **WSDL or REST contract**,
- Communication through **standard protocols** such as HTTP, SOAP, JSON,

- A **Service Registry** for discovery optional for REST essential for SOAP-based systems.

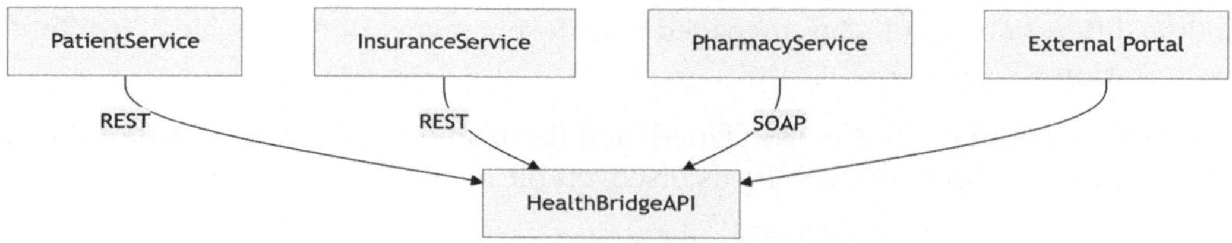

Figure 6.4: *Service-Oriented Architecture Pattern*

Define a Service Interface, Contract-First

```
public interface InsuranceService {
    ClaimStatus checkClaimStatus(String claimId);
    void notifyReimbursement(String claimId, double amount);
}
```

Expose the Service via a Controller

The service interface defines the public contract, while the controller provides the technical implementation that third-party systems consume.

```
@RestController
@RequestMapping("/insurance/")
public class InsuranceController implements InsuranceService {
    @Override
    @GetMapping("claims/{id}/status")
    public ClaimStatus checkClaimStatus(@PathVariable String id)
{
        // Simulated business logic
        return new ClaimStatus(id, "APPROVED");
    }
    @Override
    @PostMapping("claims/{id}/reimbursement")
    public void notifyReimbursement(@PathVariable String id, @
RequestParam double amount) {
        System.out.println("Reimbursed " + amount + " for claim "
+ id);
    }
}
```

Results and Benefits

With Service-Oriented Architecture, the system achieved.

Benefit	Impact
Loose coupling	Systems evolved independently without breaking others
Scalability	New consumers added without impacting Services reused across government and private portals
Interoperability	Communication between systems regardless of stack
Business alignment	Services modeled after real-world responsibilities

Table 6.4: *Service-Oriented Architecture Pattern Results and Benefits*

Service-oriented architecture enables cross-organization communication via standardized interfaces and protocols, allowing diverse systems to collaborate without sharing internal logic.

However, while Service-oriented Architecture resolves many interoperability issues, it often results in extensive services with shared state and tight infrastructure coupling. In modern cloud-native applications, a finer-grained, more agile alternative has emerged: The **Microservices Architecture**, where services are independently deployable, domain-driven, and fully autonomous.

Microservice Architecture

The Microservices Architecture pattern structures an application as a suite of small, autonomous services, each responsible for a specific business capability and independently deployable. These services communicate via lightweight protocols, such as REST, and maintain their own databases and runtime environments.

The goal is to achieve scalability, team autonomy, independent deployment, and resilience by breaking down the monolith into self-contained services.

Unlike traditional Service-Oriented Architecture, where services often share databases and infrastructures, Microservices emphasize bounded contexts, distributed ownership, and continuous delivery.

Case Study

Imagine an intelligent logistics platform *FoodFleet* designed to coordinate food deliveries for restaurants operating across multiple cities. The system manages customer orders and dynamically synchronizes restaurant menus to reflect real-time availability. It handles driver dispatch and monitors delivery progress using live tracking data. Additionally, it oversees inventory management and generates operational reports to support decision-making across the delivery network. Initially, these operations were managed through separate services with minimal integration, leading to inefficiencies and delays in fulfillment.

Initially built as a layered monolith, the application faced:

- Long deployment cycles, any change triggered a complete rebuild,
- Fragile testing pipelines a bug in delivery affected menu updates,
- Scaling challenges, such as driver tracking, required more resources than reporting.

How can *FoodFleet* evolve into a modular, resilient architecture that allows teams to work independently and deploy features at their own pace?

Note: *In this case study, we will focus on implementing useful classes to apply the design model concept.*

Applying the Microservice Architecture Pattern

We will decompose *FoodFleet* into domain-aligned microservices::

- **`OrderService`:** Manages customer orders.
- **`MenuService`:** Handles menu data and updates.
- **`DriverService`:** Tracks driver status in real-time.
- **`InventoryService`:** Monitors ingredient stock.

Each service has:

- Its own **API**,
- Its own **database**,
- Its own **codebase**, and
- Its own **deployment lifecycle.**

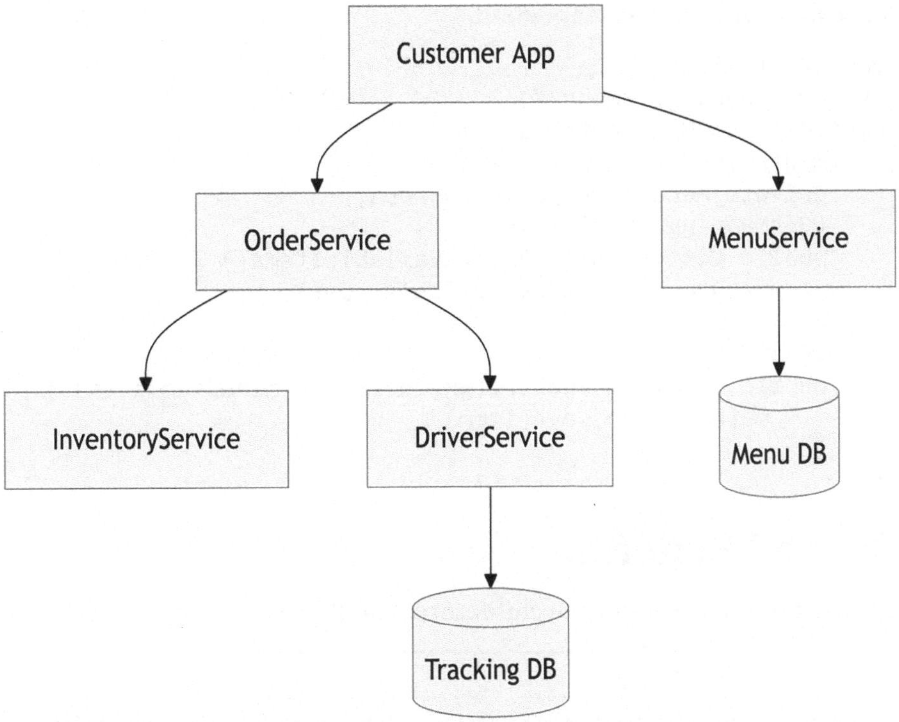

Figure 6.5: *Microservice Architecture Pattern - FoodFleet Microservices*

Java Implementation Sketch - `MenuService`

This microservice owns its domain and database. It can be deployed, scaled, and updated without impacting other services like orders or delivery.

Menu Domain Entity

```
@Entity
public class MenuItem {
    @Id
    private Long id;
    private String name;
    private double price;
    private boolean available;
}
```

Menu Repository

```
public interface MenuItemRepository extends JpaRepository
<MenuItem, Long> {
    List<MenuItem> findByAvailableTrue();
}
```

REST Controller for Menu Management

```
@RestController
@RequestMapping("/menu/")
public class MenuController {
    @Autowired
    private MenuItemRepository repo;
    @GetMapping("available")
    public List<MenuItem> getAvailableItems() {
        return repo.findByAvailableTrue();
    }
    @PostMapping
    public MenuItem addItem(@RequestBody MenuItem item) {
        return repo.save(item);
    }
}
```

Results and Benefits

After migrating to Microservices Architecture, FoodFleet achieved.

Benefit	Impact
Independent scaling	`DriverService` scaled separately for peak delivery hours
Faster deployments	Teams deployed changes to menus or drivers without blocking others
Resilience	Failures in reporting didn't affect order taking or deliveries
Technology flexibility	Each service could evolve independently such as, switch DB engines, languages

Table 6.5: *Microservices Architecture Pattern Results and Benefits*

The Microservices Architecture enables teams like those at *FoodFleet* to scale independently, deliver faster, and build resilient systems by designing around business domains rather than technical layers.

With this final pattern, we now have a comprehensive understanding of how to structure applications at the architectural level, ranging from classical monoliths with MVC and layering to event-driven, service-oriented, and cloud-native microservice systems.

Comparative Analysis – Architectural Design Patterns

Pattern	Typical Use Case	Common Pitfalls to Avoid
MVC	UI applications needing separation of logic and display	Tightly coupling controller to view logic

Layered Architecture	Enterprise systems with well-defined responsibilities	Overengineering or unnecessary layer bloat
Event-Driven Architecture	Real-time or asynchronous systems like, IoT, streaming	Lack of monitoring and event visibility
SOA	Integration across organizations or heterogeneous systems	Overhead from complex WS-* standards
Microversices	Cloud-native, scalable, independently deployable systems	Data inconsistency, service sprawl, and distributed debugging complexity

Table 6.6: *Comparative Analysis*

Conclusion

Architectural Design Patterns act as macro-level blueprints that guide the structure, boundaries, and collaboration of components within Java applications. They provide clarity in design, encourage separation of responsibilities, and support long-term growth, particularly in complex or distributed systems.

By mastering patterns such as MVC, Layered Architecture, Event-Driven SOA, and Microservices, developers, and architects gain the ability to scale software holistically, not just in code but also in team velocity, domain alignment, and system resilience.

Great architecture requires equally solid foundations in testing and diagnostics. That is why the next chapter will focus on how design patterns can make Java applications easier to test, debug, and validate.

In the next chapter, *Testing and Debugging with Design Patterns*, we will explore how design patterns can improve the quality assurance process in Java development. We will learn how to utilize patterns not only for application design but also to create testable and diagnosable systems.

Points to Remember

- Architectural patterns solve system-level structural problems and guide modular application design.
- Choose a pattern based on the domain context, team structure, and scalability requirements.
- Patterns can be combined, such as using MVC inside a microservice, but they must remain cohesive and justifiable.
- Each pattern introduces trade-offs, allowing us to understand the cost of complexity versus the benefit of flexibility.

Multiple Choice Questions

1. Which of the following is a primary benefit of using the MVC pattern?
   a. Simplifies database schema.
   b. Improves UI responsiveness.
   c. Separates concerns across data, logic, and presentation.
   d. Avoids the need for a service layer.
2. Which architectural pattern best fits real-time event handling with minimal coupling?
   a. Layered Architecture
   b. Service-Oriented Architecture
   c. Event-Driven Architecture
   d. MVC
3. In Microservices Architecture, which of the following is true?
   a. All services share a central database.
   b. Each service is tightly coupled with the others.
   c. Services are independently deployable.
   d. Services rely on a global transaction manager.

Answers

1. c
2. c
3. c

Questions

1. How does architectural layering affect testing and maintainability in a large Java application?
2. What are some of the challenges of implementing Microservices Architecture in a legacy monolithic system?

3. Compare SOA and Microservices in terms of granularity, governance, and deployment autonomy.
4. How can Event-Driven Architecture improve modularity, and what are the trade-offs?

Key Terms

- **Separation of Concerns**: Principle of dividing a program into distinct features that overlap as little as possible.
- **Service Discovery**: Mechanism used in SOA or microservices to dynamically find service instances.
- **Loose Coupling**: Design goal to reduce dependencies between system components.
- **Bounded Context**: DDD concept describing the boundary within which a model is defined and applicable.

CHAPTER 7
Testing and Debugging with Design Patterns

Introduction

Modern Java systems rarely fail due to a lack of features; they fail when hidden defects surface in production or when once-clear code becomes impenetrable under the weight of scattered bug fixes and untested edge cases. *Testing and Debugging with Design Patterns* focuses on this fragile juncture between correctness and complexity. We begin by defining the twin activities at hand:

- **Software testing** is the systematic search for evidence that code behaves as intended under all relevant conditions.
- **Debugging** is the disciplined process of locating, understanding, and removing faults revealed by those tests or by unhappy users.

While *JUnit*, *AssertJ*, or *Mockito* provide us with the tools for exercising code, design patterns offer us the structures that keep those exercises focused, repeatable, and maintainable. Our objective in this chapter is to demonstrate how a concise portfolio of classic patterns, including Stub, Mock Object, Singleton, Strategy, and Decorator, can transform an ordinary test suite into a living specification, making production defects both rarer and easier to diagnose.

After a brief survey of each pattern, we will explore a realistic testing problem that would typically hinder a conventional unit-testing approach. We will then refactor the scenario using the relevant design pattern, illustrating the transformation with side-by-side code snippets to clarify the improved flow of control and distribution of responsibilities. This will also allow us to highlight debugging advantages, for instance, how a well-placed Strategy pattern can eliminate complex if-ladders that obscure edge-case bugs, or how the Decorator pattern can trace live objects without relying on invasive logging techniques.

By the end of the chapter, we will have a tested, debug-friendly mini-project in our toolbox and a checklist of best practices that we can copy and paste into any team culture. More importantly, we will have internalized a mindset in which *design for testability* is not bolted on later, but woven into the very class structure we craft on day one.

Structure

In this chapter, we will cover:

- Test Stub Pattern
- Mock Object Pattern
- Singleton Pattern
- Strategy Pattern
- Decorator Pattern for Test Data Setup

Test Stub Pattern

The Test Stub Pattern is a structural testing pattern that provides controlled, simplified replacements for real objects that a class under test depends on. Unlike mocks, which verify behavior, stubs simply return pre-defined results to isolate the test subject from complex, slow, or unreliable collaborators.

In real applications, we often interact with:

- Databases or external APIs;
- File systems or network I/O;
- Time-sensitive components like clocks;
- Services with complex business logic.

These dependencies make our unit tests slow, as they involve real-world calls; flaky, since results can vary based on external conditions; and hard to debug, due to unrelated noise in logs and stack traces.

With Test Stubs, we can simulate these collaborators using simple, local, predictable code, allowing us to test a unit in isolation.

Case Study

Consider an e-commerce platform where every customer order must be verified against the current stock in the warehouse. This verification is handled by a class called **`OrderValidator`**, which calls the **`InventoryService`** backend service to check product availability.

However, **InventoryService** reaches out to a remote REST API connected to a distributed warehouse system. This introduces real-world problems in a test environment:

- The API might be down or slow.
- Responses might vary, depending on live inventory fluctuations.
- External calls make the tests unreliable and slow.

Testing Challenges: Suppose we attempt to write tests directly using the real **InventoryService**. In that case, we encounter inconsistent results from time-based logic or randomness, delays caused by actual HTTP requests or I/O, and fragile assertions that break depending on the current state of the inventory.

These issues violate the key testing principles of repeatability, determinism, and isolation.

Note: *In this case study, we will focus on implementing useful classes to apply the design model concept.*

Applying the Test Stub Pattern

To simulate the **InventoryService**, we replace the real service with a test-specific implementation that returns fixed, predictable results, enabling us to test the **OrderValidator** logic in complete isolation.

Define a Substitutable Interface

Introduce an interface to abstract away the concrete **InventoryService** logic.

```
public interface InventoryService {
   boolean isProductAvailable(String productId);
}
```

Interfaces enable polymorphism, allowing us to inject a stub implementation without changing the production code.

Provide the Real Implementation for InventoryService

The production version still does the actual remote call, introducing latency and randomness.

```
public class RealInventoryService implements InventoryService {
   @Override
   public boolean isProductAvailable(String productId) {
       // Simulate a real inventory check
```

```
            return Math.random() > 0.5; // Unpredictable result
        }
    }
```

This version is **not test-friendly**. Its behavior changes with each call and introduces uncontrollable dependencies.

Create the Stub for Testing

We now write a lightweight stub that returns a constant value to simulate the availability of a product.

```
public class StubInventoryService implements InventoryService {
    private final boolean fixedAvailability;

    public StubInventoryService(boolean fixedAvailability) {
        this.fixedAvailability = fixedAvailability;
    }

    @Override
    public boolean isProductAvailable(String productId) {
        return fixedAvailability;
    }
}
```

Design Tip: *The stub is configured externally. This allows us to test both available and unavailable scenarios by passing true or false.*

Use the Stub in Unit Tests

Inject the stubbed version into the **`OrderValidator`** to isolate the unit logic.

```
public class OrderValidator {
    private final InventoryService inventoryService;
    public OrderValidator(InventoryService inventoryService) {
        this.inventoryService = inventoryService;
    }
    public boolean canFulfillOrder(String productId) {
        return inventoryService.isProductAvailable(productId);
    }
}
```

And then test it as follows:

```
public class OrderValidatorTest {
    @Test
    public void testOrderFulfilledWhenProductIsAvailable() {
        // Using a stub to simulate the inventory service
        InventoryService stub = new StubInventoryService(true);
```

```
        // Injecting the stub into the OrderValidator
        OrderValidator validator = new OrderValidator(stub);
        assertTrue(validator.canFulfillOrder("PROD-123"));
    }
    @Test
    public void testOrderNotFulfilledWhenProductIsUnavailable() {
        // Using a stub to simulate the inventory service with
product unavailable
        InventoryService stub = new StubInventoryService(false);
        // Injecting the stub into the OrderValidator
        OrderValidator validator = new OrderValidator(stub);
        assertFalse(validator.canFulfillOrder("PROD-123"));
    }
}
```

Now, each test becomes **deterministic**, producing the same result every time, **isolated**, free from external dependencies, and **fast** executing instantly with no genuine I/O.

Using the Test Stub Pattern in this scenario has:

- Freed the test suite from real-world unpredictability.
- Allowed simulation of edge cases always available or never available.
- Reduced test fragility and execution time.
- Improved developer confidence during TDD and refactoring.

Design Insight: *Test Stubs encourage writing interface-based code, which is inherently more modular and adaptable, a win for both testing and architecture.*

The Test Stub Pattern is ideal when we are only concerned with predefined responses, but what if we need to verify **how a method was used**, such as whether it was called, how many times, or with which parameters?

That is where the **Mock Object Pattern** comes in, a topic we will explore in the next section.

Mock Object Pattern

The Mock Object Pattern is a testing pattern used to replace real dependencies with controllable, programmable objects that not only simulate responses but also track and verify how they are used.

Unlike stubs, which focus on what is returned, mocks focus on what is done: whether a method was called, how many times, with what arguments, and in what sequence.

Note: *A mock object is like a silent observer sitting in on a method call, recording everything and allowing us to test that the interaction occurred exactly as expected.*

This makes mocks invaluable in **behavior verification**, especially in **interaction-rich systems** like service orchestration, messaging, or event publishing.

Case Study

Let us say we are developing a user registration service. After a new user successfully signs up, the system should:

1. Create the user in the database.
2. Send a welcome notification via **NotificationService**.

We want to test the behavior of **UserRegistrationService**. However, the focus of our test is not whether the notification was delivered; we want to verify that the service called the notification method correctly after the user was saved.

```
public interface NotificationService {
   void sendWelcomeEmail(String userEmail);
}

public class UserRegistrationService {
   private final NotificationService notifier;

   public UserRegistrationService(NotificationService notifier) {
       this.notifier = notifier;
   }

   public void register(String email) {
       // Simulate saving user to the database
       notifier.sendWelcomeEmail(email);
   }
}
```

If we use a stub, we can only simulate what the notification would do; we cannot **verify** whether the notification method was called or not. This leaves us blind to:

- Logic that skips the call.
- Calls to the wrong method or with wrong parameters.
- Multiple invocations when only one was expected.

What we need is a **test double** that records these method interactions.

Applying the Layered Architecture Pattern

We will implement a manual mock that captures method calls and allows assertions after the execution.

Define the Interface

We reuse the **NotificationService** interface.

```
public interface NotificationService {
   void sendWelcomeEmail(String userEmail);
}
```

Create the Manual Mock

Here is a mock implementation that records whether the method was called and with which value:

```
public class MockNotificationService implements NotificationService {
   private boolean called = false;
   private String calledWith = null;

   @Override
   public void sendWelcomeEmail(String userEmail) {
       called = true;
       calledWith = userEmail;
   }

   // Getters for assertions
   public boolean wasCalled() {
       return called;
   }

   public String getCalledWith() {
       return calledWith;
   }
}
```

This mock does not return a value; it **verifies usage** after the fact.

Write the Behavior-Focused Test

We inject the mock into the **UserRegistrationService** and assert behavior after the method call.

```
public class UserRegistrationServiceTest {

   @Test
   public void testWelcomeEmailIsSentOnRegistration() {
       MockNotificationService mockNotifier = new MockNotification-
Service();
       UserRegistrationService service = new UserRegistration
Service(mockNotifier);
```

```
        service.register("test@example.com");

        assertTrue(mockNotifier.wasCalled());
        assertEquals("test@example.com", mockNotifier.get
CalledWith());
    }
}
```

With this test, we are validating that the **sendWelcomeEmail** method was invoked and that it was called with the correct argument.

Using the Mock Object Pattern allows us to:

- Verify interactions, not just outputs.
- Catch missing or incorrect method calls.
- Test logic without requiring actual side effects.
- IFocus tests on expected behavior, especially in messaging, logging, and communication systems.

Design Insight: *Mocks are ideal for testing orchestration logic places where our code does not compute a result but delegates responsibilities to others.*

Mocks work great for observing behavior, but what happens when the system under test contains shared state, like a global object or singleton?

That is where we will encounter testing pains with the **Singleton Design**, and we will show how to manage them cleanly.

Singleton Pattern in Testing

The Singleton Pattern ensures that a class has only one instance, and provides a global point of access to it. While this can be useful for shared resources such as loggers, caches, or configuration managers, it introduces challenges for testing due to its tight coupling, hidden state, and global reach.

Note: *A Singleton is like a global variable in disguise. It is convenient in production, but in tests, it can cause chaos by sharing state across test cases or resisting replacement.*

In test scenarios, the Singleton pattern must be **controlled or replaced** to ensure proper isolation and avoid unpredictable side effects.

Case Study

To suppose, we are building an application where configuration properties, such as maximum retries and logging flags, are fetched via a central **AppConfig** class. This configuration is loaded once and accessed everywhere through a static singleton.

```
public class AppConfig {
   private static final AppConfig instance = new AppConfig();

   private boolean loggingEnabled = true; // default

   private AppConfig() {}

   public static AppConfig getInstance() {
       return instance;
   }

   public boolean isLoggingEnabled() {
       return loggingEnabled;
   }

   public void setLoggingEnabled(boolean value) {
       this.loggingEnabled = value;
   }
}
```

You have a service *DataProcessor* that relies on *AppConfig*:

```
public class DataProcessor {
   public String process(String input) {
       if (AppConfig.getInstance().isLoggingEnabled()) {
           System.out.println("Processing input: " + input);
       }
       return input.toUpperCase();
   }
}
```

Now, we want to test the **DataProcessor** behavior:

- When logging is **enabled**, it should print a message.
- When logging is **disabled**, it should remain silent.

However, because **AppConfig** is a Singleton with global state:

- Its state persists between test runs.
- Tests interfere with each other if one modifies them.
- We cannot inject a different configuration for different test cases.

Applying the Singleton Pattern in Testing

We can tame Singleton behavior during testing using one of two main strategies:

1. **Expose a reset method** only in test scope to clear or reinitialize the singleton.
2. **Refactor to inject the dependency**, even if it is a singleton under the hood.

Note: *For most use cases, the recommended strategy is to refactor the design to inject the dependency, treating the singleton as an internal implementation detail.*

Resettable Singleton for Test Isolation

Modify the Singleton to allow resetting for tests:

```
public class AppConfig {
    private static AppConfig instance = new AppConfig();

    private boolean loggingEnabled = true;

    private AppConfig() {}

    public static AppConfig getInstance() {
        return instance;
    }

    public static void reset() {
        instance = new AppConfig();
    }

    public boolean isLoggingEnabled() {
        return loggingEnabled;
    }

    public void setLoggingEnabled(boolean value) {
        this.loggingEnabled = value;
    }
}
```

Your test class now includes setup and teardown to reset state:

```
public class DataProcessorTest {

    @BeforeEach
    public void resetSingleton() {
        AppConfig.reset();
    }
```

```
    @Test
    public void testLoggingEnabled() {
        AppConfig.getInstance().setLoggingEnabled(true);
        DataProcessor processor = new DataProcessor();
        String result = processor.process("test");
        assertEquals("TEST", result);
        // Output would be printed (not asserted here)
    }

    @Test
    public void testLoggingDisabled() {
        AppConfig.getInstance().setLoggingEnabled(false);
        DataProcessor processor = new DataProcessor();
        String result = processor.process("test");
        assertEquals("TEST", result);
        // No logging expected
    }
}
```

Now that we have tamed the global state, let us explore how to test **variant behaviors** dynamically without rewriting logic or duplicating test cases.

That is precisely what the **Strategy Pattern** enables, especially in testing multiple business rules.

Strategy Pattern for Variant Testing

The Strategy Pattern defines a family of interchangeable algorithms or behaviors, encapsulates each one, and makes them swappable at runtime without altering the clients that use them.

In the context of testing, this pattern is handy when the logic being tested depends on variable business rules. Instead of duplicating test classes or relying on brittle conditionals, the Strategy Pattern enables us to inject the behavior under test, allowing for focused, reusable, and clean test scenarios.

Note: *Think of the Strategy Pattern as a behavioral plug-in: it lets us test how our system reacts to different logics without rewriting core test logic.*

Case Study

In a shopping application, customers may be eligible for different **discount rules** depending on:

- Whether they are VIPs;
- Whether they buy more than five items; or,

- Whether their total amount exceeds a threshold.

The checkout logic uses a **DiscountStrategy** to calculate the final price based on the selected rule.

Here is the abstraction:

```
public interface DiscountStrategy {
    double applyDiscount(double originalAmount);
}
```

Moreover, a *CheckoutService* that delegates to the strategy:

```
public class CheckoutService {
    private final DiscountStrategy discountStrategy;

    public CheckoutService(DiscountStrategy discountStrategy) {
        this.discountStrategy = discountStrategy;
    }

    public double checkout(double totalAmount) {
        return discountStrategy.applyDiscount(totalAmount);
    }
}
```

Without the Strategy Pattern, our test logic would be cluttered with:

- If conditions to simulate VIP, bulk, or promo scenarios.
- Complex switch logic embedded inside the **CheckoutService**.
- Hard-to-maintain test cases for each combination.

Worse, we would have to repeat setup and assertions across multiple tests.

Applying the Strategy Pattern

Using the Strategy Pattern, we decouple the **discount logic** from the **checkout logic**. In our tests, we can now inject different discount strategies to simulate edge cases.

Define Several Discount Strategies

The following code defines multiple implementations of the **DiscountStrategy** interface, each encapsulating a different discount policy that can be applied to a purchase amount.

```
public class NoDiscountStrategy implements DiscountStrategy {
    @Override
    public double applyDiscount(double originalAmount) {
        return originalAmount;
    }
```

```
}

public class FixedPercentageStrategy implements DiscountStrategy
{
    private final double percentage;

    public FixedPercentageStrategy(double percentage) {
        this.percentage = percentage;
    }

    @Override
    public double applyDiscount(double originalAmount) {
        return originalAmount * (1 - percentage);
    }
}

public class ThresholdDiscountStrategy implements Discount
Strategy {
    @Override
    public double applyDiscount(double originalAmount) {
        return originalAmount > 100 ? originalAmount - 15
: originalAmount;
    }
}
```

Use Strategies in Unit Tests

We inject a specific discount rule into the **CheckoutService**, making the test concise and focused.

```
public class CheckoutServiceTest {
    @Test
    public void testCheckoutWithNoDiscount() {
        DiscountStrategy noDiscount = new NoDiscountStrategy();
        CheckoutService checkout = new CheckoutService(noDis-
count);

        double result = checkout.checkout(100.0);

        assertEquals(100.0, result);
    }

    @Test
    public void testCheckoutWithPercentageDiscount() {
        DiscountStrategy percentage = new FixedPercentage
Strategy(0.10); // 10%
```

```
        CheckoutService checkout = new CheckoutService(percentage);

        double result = checkout.checkout(200.0);

        assertEquals(180.0, result, 0.01);
    }

    @Test
    public void testCheckoutWithThresholdDiscount() {
        DiscountStrategy threshold = new ThresholdDiscountStrate-
gy();
        CheckoutService checkout = new CheckoutService(threshold);

        double result = checkout.checkout(120.0);

        assertEquals(105.0, result);
    }
}
```

Note: *These tests are fully isolated, with no conditionals, shared setup, or duplicated logic.*

With the Strategy Pattern in testing, we can:

- Test multiple behaviors without modifying test code.
- Isolate and reuse discount algorithms.
- Reduce complexity in test scenarios.
- Make the system more open for extension, closed for modification.

Design Insight: *In testing, Strategy helps our model* ***variability as an interface****, enabling focused assertions and clean test flows.*

So far, we have controlled responses, observed behaviors, and varied injected logic. However, what if our tests require building complex objects with slightly different properties, without duplicating boilerplate?

That is where the **Decorator Pattern** shines, especially for setting up test data.

Decorator Pattern

The Decorator Pattern allows behavior to be added to an individual object, dynamically and transparently, without affecting other objects of the same class. It achieves this by wrapping objects inside other objects, layering responsibilities in a flexible, modular way.

In testing, this pattern is ideal for building complex test data with variations without duplicating constructors, using inheritance, or writing dozens of setup methods. By wrapping test objects in decorators, we can enrich them with additional properties, behaviors, or traits that are specific to a particular test case.

Case Study

Imagine an online system that manages user profiles. A customer can be:

- Email-verified
- Located in a specific region
- A VIP or regular member
- Opted in for promotions
- Assigned a loyalty level

Each of these traits affects how the system interacts with the customer. Now, our Customer Service process handles customers differently depending on those attributes.

In tests, we often need a base customer object, but sometimes with just a few of these traits added.

Hardcoding multiple constructors or creating specific test subclasses **`VerifiedCustomer`**, **`VipCustomer`**, **`PremiumCustomerWithLocation`** leads to:

- Class explosion;
- Boilerplate duplication; and,
- Hard-to-maintain test fixtures.

We want to:

- Compose customer test objects with various combinations of attributes.
- Keep the setup code concise, clear, and expressive.
- Avoid inheritance or duplication for each test case.

That is precisely what the **Decorator Pattern** provides.

Applying the Decorator Pattern

By decorating a base customer with trait-specific decorators, each test composes the data it needs cleanly and fluently.

Define the Customer Interface:

```
public interface Customer {
    String getProfile();
}
```

Implement the `BaseCustomer`:

```
public class BaseCustomer implements Customer {
    private final String name;

    public BaseCustomer(String name) {
        this.name = name;
    }

    @Override
    public String getProfile() {
        return "Customer: " + name;
    }
}
```

Create Trait Decorators

Each decorator wraps a Customer and adds one additional trait.

```
public abstract class CustomerDecorator implements Customer {
    protected final Customer delegate;

    public CustomerDecorator(Customer delegate) {
        this.delegate = delegate;
    }

    @Override
    public String getProfile() {
        return delegate.getProfile();
    }
}
Example decorators:
public class VipCustomer extends CustomerDecorator {
    public VipCustomer(Customer delegate) {
        super(delegate);
    }

    @Override
    public String getProfile() {
        return delegate.getProfile() + " | VIP";
    }
}

public class LocatedCustomer extends CustomerDecorator {
    private final String location;

    public LocatedCustomer(Customer delegate, String location) {
```

```
            super(delegate);
            this.location = location;
        }

        @Override
        public String getProfile() {
            return delegate.getProfile() + " | Location: " + location;
        }
    }

    public class VerifiedCustomer extends CustomerDecorator {
        public VerifiedCustomer(Customer delegate) {
            super(delegate);
        }

        @Override
        public String getProfile() {
            return delegate.getProfile() + " | Verified Email";
        }
    }
```

Use Decorators in Test Setup

```
    public class CustomerServiceTest {
        @Test
        public void testProcessVipCustomer() {
            Customer customer = new VipCustomer(new BaseCustomer
    ("Alice"));
            String profile = customer.getProfile();

            assertTrue(profile.contains("VIP"));
        }
        @Test
        public void testProcessVerifiedCustomerWithLocation() {
            Customer customer = new LocatedCustomer(
                                      new VerifiedCustomer(
                                          new BaseCustomer("Bob")),
                                      "Paris");
            String profile = customer.getProfile();

            assertTrue(profile.contains("Verified Email"));
            assertTrue(profile.contains("Location: Paris"));
        }
    }
```

Note: *The result is expressive, readable, and avoids combinatorial class overload.*

The Decorator Pattern for test data setup:

- Enables composable and reusable fixtures.
- Keeps test setup clean, DRY, and intention-revealing.
- Avoids rigid class hierarchies and constructor overloads.
- Makes tests easier to maintain as requirements grow.

Design Insight: *Decorators help model test complexity as layers of traits, not as subclasses, making test maintenance smoother and more expressive.*

Conclusion

In this chapter, we have explored how design patterns not only shape production code but also shape the way we test, debug, and reason about our systems. From isolating unpredictable dependencies with **Test Stubs** to validating critical interactions using **Mock Objects**, to managing shared state via **Singleton** refactoring, each pattern we have examined contributes to a broader strategy of making our codebase robust, resilient, and maintainable.

We then extended our capabilities with the **Strategy Pattern**, which enabled us to test behavioral variations without having to rewrite the logic. Finally, the **Decorator Pattern** empowered us to generate clean, modular, and reusable test data compositions without bloating our fixture setups.

In the next chapter, ***Design Patterns in Java Frameworks***, we will explore how popular Java frameworks embed core design patterns into their architecture to promote scalability, modularity, and maintainability. We will learn how to recognize and leverage these patterns, such as Dependency Injection in Spring, DAO in Hibernate, and the Front Controller in JSF, to write cleaner, framework-aligned code. Through practical examples, we will see how understanding these built-in patterns can enhance productivity and lead to more robust enterprise applications.

Points to Remember

- The **Test Stub Pattern** is used to isolate units from non-deterministic or slow dependencies by replacing them with predictable stand-ins.
- The **Mock Object Pattern** focuses on **verifying interactions**, not return values. It is ideal for behavior-driven testing.
- The **Singleton Pattern** can **hurt test isolation** unless refactored to support injection or reset mechanisms.
- The **Strategy Pattern** helps test different business rules or behaviors by injecting variations, instead of hardcoding logic.

- The **Decorator Pattern** enables clean and composable test data setups by wrapping a base object with dynamic traits.
- Well-designed tests reflect good system design. **Pattern-aware testing** leads to improved modularity, traceability, and clearer debugging.
- Avoid over-mocking, deep decorator nesting, and rigid test setups. Focus on **expressiveness, reusability, and independence**.

Multiple Choice Questions

1. Which of these is the primary advantage of using a stub in testing?
   a. To verify method calls and arguments.
   b. To simulate different user inputs.
   c. To isolate the system under test from external dependencies.
   d. To replace constructors with factories.
2. Which pattern is best suited for verifying whether a method was called with specific arguments?
   a. Strategy Pattern
   b. Test Stub Pattern
   c. Singleton Pattern
   d. Mock Object Pattern
3. The Strategy Pattern allows us to:
   a. Simulate APIs with canned responses.
   b. Test variant behaviors by injecting logic dynamically.
   c. Replace singletons with stateless services.
   d. Wrap test data with traits.
4. Which of the following is one of the benefits of using the Decorator Pattern in test data setup?
   a. Ensures concurrency in test runs.
   b. Injects services via reflection.
   c. Composes traits without subclassing.
   d. Guarantees test parallelism.

Answers

1. c
2. d
3. b
4. c

Questions

1. In what scenarios would we choose a stub over a mock, and what are the reasons for this choice?
2. How can we safely refactor a legacy singleton to make it test-friendly and maintain its original functionality?
3. Describe a real-world use case where the Strategy Pattern improved the readability or reusability of our test suite.
4. How would we avoid decorator overuse in a complex test data setup while still maintaining flexibility?
5. What design decisions in our application today might hinder future testability, and how can we use design patterns to mitigate that?
6. In which situations does the Decorator Pattern offer better flexibility than the Builder Pattern for complex test configurations?

Key Terms

- **Test Stub**: A controlled replacement for a real dependency that returns fixed data.
- **Mock Object**: A test double that records and verifies how it was interacted with.
- **Singleton Pattern**: Ensures only one instance exists, but often causes state-related test issues.
- **Strategy Pattern**: Encapsulates a behavior or algorithm and allows it to be replaced at runtime.
- **Decorator Pattern**: Wraps an object to add functionality or attributes dynamically.
- **Behavioral Testing**: Verifying the outcome and sequence of actions performed by the system.

- **Test Isolation**: Ensuring a test runs independently of others, without shared side effects.
- **Fixture Setup**: The process of preparing test data before test execution.
- **Dependency Injection**: Providing external resources to a class through its constructor or setter.
- **Test Smell**: A symptom in test code that may indicate deeper problems in design or coverage.

CHAPTER 8
Design Patterns in Java Frameworks

Introduction

Java frameworks are far more than mere utility libraries; they serve as comprehensive architectural foundations that structurally embed design patterns, often without the developer being aware. These patterns, though hidden behind the abstractions they provide, do form the core of modularity, dependency injection, request routing, and separation of concerns. Gaining insight into how these patterns are implemented in frameworks such as Spring, Hibernate, or JSF enables developers to better leverage their capabilities and build applications that are more robust, testable, and maintainable.

This chapter examines how classic design patterns are integrated into the most widely used Java frameworks. We will analyze injection and decoupling mechanisms with **Spring**, the **DAO** architecture in **Hibernate**, **front controller** logic in **JSF**, and **interception filters** in **Struts**. Each section will not only explain the underlying design pattern, but also provide concrete examples through original, well-commented code, real-world business scenarios, and explanatory diagrams.

By the end of this chapter, we will be able to identify the design patterns implicitly used within Java frameworks, apply them consciously in their own modules, design components that align more closely with architectural best practices, and improve their ability to diagnose, test, and maintain Java applications effectively.

Structure

In this chapter, we will cover the following topics:

- Spring Framework: Dependency Injection and Aspect-Oriented Programming
- Hibernate: Data Access Object Pattern

- JakartaServer Faces: Front Controller Pattern
- Apache Struts: Intercepting Filter Pattern

Spring Framework: Dependency Injection and Aspect-Oriented Programming

The Spring Framework is one of the most influential platforms in the Java ecosystem. At its core, it leverages several design patterns to promote **loose coupling**, **modularity**, and **testability**. Two central patterns shape the Spring architecture:

- **Dependency Injection Pattern**: It is responsible for decoupling components and facilitating easy testing and substitution.
- **Proxy Pattern**: This is used extensively in Aspect-Oriented Programming AOP for cross-cutting concerns such as logging, transaction management, and caching.

This section explores how these patterns operate within the Spring core and how we can leverage them effectively.

Dependency Injection Pattern

Dependency Injection, known as *DI*, is a **creational pattern** that separates the construction of an object from its dependencies. Rather than an object creating or finding its collaborators, they are provided to it, typically injected by a container.

In Spring, *DI* is at the heart of the **IoC, Inversion of Control Container**, which manages the lifecycle and relationships of objects.

Let us consider an e-commerce scenario where we inject different payment processors.

This diagram illustrates the runtime binding of an interface to an implementation. The consumer `CheckoutService` does not know about the actual class being injected, a clear case of **loose coupling**.

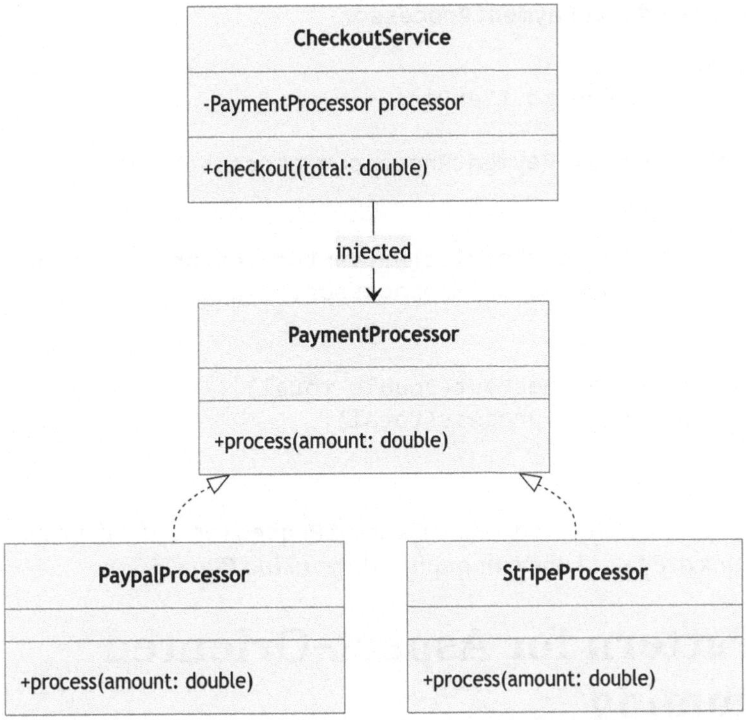

Figure 8.1: *Dependency Injection - Payment Service Injection*

Interface

```
public interface PaymentProcessor {
    void process(double amount);
}
```

Concrete Implementation 1

```
@Component
public class PaypalProcessor implements PaymentProcessor {
    public void process(double amount) {
        System.out.println("Processing via PayPal: " + amount);
    }
}
```

Concrete Implementation 2

```
@Component
public class StripeProcessor implements PaymentProcessor {
    public void process(double amount) {
        System.out.println("Processing via Stripe: " + amount);
    }
}
```

Service That Depends on `PaymentProcessor`

```
@Service
public class CheckoutService {

    private final PaymentProcessor processor;

    @Autowired
    public CheckoutService(PaymentProcessor processor) {
        this.processor = processor;
    }

    public void checkout(double total) {
        processor.process(total);
    }
}
```

Note: *Spring injects the correct* **`PaymentProcessor`** *at runtime. If multiple implementations are found, we can qualify them using* **`@Qualifier`**.

Proxy Pattern for Aspect-Oriented Programming

The **Proxy Pattern** is a **structural pattern**. A proxy acts as a substitute or placeholder for another object, managing access to that object. Spring uses proxies extensively in AOP to apply behaviors such as:

- Logging
- Transaction Management
- Caching
- Security

Note: *In Spring AOP, proxies wrap target objects to add behavior* ***before***, ***after***, *or* ***around*** *method calls.*

For instance, we want to log method calls across several services without polluting the business logic.

This diagram illustrates how the Spring proxy intercepts the call to add behavior like logging before reaching the target service. This dynamic redirection implements the **Proxy Pattern** behind the scenes.

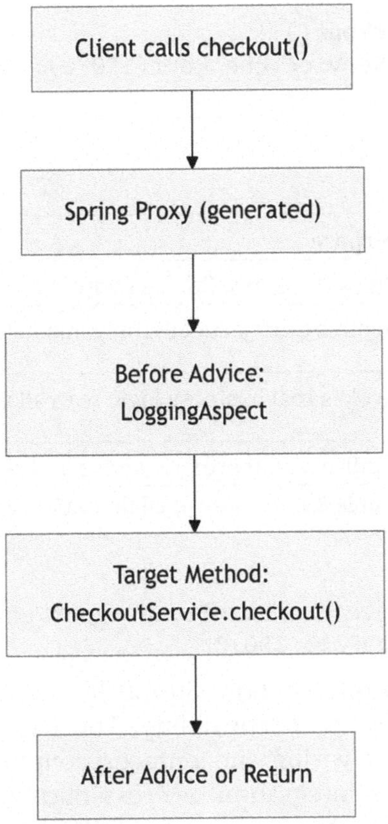

Figure 8.2: *AOP - Logging Aspect*

The `LoggingAspect` Class Implementation

```
@Aspect
@Component
public class LoggingAspect {

    @Before("execution(* com.rickenbazolo.*.*(..))")
    public void logBeforeMethod(JoinPoint joinPoint) {
        System.out.println("Calling: " + joinPoint.getSignature());
    }
}
```

Code Integration Test

```
@SpringBootTest
class CheckoutServiceTest {

    @Autowired
    CheckoutService checkoutService;
```

```
        @Test
        void testCheckout() {
            checkoutService.checkout(150.0);
        }
    }
```

What This Test Validates

Aspect	**Purpose**
`@SpringBootTest`	Starts the entire Spring context for a full-stack integration test
`@Autowired CheckoutService`	Ensures Spring successfully injects all dependencies
`checkoutService.checkout(...)`	Invokes real business logic with all wiring DI + AOP in place
Console output	Confirms AOP proxy is active and real implementation works

Table 8.1: *Purpose of DI and AOP Test*

When Running the Test

```
Calling: void com.rickenbazolo.CheckoutService.checkout(double)
Processing via PayPal: 150.0
```

In this section, we have explored how Spring leverages two fundamental design patterns to achieve modularity and flexibility: The **Dependency Injection Pattern**, which simplifies component wiring and reduces coupling, and the **Proxy Pattern**, which enables the seamless integration of cross-cutting concerns such as logging or security without polluting core business logic. These patterns form the backbone of the Spring framework, and mastering them empowers developers to write clean, scalable, and testable applications.

We will now turn our attention to **Hibernate**, where design patterns also play a central role, particularly the **Data Access Object Pattern** and its relationship with **lazy loading**. These mechanisms are the key in managing persistence logic efficiently in Java enterprise applications.

Hibernate: Data Access Object Pattern

Hibernate is a robust Object-Relational Mapping ORM framework that bridges the gap between the object-oriented world of Java and relational databases. Beyond data persistence, Hibernate encapsulates multiple design patterns that make data access **modular**, **maintainable**, and **efficient**.

Two major patterns are inherently present in Hibernate:

- **DAO Pattern**: This encapsulates database access logic in dedicated classes.
- **Proxy Pattern**: It enables *lazy loading* of entities using runtime-generated proxies.

In this section, we explore how Hibernate leverages these patterns and how we can apply them effectively in real-world scenarios.

Data Access Object Pattern in Hibernate

The Data Access Object Pattern is a structural design pattern that abstracts and encapsulates all interactions with the data source, providing a clean separation between persistence logic and business logic. By isolating database operations within dedicated DAO classes, this pattern ensures that the service layer remains agnostic to how data is retrieved or stored. This separation not only enhances code reusability but also facilitates unit testing, as DAOs can easily be mocked or stubbed to simulate data access in isolation.

Note: *Spring Data JPA can generate DAO implementations automatically, but understanding the manual approach helps in customizing complex queries.*

This class diagram illustrates the application of the **DAO Pattern** in a typical Hibernate-based persistence layer. The Userclass represents the domain entity with basic fields. The **`UserDao`** interface defines the contract for data access operations. The **`UserDaoImpl`** class provides the concrete implementation of this interface and uses an **`EntityManager`** to perform the actual database operations.

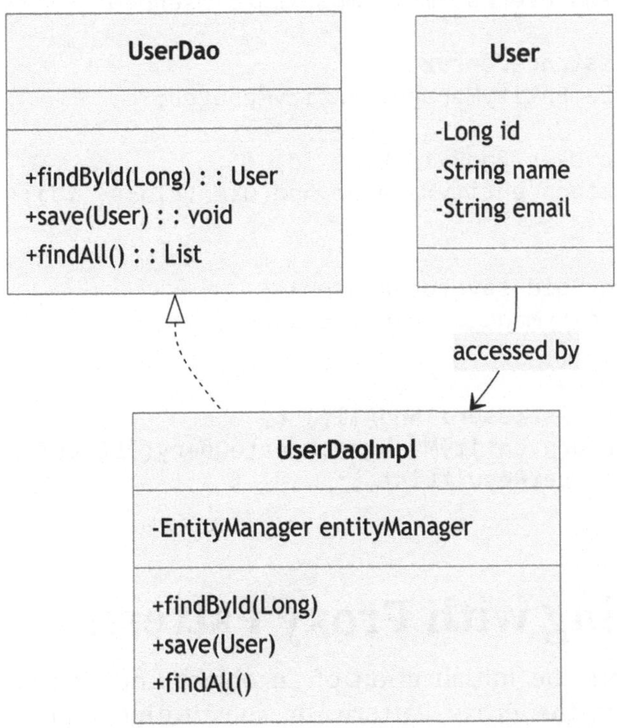

Figure 8.3: *Hibernate - DAO Pattern with Hibernate*

Entity

```
@Entity
public class User {
    @Id @GeneratedValue
    private Long id;

    private String name;
    private String email;

    // Getters and Setters
}
```

DAO Interface

```
public interface UserDao {
    User findById(Long id);
    void save(User user);
    List<User> findAll();
}
```

Implementation

```
@Repository
public class UserDaoImpl implements UserDao {

    @PersistenceContext
    private EntityManager entityManager;

    public User findById(Long id) {
        return entityManager.find(User.class, id);
    }

    public void save(User user) {
        entityManager.persist(user);
    }

    public List<User> findAll() {
        return entityManager.createQuery("SELECT u FROM User u",
User.class).getResultList();
    }
}
```

Lazy Loading with Proxy Pattern

Lazy loading defers the initialization of an object until it is needed. Hibernate achieves this using the Proxy Pattern, by substituting real entities with proxy instances that only fetch data when accessed.

This optimization prevents unnecessary database queries and improves performance in *many-to-one* or *one-to-many* relationships.

Use Case: User and Orders

```
@Entity
public class Order {
    @Id @GeneratedValue
    private Long id;

    @ManyToOne(fetch = FetchType.LAZY)
    private User user;
}
```

By default, the *user* is a **proxy**. The associated user will only be fetched when explicitly accessed:

```
Order order = entityManager.find(Order.class, 7L);
User u = order.getUser(); // No query yet
String email = u.getEmail(); // Now triggers query
```

This sequence diagram demonstrates how the **Hibernate lazy loading mechanism** works when accessing an associated entity. The application calls **`order.getUser()`**, but instead of fetching the full User from the database immediately, Hibernate returns a **proxy instance**. When the application later calls **`user.getEmail()`**, the proxy triggers a query to the **database**, retrieves the real User object, and returns the requested email field. This approach optimizes performance by delaying database access until the data is needed.

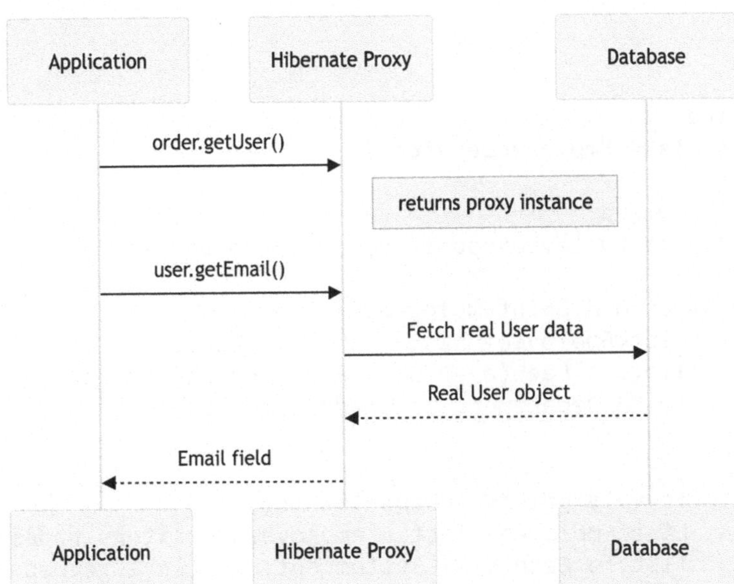

Figure 8.4: *Hibernate - DAO Pattern with Hibernate*

Note: *Accessing proxies outside of a session is a common pitfall that usually results in a lazy loading exception.*

Case Study

Imagine a company that tracks employees and their assigned departments. Departments are rarely accessed when retrieving employee lists, so lazy loading is preferred.

Entities

```
@Entity
public class Employee {
    @Id @GeneratedValue
    private Long id;

    private String name;

    @ManyToOne(fetch = FetchType.LAZY)
    private Department department;
}

@Entity
public class Department {
    @Id @GeneratedValue
    private Long id;
    private String name;
}
```

Service Layer

```
@Service
public class EmployeeService {

    @Autowired
    private EmployeeRepository employeeRepository;

    public void printEmployees() {
        List<Employee> list = employeeRepository.findAll();
        list.forEach(e -> System.out.println(e.getName()));
        // No Department is loaded at this point
    }

    public void printWithDepartments() {
        List<Employee> list = employeeRepository.findAll();
        list.forEach(e -> System.out.println(e.getDepartment().
getName()));
```

```
            // Department gets lazily loaded here
        }
    }
```

Integration Testing with Lazy Load Awareness

```
    @SpringBootTest
    @Transactional
    class EmployeeServiceTest {

        @Autowired
        EmployeeService employeeService;

        @Test
        void testLazyLoadingInTransaction() {
            employeeService.printWithDepartments();
        }
    }
```

Note: *Why* **`@Transactional?`** *Without an active transaction, lazy loading will fail because the Hibernate session closes too early.*

Hibernate leverages several key design patterns to manage data persistence in a clean and maintainable way. It uses the Data Access Object Pattern to separate persistence logic from business logic, allowing us to encapsulate database interactions in dedicated classes. Additionally, it employs the Proxy Pattern to implement lazy loading for associated entities, enabling on-demand data retrieval and improving performance. Understanding these patterns is essential for building efficient, decoupled, and scalable data access layers.

In the next section, we will explore **Jakarta Server Faces**, and how it incorporates the **Front Controller Pattern** to centralize request handling and streamline user interface logic in Java web applications.

Jakarta Server Faces - Front Controller Pattern

Jakarta Server Faces (JSF) is a component-based UI framework for building Java web applications. It follows the Model-View-Controller or MVC architectural pattern and heavily relies on the Front Controller Pattern to centralize request handling.

In JakartaServer Faces, several design patterns work together to structure the framework's request processing and user interaction model. At its core, JSF implements the **Front Controller Pattern** through the FacesServlet, which acts as a central entry point for all incoming HTTP requests. This servlet delegates processing to the appropriate managed beans, thus, effectively decoupling request handling from presentation logic. Additionally, JSF applies the **Command Pattern** in a secondary role, where user actions such as button clicks or form submissions invoke methods on managed beans, encapsulating user-initiated behavior as commands. This architecture promotes a clean separation of concerns, facilitates the reuse of UI components, and supports centralized navigation and configuration through declarative rules.

The Front Controller Pattern is a **behavioral pattern** that centralizes control logic in a single handler controller. This controller intercepts all requests and dispatches them to specific components.

In JSF, the front controller is the **`FacesServlet`**, configured in *web.xml* or via annotations. This central servlet processes every HTTP request targeting an **`.xhtml`** page.

Example of JSF Flow

All **`.xhtml`** files are routed through **`FacesServlet`**, making it the single entry point just like any good front controller.

```
<servlet>
    <servlet-name>Faces Servlet</servlet-name>
    <servlet-class>jakarta.faces.webapp.FacesServlet</servlet
-class>
</servlet>

<servlet-mapping>
    <servlet-name>Faces Servlet</servlet-name>
    <url-pattern>*.xhtml</url-pattern>
</servlet-mapping>
```

JSF Front Controller

Each JSF request follows a strict lifecycle handled by the central servlet. The front controller ensures uniform processing, validation, and navigation.

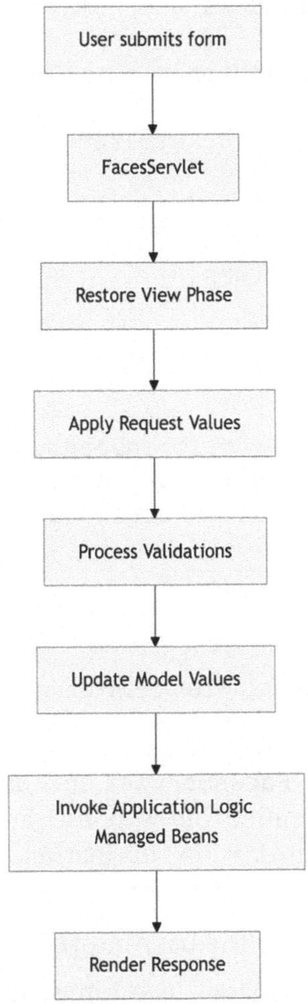

Figure 8.5: *Jakarta Server Faces - JSF Front Controller*

JSF with Managed Beans and Navigation

When the user clicks **`Login`**, the action triggers the **`login()`** method in **`LoginBean`**. This is analogous to the **Command Pattern**, where behavior is encapsulated as a method and passed to the controller.

```
@Named
@RequestScoped
public class LoginBean {

    private String username;
    private String password;

    public String login() {
```

```
        if ("admin".equals(username) && "secret".equals
(password)) {
            return "dashboard.xhtml?faces-redirect=true";
        } else {
            return "login.xhtml?error=true";
        }
    }

    // Getters and Setters
}
```

Login.xml

```
<h:form>
    <h:inputText value="#{loginBean.username}" />
    <h:inputSecret value="#{loginBean.password}" />
    <h:commandButton value="Login" action="#{loginBean.login}" />
</h:form>
```

Case Study

Imagine a customer portal that requires centralized request processing and secure, user-friendly login workflows.

In a JSF-based application, the **FacesServlet** acts as the central controller, routing all page requests through a unified entry point. From there, **managed beans** are responsible for handling authentication, navigation, and business logic. This setup enables a well-defined separation of concerns:

- **View**: **login.xhtml** defines the user interface.
- **Controller**: **LoginBean** manages user input and interaction.
- **Model**: The User entity represents the domain data.

This architecture follows the principles of the **Model-View-Controller** pattern, enhanced by JSF's declarative and component-driven capabilities.

LoginBean and View Diagram

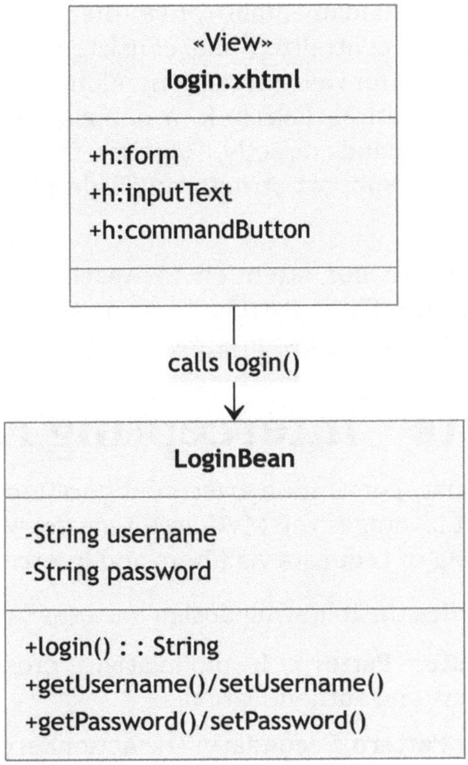

Figure 8.6: *Jakarta Server Faces - LoginBean and View*

Integration Testing

JSF is often tested via **integration or functional tests** such as with Selenium, but mock tests can also verify controller logic.

```
class LoginBeanTest {
    @Test
    void loginShouldRedirectIfValid() {
        LoginBean bean = new LoginBean();
        bean.setUsername("admin");
        bean.setPassword("secret");
        String outcome = bean.login();
        assertEquals("dashboard.xhtml?faces-redirect=true",
outcome);
    }
}
```

Note: *While this test does not require the JSF container, it validates the action method logic, which is vital in Command Pattern design.*

Two key design patterns fundamentally drive the JSF architecture. The **Front Controller Pattern** enables centralized and consistent handling of user requests, ensuring a unified entry point for web interactions. Alongside it, the **Command Pattern** allows user actions such as button clicks or form submissions to invoke managed bean methods as executable commands directly. Together, these patterns promote a clean separation of concerns and support structured UI development in large-scale Java web applications.

In the next section, we turn our attention to **Apache Struts** and explore how it implements the **Intercepting Filter Pattern** to manage cross-cutting concerns such as logging, authentication, and request preprocessing.

Apache Struts - Intercepting Filter Pattern

Apache Struts is a robust, convention-over-configuration framework for building Java web applications. It leverages the MVC architecture, with a strong emphasis on **pre- and post-processing of requests** via filters and interceptors.

At its core, Struts embodies the following design patterns:

- **Intercepting Filter Pattern**: It modularizes cross-cutting concerns like validation, logging, and authentication.
- **Front Controller Pattern, Secondary:** The ActionServlet acts as the centralized entry point for all HTTP requests.

This section examines how Struts structures request processing through these patterns, enhancing modularity and maintainability.

Intercepting Filter Pattern in Struts

The Intercepting Filter Pattern is a structural pattern that allows standard services such as logging, authentication, or input validation to be applied to requests or responses before and after the main request handler executes.

In Struts, this is achieved via:

- **`RequestProcessor` in Struts 1:**

  Request processing is centralized in the **`RequestProcessor`**, which coordinates the execution flow before delegating to action classes. This approach relies on a tightly coupled lifecycle and a rigid processing pipeline.

- **Interceptors in Struts 2 `InterceptorStack`:**

  Cross-cutting concerns such as validation, authentication, and logging are applied declaratively around action execution. While more flexible than Struts

1, this model still requires explicit configuration and framework-specific abstractions.

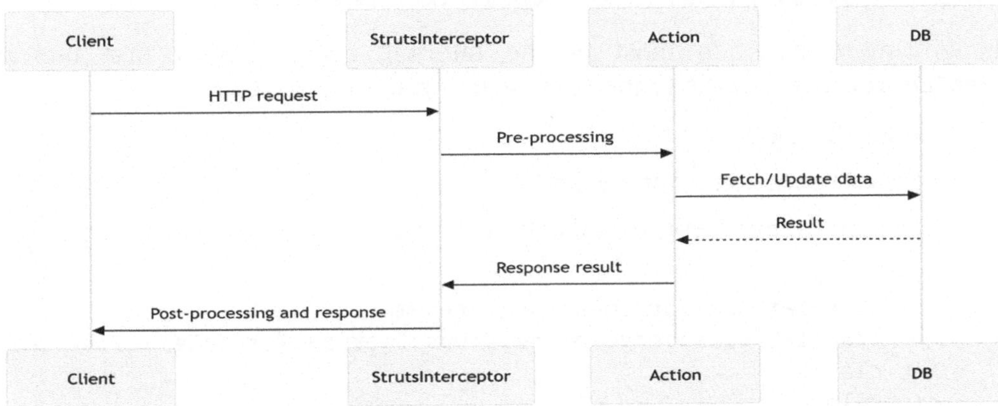

***Figure 8.7**: Apache Struts - Intercepting Filter*

Logging Interceptor

```
public class LoggingInterceptor extends AbstractInterceptor {
    public String intercept(ActionInvocation invocation) throws
Exception {
        System.out.println("Before action: " + invocation.get
Action().getClass().getName());
        String result = invocation.invoke();
        System.out.println("After action: " + result);
        return result;
    }
}
```

struts.xml Configuration

```
<interceptors>
    <interceptor name="logging" class="com.example.Logging
Interceptor" />
    <interceptor-stack name="defaultStack">
        <interceptor-ref name="logging"/>
        <interceptor-ref name="defaultStack"/>
    </interceptor-stack>
</interceptors>

<action name="login" class="com.example.LoginAction">
    <interceptor-ref name="defaultStack" />
    <result name="success">/dashboard.jsp</result>
</action>
```

Note: *The interceptor wraps the action method, allowing pre/post-processing around it.*

Front Controller Pattern in Struts

Although Interceptors do most of the filtering, every request first hits the **`ActionServlet`**, which is the Front Controller of the framework. It:

- Parses the URL;
- Locates the action mapping; and,
- Delegates to interceptors and action classes.

```
<servlet>
    <servlet-name>action</servlet-name>
    <servlet-class>org.apache.struts.action.ActionServlet</serv-
let-class>
</servlet>

<servlet-mapping>
    <servlet-name>action</servlet-name>
    <url-pattern>*.do</url-pattern>
</servlet-mapping>
```

All *.do* requests go through a single servlet, the very definition of a Front Controller.

Case Study

Imagine an IT company requires a support portal to manage incoming user requests efficiently and securely. Each request must be **authenticated** to verify the user's session or access token, **validated** to ensure all necessary input fields are correctly provided, and **logged** to track user actions for auditing and analytical purposes. Embedding these concerns directly within every action class would not only result in significant code duplication but also violate the principle of separation of concerns, making the system harder to maintain and evolve.

To address the duplication of cross-cutting concerns, the system introduces a modular approach using interceptors. The **`AuthenticationInterceptor`** verifies the user session or access token before any request is processed, ensuring that only authorized users can proceed. The **`ValidationInterceptor`** checks that all required input fields are present and correctly formatted, reducing the risk of processing invalid data. Meanwhile, the **`LoggingInterceptor`** captures and records each request and user action, supporting auditability and debugging. This interceptor-based design centralizes essential concerns, promotes code reuse, and enhances maintainability, while allowing action classes to remain focused solely on their core business responsibilities.

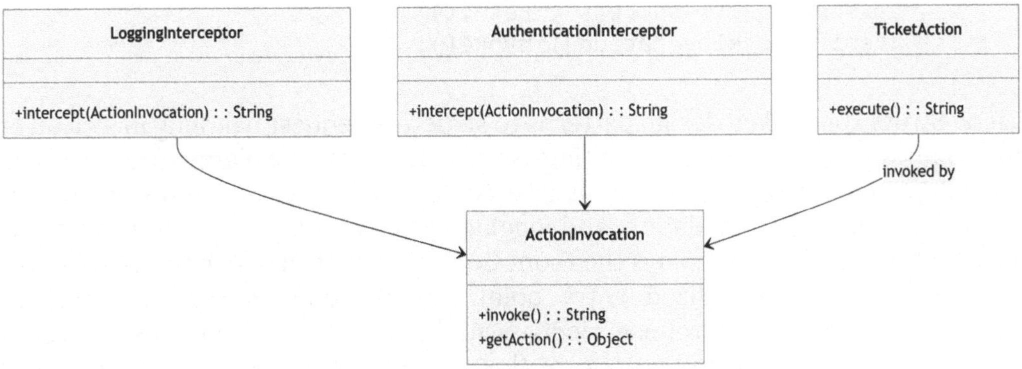

Figure 8.8: *Apache Struts - Interceptor Stack*

struts.xml

```
<interceptor-stack name="secureStack">
    <interceptor-ref name="authentication"/>
    <interceptor-ref name="validation"/>
    <interceptor-ref name="logging"/>
    <interceptor-ref name="defaultStack"/>
</interceptor-stack>

<action name="createTicket" class="com.company.TicketAction">
    <interceptor-ref name="secureStack"/>
    <result name="success">/success.jsp</result>
</action>
```

Note: *Each cross-cutting concern is handled separately, in sequence, with full modularity.*

Testing Interceptors

Struts 2 allows unit testing of interceptors and actions using its mock framework or JUnit with Mockito.

```
@Test
void testLoggingInterceptor() throws Exception {
    LoggingInterceptor interceptor = new LoggingInterceptor();
    ActionInvocation mockInvocation = mock(ActionInvocation.
class);

    when(mockInvocation.getAction()).thenReturn(new LoginAction());
    when(mockInvocation.invoke()).thenReturn("success");

    String result = interceptor.intercept(mockInvocation);
```

```
        assertEquals("success", result);
        verify(mockInvocation).invoke();
    }
```

Apache Struts applies key design patterns to structure request handling in a clean and extensible way. It uses the Intercepting Filter Pattern to modularize pre- and post-processing logic through configurable interceptors, allowing cross-cutting concerns such as authentication, validation, and logging to be handled consistently across the application. In parallel, it employs the Front Controller Pattern via the **`ActionServlet`**, which serves as a centralized entry point for all incoming requests. Together, these patterns provide a robust mechanism for separating concerns, enhancing maintainability, and ensuring a uniform flow of request processing throughout the framework.

Conclusion

Design patterns are not just abstract ideas; they are deeply embedded into the structure and philosophy of the most widely used Java frameworks. Whether it is the Spring's powerful use of Dependency Injection and Proxy, Hibernate's clean DAO abstraction and Lazy Loading, the JSF Front Controller lifecycle and Command mapping, or the Struts Flexible Intercepting Filters, patterns are everywhere.

This chapter has shown how understanding these underlying patterns allow developers to:

- Read and structure framework-based code with better clarity;
- Extend or customize behavior without breaking architectural principles; and,
- Make better decisions about **testability**, **modularity**, and **reuse.**

Frameworks like Spring, Hibernate, JSF, and Struts are not just toolkits; they are pattern-driven ecosystems. Mastering the patterns behind them unlocks their full potential.

In real-world enterprise applications, Java frameworks are rarely used in isolation. A typical architecture often combines multiple frameworks to handle different layers of the application. For example, the **Spring Framework** may be used for orchestrating business logic and managing dependencies, **Hibernate** for object-relational mapping ORM and database persistence, and **JSF** for building the web-based presentation layer and managing user interactions. Each of these frameworks embeds powerful design patterns, working together to create a cohesive, modular, and maintainable system architecture.

In the next chapter, ***Distributed System Design Patterns***, we will explore how essential architectural patterns enable communication, coordination, and scalability in distributed environments. We will examine how models such as Client-Server, Broker, and Peer-to-Peer provide structured approaches to building resilient and modular distributed systems. Through practical examples, we will learn how these patterns form the foundation of modern architectures ranging from cloud-native applications to microservices and decentralized networks, and how applying them can improve the reliability and maintainability of large-scale systems.

Points to Remember

- Design patterns are structural and behavioral blueprints applied across frameworks.
- Spring uses **Dependency Injection** to decouple classes and **Proxy Pattern** for AOP.
- JSF structures request flow using the **Front Controller Pattern**, and action binding via the **Command Pattern**.
- Apache Struts handles cross-cutting concerns using the **Intercepting Filter Pattern**.
- Combining frameworks in a real-world application requires understanding how their patterns interact.
- Always ensure active session when accessing lazy-loaded fields.
- The Proxy Pattern enables features like logging, security, and transaction management.

Multiple Choice Questions

1. Which pattern is common between JSF and Struts?
    a. Strategy
    b. Front Controller
    c. Decorator
    d. Builder
2. Which of the following pattern is used for separating data access logic in Hibernate?
    a. Factory
    b. DAO
    c. Proxy
    d. Command

3. Which of these allows Spring to apply logging or security without modifying business code?
    a. Factory
    b. Singleton
    c. Proxy
    d. Bridge
4. Which of these is NOT typically a cross-cutting concern handled by Interceptors?
    a. Logging
    b. Security
    c. Navigation
    d. Input validation

Answers

1. b
2. b
3. c
4. c

Questions

1. Why is it important to recognize the design patterns in a framework you use daily?
2. How can understanding Proxy Pattern improve debugging and testing in Spring or Hibernate?
3. If your application grows in size, which patterns help manage complexity across layers?
4. How would you replace one persistence framework with another such as Hibernate to JOOQ without rewriting the entire business logic?
5. In a microservice-based system, how do the patterns presented in this chapter apply differently than in monoliths?

Key Terms

- **DAO (Data Access Object)**: Encapsulates all database access logic into a separate layer.
- **Front Controller**: Central controller that handles all requests in a web framework.
- **Intercepting Filter**: Inserts reusable logic like logging, validation before/after request flow.
- **`EntityManager`**: JPA interface used to persist and manage entities.
- **`FacesServlet`**: The front controller for all JSF page requests.
- **Interceptors**: Middleware logic in frameworks like Struts that wraps around action methods.
- **`@Aspect/@Before`**: Spring AOP annotations used to define proxies and behavior injection.
- **Lazy Loading**: Defers object loading until it is accessed; implemented using proxies.

CHAPTER 9
Patterns for Distributed System

Introduction

Distributed systems have become the cornerstone of scalable and resilient software architectures. Whether powering cloud-native applications, microservices, messaging platforms, or decentralized networks, they allow components to communicate and collaborate across machines, processes, or even continents. However, this distribution comes at a cost: systems must now handle latency, partial failures, service discovery, synchronization, and consistency. These challenges demand structured solutions that abstract complexity while preserving performance and reliability.

Design patterns for distributed systems offer time-tested strategies to structure interactions, manage complexity, and ensure predictable behavior across remote components. In this chapter, we explore three foundational patterns: The **Client-Server Pattern**, which defines a clear division of roles between service providers and consumers; the **Broker Pattern**, which decouples communication through intermediaries that mediate service invocations; and the **Peer-to-Peer Pattern**, which distributes responsibilities evenly across nodes, supporting decentralized collaboration and scalability. Each pattern is contextualized with a real-world scenario and explained through detailed UML-style diagrams and well-commented Java implementations.

By the end of this chapter, readers will be equipped to recognize and apply distributed design patterns in their Java systems. They will learn how to architect solutions that remain maintainable under scale, resilient to failure, and modular in structure. Beyond the theoretical understanding, this chapter fosters practical intuition through annotated code, architectural guidance, and illustrative examples, allowing developers, engineers, and architects to build distributed applications aligned with the best practices confidently.

Structure

In this chapter, we will cover:

- Client-Server Pattern
- Broker Pattern
- Peer-to-Peer Pattern

Client-Server Pattern

The Client-Server Pattern is the foundational architecture model for distributed systems. It divides a system into two distinct roles: the **client**, which initiates requests, and the **server**, which processes and responds to those requests. This separation allows for modularity, reuse, centralized data access, and scalability through replication or load balancing on the server side. Most web applications, mobile backends, and service-based architectures begin with this pattern.

At its core, the Client-Server Pattern introduces **directionality**: clients depend on services exposed by servers, but not vice versa. Communication often follows a synchronous request-response model, such as HTTP, but can also be extended to asynchronous models via messaging protocols. This pattern becomes especially powerful when clients are lightweight and stateless, and servers are designed to scale horizontally.

Case Study

Consider a nationwide online movie booking system. Users interact via a web or mobile interface to search for shows, reserve seats, and make payments. These requests are sent to a backend server, which hosts the business logic, connects to the movie catalog, checks seat availability, handles transactions, and sends back confirmations. The client is only responsible for rendering the UI and relaying user input, while the server centralizes data integrity, validation, and rules enforcement.

This scenario illustrates the benefits of the Client-Server model: centralized control over ticket inventory, uniform business rules, and the possibility to horizontally scale the server under peak loads such as blockbuster releases.

Note: *In this case study, we will focus on implementing useful classes to apply the design model concept.*

Applying the Client-Server Pattern

This sequence diagram shows a typical interaction flow: the client initiates requests, the server processes and responds, with no direct dependence in the opposite direction.

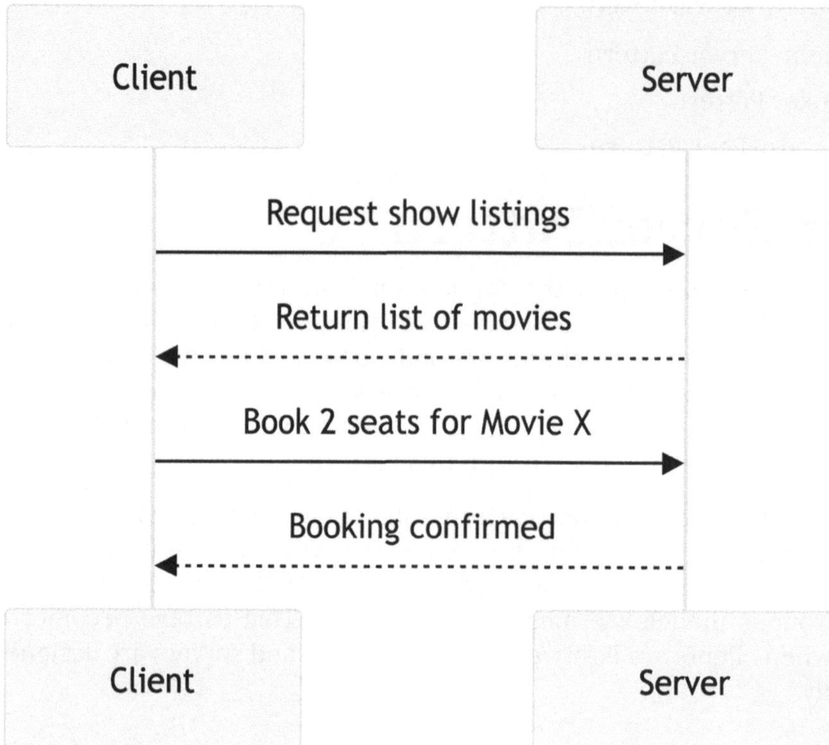

Figure 9.1: *Client-Server Pattern - Interaction Flow*

Define the Data Model

This class represents a movie with a title and a number of available seats. It provides a method to book seats while ensuring that availability is respected.

```
public class Movie {
    private String title;
    private int availableSeats;

    public Movie(String title, int availableSeats) {
        this.title = title;
        this.availableSeats = availableSeats;
    }

    public boolean bookSeats(int seats) {
        if (availableSeats >= seats) {
            availableSeats -= seats;
```

```
            return true;
        }
        return false;
    }

    // Getters omitted for brevity
}
```

Create the Server Component

This class simulates the server-side logic: it holds a movie catalog, lists available movies, and handles booking requests by validating seat availability.

```
public class MovieServer {
    private Map<String, Movie> movies = new HashMap<>();

    public MovieServer() {
        movies.put("Interstellar", new Movie("Interstellar",
100));
        movies.put("Inception", new Movie("Inception", 80));
    }

    public List<String> listAvailableMovies() {
        return new ArrayList<>(movies.keySet());
    }

    public String bookMovie(String title, int seats) {
        Movie movie = movies.get(title);
        if (movie != null && movie.bookSeats(seats)) {
            return "Booking confirmed for " + title;
        }
        return "Booking failed. Not enough seats or movie not
found.";
    }
}
```

Simulate the Client

This component acts as the client, interacting with the server to list movies and perform a booking request. It shows how the client remains decoupled from business logic.

```
public class MovieClient {
    private MovieServer server;

    public MovieClient(MovieServer server) {
        this.server = server;
```

```
    }

    public void performBooking() {
        System.out.println("Available movies: " + server.
listAvailableMovies());
        String response = server.bookMovie("Interstellar", 2);
        System.out.println("Server response: " + response);
    }

    public static void main(String[] args) {
        MovieServer server = new MovieServer();
        MovieClient client = new MovieClient(server);
        client.performBooking();
    }
}
```

Output Console:

```
Available movies: [Interstellar, Inception]
Server response: Booking confirmed for Interstellar
```

Applying the Client–Server Pattern lays the groundwork for structured communication in distributed systems. By clearly separating roles and responsibilities, it enhances modularity, simplifies testing, and enables independent scaling of server components. As systems grow, however, direct client–server interactions become harder to manage.

The pattern promotes centralized control, making it easier to secure, monitor, and scale the server side. At the same time, it can introduce latency bottlenecks and single points of failure. In practice, teams mitigate these risks with load balancers, caching proxies, and failover clusters to achieve high availability and performance at scale.

For developers, it is essential to ensure stateless client interactions wherever possible, gracefully handle server failures and timeouts, define clear API boundaries and contracts between clients and servers, and implement robust logging and observability on both sides.

This pattern remains a foundational starting point for distributed architectures and often underpins microservices as well as cloud-native applications. Next, we will explore the **Broker Pattern**, which introduces an intermediary to route requests, decouple services, and simplify integration across distributed components.

Broker Pattern

In distributed systems, as the number of services and clients grows, direct communication between each component becomes complex and challenging to scale. **The Broker Pattern** solves this by introducing an intermediary called a broker that decouples clients from service providers. Instead of sending requests directly, clients communicate with the broker, which is responsible for locating the appropriate service, forwarding the request, and returning the response.

This pattern introduces a level of indirection that promotes loose coupling, simplifies service discovery, and facilitates runtime flexibility. It is instrumental in service-oriented architectures, microservices, and event-driven systems, where many components interact without being tightly bound.

Case Study

Imagine an e-commerce platform where multiple microservices handle different business responsibilities, such as order processing, inventory checks, payment validation, and notifications. Without a broker, each client would need to know the location and interface of each service. By introducing a `ServiceBroker`, we enable the client to send a generic request, such as process order, and the broker takes care of routing it to the correct service.

This architecture simplifies integration, supports dynamic service registration and removal, and provides a central point for monitoring, logging, or even applying cross-cutting concerns like authentication or rate limiting.

Applying the Broker Pattern

This interaction flow demonstrates how the broker mediates between the client and backend services without exposing internal architecture to the client.

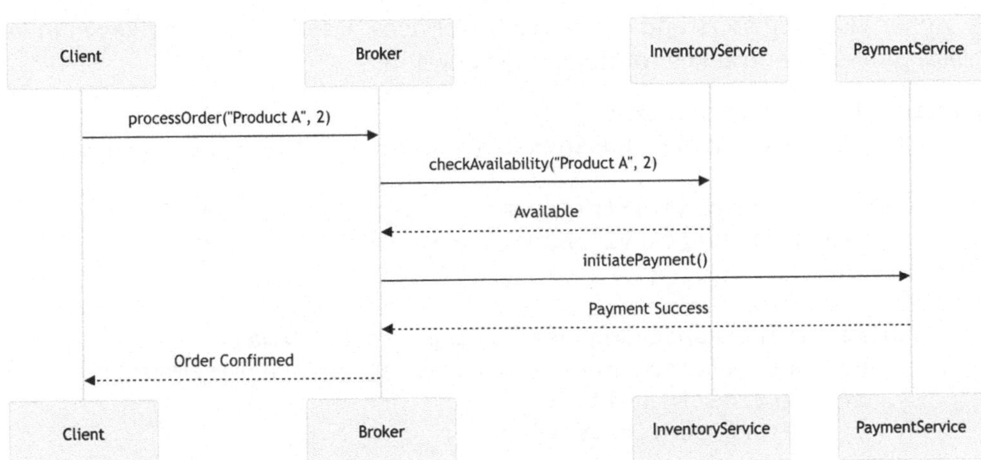

Figure 9.2: *Broker Pattern - Service Mediation*

Define the Service Interface

We begin by defining a common interface that all services will implement, enabling the broker to interact with them polymorphically.

```
public interface BusinessService {
    String execute();
}
```

Create Concrete Services

These are the backend services, such as inventory and payment, which encapsulates business logic.

```
public class InventoryService implements BusinessService {
    @Override
    public String execute() {
        return "Inventory checked: Product available.";
    }
}
public class PaymentService implements BusinessService {
    @Override
    public String execute() {
        return "Payment processed successfully.";
    }
}
```

Implement the Broker

This broker class registers and delegates to services based on a string key *simulating a service name*. It centralizes routing and execution.

```
public class ServiceBroker {
    private Map<String, BusinessService> registry = new HashMap<>();

    public void register(String serviceName, BusinessService service) {
        registry.put(serviceName, service);
    }

    public String handleRequest(String serviceName) {
        BusinessService service = registry.get(serviceName);
        if (service != null) {
            return service.execute();
        }
        return "Service not found.";
    }
}
```

Simulate the Client

The client interacts only with the broker, unaware of which services are behind it. This allows flexibility and low coupling.

```
public class BrokerClient {
    public static void main(String[] args) {
        ServiceBroker broker = new ServiceBroker();
        broker.register("inventory", new InventoryService());
        broker.register("payment", new PaymentService());

        System.out.println("Client request: Check Inventory");
        System.out.println("Response: " + broker.handleRequest
("inventory"));

        System.out.println("Client request: Process Payment");
        System.out.println("Response: " + broker.handleReq-
uest("payment"));
    }
}
```

Output Console:

```
Client request: Check Inventory
Response: Inventory checked: Product available.
Client request: Process Payment
Response: Payment processed successfully.
```

The **Broker Pattern** provides a powerful abstraction for mediating service interactions in distributed architectures. It enhances flexibility, promotes decoupling, and supports dynamic service discovery, key traits for modern microservice ecosystems, while still introducing a dependency on a central mediator.

It is ideal for systems that need dynamic lookup, extensibility, and runtime binding. The broker central vantage point can also host cross-cutting concerns such as logging, metrics, authentication, rate limiting, and load balancing.

However, brokers can become bottlenecks or single points of failure. High-availability deployments should distribute or replicate the broker itself, and observability must be strong because debugging requires tracing requests through the broker's routing path.

Best practices include keeping brokers stateless and horizontally scalable, supporting dynamic service registration/deregistration, continuously monitoring latency and failure modes, and resisting overly complex routing logic within the broker.

In the next section, we will examine the **Peer-to-Peer Pattern**, which distributes responsibilities symmetrically among nodes to enable decentralized communication, improve fault tolerance, and eliminate single points of failure.

Peer-to-Peer Pattern

The Peer-to-Peer Pattern represents a decentralized architecture where all participating nodes, called peers, can act as both clients and servers. Unlike the Client-Server or Broker models, no central authority exists; instead, each peer communicates directly with others to share resources, coordinate actions, or propagate data. This pattern is particularly useful in scenarios requiring scalability, fault tolerance, and autonomy.

Peer-to-peer architectures eliminate the dependency on a single point of failure. When designed properly, they distribute workload evenly, allowing systems to scale naturally as more peers join. However, this comes at the cost of increased complexity in discovery, consistency, and communication protocols.

Case Study

Consider a file-sharing application where users contribute storage and bandwidth to host and retrieve files collaboratively. Each user peer maintains a portion of the shared content. When a peer wants to download a file, it queries the network to locate peers who hold the desired parts. As peers join or leave, the system self-adjusts to rebalance data distribution and availability.

This decentralized model ensures that content remains accessible even when individual nodes go offline. It exemplifies Peer-to-Peer strengths: **resilience**, **collaboration**, and **horizontal scalability**.

Applying the Peer-to-Peer Pattern

This diagram shows how peers interact directly to exchange file segments, each serving and requesting as needed.

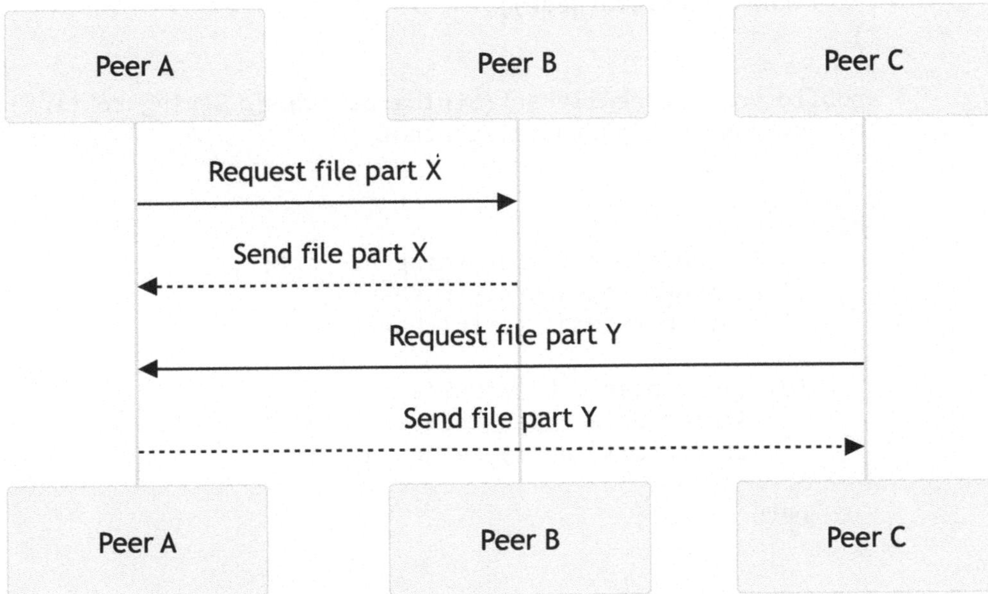

Figure 9.3: *Peer-to-Peer Pattern - File Sharing*

Define the Peer Interface

This interface defines a common contract for peer behavior: sending and requesting data.

```
public interface Peer {
    String requestData(String filePart);
    void provideData(String filePart, String data);
}
```

Implement a Concrete Peer Node

This interface defines a common contract for peer behavior: sending and requesting data.

```
public class FileSharingPeer implements Peer {
    private String name;
    private Map<String, String> storage = new HashMap<>();
    private List<Peer> knownPeers = new ArrayList<>();

    public FileSharingPeer(String name) {
        this.name = name;
    }
```

```
    public void addPeer(Peer peer) {
        knownPeers.add(peer);
    }

    public void storeFilePart(String partName, String content) {
        storage.put(partName, content);
    }

    @Override
    public String requestData(String filePart) {
        if (storage.containsKey(filePart)) {
            return storage.get(filePart);
        }
        for (Peer peer : knownPeers) {
            String data = peer.requestData(filePart);
            if (data != null) return data;
        }
        return null;
    }

    @Override
    public void provideData(String filePart, String data) {
        storage.put(filePart, data);
    }

    public String getName() {
        return name;
    }
}
```

Simulate Peer-to-Peer Communication

We create multiple peers and demonstrate decentralized data retrieval.

```
public class P2PSimulation {
    public static void main(String[] args) {
        FileSharingPeer alice = new FileSharingPeer("Alice");
        FileSharingPeer bob = new FileSharingPeer("Bob");
        FileSharingPeer carol = new FileSharingPeer("Carol");

        // Establish peer relationships
        alice.addPeer(bob);
        bob.addPeer(carol);
        carol.addPeer(alice);

        // Store data in a remote peer
        carol.storeFilePart("part-1", "This is file part 1");
```

```
            // Request file from another peer
            String result = alice.requestData("part-1");
            System.out.println("Alice received: " + result);
        }
    }
```

Output Console:

```
    Alice received: This is file part 1
```

Note: *This simplified peer-to-peer example may lead to unbounded recursion if the request propagation logic does not include proper termination conditions. Because peers can form cyclic relationships (for example, Alice → Bob → Carol → Alice), a data request that is forwarded from one peer to another may loop indefinitely, eventually resulting in a* **`StackOverflowError`**.

The Peer-to-Peer Pattern decentralizes responsibility, enabling dynamic, fault-tolerant, and scalable communication among distributed nodes. By removing single points of control, it supports autonomy and resilience across the system. In the next section, we shall conclude this chapter by summarizing the comparative strengths of each distributed pattern, thereby helping developers select the right approach based on system goals and constraints.

Conclusion

In this chapter, we explored three foundational design patterns that provide structure and reliability in distributed systems: The **Client-Server Pattern**, the **Broker Pattern**, and the **Peer-to-Peer Pattern**. Each pattern addresses a distinct mode of communication and control, from centralized service delivery to fully decentralized collaboration.

The **Client-Server Pattern** established the baseline for remote interaction through clear role separation, enabling modularity and centralized business logic. The **Broker Pattern** introduced an intermediary to decouple service invocation and streamline integration across heterogeneous services, increasing flexibility and service discovery capabilities. Finally, the **Peer-to-Peer Pattern** demonstrated how distribution can be symmetric and autonomous, promoting scalability and fault tolerance while demanding greater coordination and resilience strategies.

Together, these patterns provide a toolkit for designing distributed Java applications that are scalable, resilient, and maintainable. Choosing the appropriate pattern depends on the specific system goals—whether the priority is control, flexibility, or decentralization.

In the next chapter, **Design Patterns for Security and Scalability**, we will shift focus to architectural patterns that protect distributed applications and ensure they can scale under heavy load. We will study **Security Design Patterns**, which help prevent common vulnerabilities and enforce robust access control, and **Scalability Design Patterns**, which optimize system behavior under increasing demands. These patterns are essential to move from functional distributed systems to **reliable and enterprise-grade platforms**.

Points to Remember

- Distributed systems involve multiple nodes or services that interact across a network to accomplish shared goals.
- The **Client-Server Pattern** separates consumer *clients* and service providers *servers*, establishing a clear communication contract.
- The **Broker Pattern** introduces an intermediary that routes client requests to the appropriate backend service, enabling loose coupling and dynamic service discovery.
- The **Peer-to-Peer Pattern** eliminates centralized control by allowing each node to act as both client and server, supporting fault tolerance and scalability.
- Choosing the right pattern depends on system complexity, communication needs, fault tolerance requirements, and performance constraints.
- UML Diagrams and code examples in Java help illustrate the structural dynamics and implementation practices for each pattern.
- Combining multiple distributed patterns is common in real-world systems, for instance, using brokers for service mediation over a client-server foundation.
- Distributed systems must account for latency, failures, synchronization, and consistency each pattern addresses these trade-offs differently.
- These patterns serve as architectural blueprints for scalable microservices, messaging systems, collaborative platforms, and decentralized networks.

Multiple Choice Questions

1. Which pattern is best suited for decentralizing communication among nodes?

   a. Client-Server Pattern

   b. Broker Pattern

   c. Peer-to-Peer Pattern

   d. MCV Pattern

2. In the Broker Pattern, the broker is responsible for:
    a. Caching client data
    b. Forwarding requests and locating services
    c. Executing business logic
    d. Encrypting messages
3. One limitation of the Client-Server Pattern is:
    a. Peer discovery is complex.
    b. Data replication is uncontrolled.
    c. The server can become a single point of failure.
    d. Clients cannot scale independently.
4. Which of the following is a major advantage of the Peer-to-Peer Pattern?
    a. Simplifies server logic
    b. Enables centralized control
    c. Increases scalability and resilience
    d. Reduces client requests
5. Which pattern introduces a centralized communication intermediary?
    a. Factory Pattern
    b. Singleton Pattern
    c. Observer Pattern
    d. Broker Pattern

Answers

1. c
2. b
3. c
4. c
5. d

Questions

1. In which of the scenarios would the Client-Server Pattern become insufficient, and how might you extend or combine it with other patterns?
2. What are the trade-offs involved in introducing a broker between clients and services in a microservices architecture?
3. How does the Peer-to-Peer Pattern handle data availability and fault tolerance in the absence of a central server?
4. What challenges might arise in managing security and authentication in a Peer-to-Peer network?
5. How can understanding the differences between the three distributed patterns help guide your design choices when scaling a Java application?

Key Terms

- **Distributed System**: A system where components are located on different networked computers and communicate by passing messages.
- **Client-Server Pattern**: A pattern where clients send requests and servers respond with services or data.
- **Broker Pattern**: A pattern that introduces an intermediary to manage and forward service requests.
- **Peer-to-Peer**: A model where each node can act as both client and server, without central coordination.
- **Service Discovery**: The process by which a client dynamically finds a service provider, often facilitated by a broker.
- **Fault Tolerance**: The ability of a system to continue functioning in the presence of failures.
- **Service Registry**: A component used in brokers that keeps track of available services and their endpoints.
- **Decentralization**: The absence of a central point of control, often leading to improved resilience and autonomy.
- **Message Routing**: The process by which a broker directs client requests to the appropriate service.
- **Scalability**: The capacity of a system to handle increased load by adding more nodes or resources.

CHAPTER 10
Design Patterns for Security and Scalability

Introduction

Design patterns for security and scalability are essential tools for building reliable distributed Java systems. Security ensures that applications can resist threats and protect sensitive data, while scalability guarantees that systems remain responsive and efficient as workloads increase. When combined, these patterns provide a framework for designing software that is both trustworthy and resilient under pressure.

This chapter introduces patterns that address the most common vulnerabilities and performance bottlenecks encountered in real-world applications. Security patterns cover issues such as input validation, authentication, authorization, secrets management, and abuse prevention. Scalability patterns focus on techniques like caching, circuit breaking, bulkheading, sharding, and asynchronous messaging.

To make these ideas concrete, each pattern is explained through its problem context, the forces that shape its solution, and the trade-offs it implies. Visual diagrams help illustrate how components interact, while Java examples show how the patterns can be implemented in practice. The goal is to give developers and architects practical tools they can apply directly in their projects.

By the end of this chapter, the reader will not only recognize recurring challenges in security and scalability but also know how to respond to them systematically. The benefits are twofold: firstly, fewer vulnerabilities that can compromise the system, and secondly, greater resilience when demand or failures put stress on the infrastructure. The result is an application that inspires trust and adapts to growth without losing stability.

Structure

In this chapter, we will cover the following topics:

- Security Design Patterns
- Scalability Design Patterns

Security Design Patterns

Security in software design is not an afterthought but a fundamental aspect of building distributed Java applications. Every new service, endpoint, or integration expands the potential attack surface and creates opportunities for exploitation. Without a systematic approach, developers risk leaving gaps that malicious actors can exploit.

Security design patterns provide structured solutions to recurring problems in protecting systems. They allow teams to handle authentication, authorization, input handling, and data protection in a consistent and reusable way. Instead of reinventing solutions for each project, these patterns capture proven strategies that strengthen trust across all layers of the system.

In this section, we will explore a set of patterns that directly address the most common vulnerabilities in distributed environments. Each pattern begins with the problem it solves and the context where it applies, followed by its implementation principles, an illustration that shows how security flows through the system, and a Java code example that demonstrates the idea in practice.

Input Validation and Canonicalization

Input validation and canonicalization form the first shield that protects an application from malicious data. Every request entering the system carries potential risks, whether it comes from a user, an API client, or another service. By validating input against strict rules and normalizing its representation, we ensure that only legitimate and predictable data is processed. This simple but crucial step prevents a wide range of attacks before they can reach the deeper layers of the application.

Attackers often exploit weak input handling to inject malicious commands, bypass filters, or manipulate business logic. For example, a string representing `../etc/passwd` may be encoded in different ways to escape naive filters. Without proper validation and canonicalization, distributed systems become vulnerable to SQL injection, cross-site scripting (XSS), path traversal, and logic bypass.

Applying Input Validation and Canonicalization

The pattern enforces two steps:

1. **Validation**: Checking that the input matches predefined formats, ranges, and constraints.
2. **Canonicalization**: Normalizing input to a single, standard representation before applying validation rules.

Together, these measures ensure that ambiguous encodings or unexpected data never reach the core business logic.

This diagram shows the validator acting as a gatekeeper between the outside world and internal services.

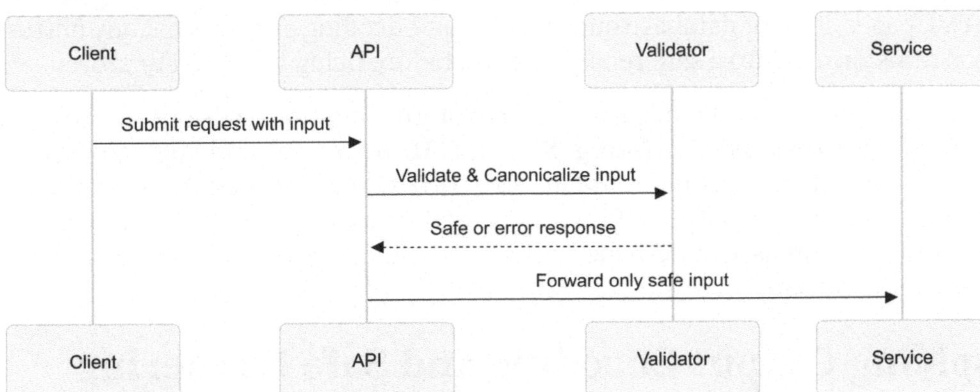

Figure 10.1: *Security Pattern - Input Validation and Canonicalization*

Here, usernames are constrained to a safe format, while file paths are normalized to their canonical representation to prevent traversal exploits.

```
public record UserInput(
    @NotBlank(message = "Username cannot be blank")
    @Pattern(regexp = "^[a-zA-Z0-9_]{3,20}$",
             message = "Invalid username format")
    String username
) {}

// Example of canonicalization
public class Canonicalizer {
    public static String normalizePath(String input) throws
IOException {
        return new File(input).getCanonicalPath();
    }
}
```

Trade-Offs

Input validation comes with clear advantages and some trade-offs. On the positive side, it blocks many injection and traversal attacks, ensures predictable data, and integrates seamlessly with frameworks such as Spring Validation. However, it also has limitations: strict validation may reject inputs that are valid but unexpected, canonicalization can introduce additional processing overhead, and validation rules must evolve in line with the application's changing requirements.

Output Encoding and Safe Rendering

If input validation protects the system at the entry point, output encoding protects users and downstream systems at the exit point. Many security vulnerabilities arise not from malicious input alone but from the way this input is later displayed or embedded in HTML pages, logs, or database queries. Output encoding ensures that any untrusted data is transformed into a safe representation before being rendered or stored.

Applications that directly display user-generated content without encoding are vulnerable to **Cross-Site Scripting XSS**, **HTML injection**, and **log injection**. For instance, an attacker could submit `<script>alert('hacked')</script>` as a comment. If the system outputs this string directly in a web page, the browser executes it as JavaScript. Similarly, unescaped values in SQL queries or logs can corrupt data and create backdoors.

Applying Output Encoding and Safe Rendering

The pattern mandates that all untrusted data be **encoded or escaped** before being used in a different context:

- Encode HTML characters before rendering in web pages.
- Use parameterized queries instead of concatenated SQL strings.
- Apply structured logging instead of concatenated log entries.

This guarantees that malicious input is treated as data, not as executable code.

The following diagram shows the encoder acting as a shield, transforming dangerous characters into harmless equivalents before the data is returned to the client.

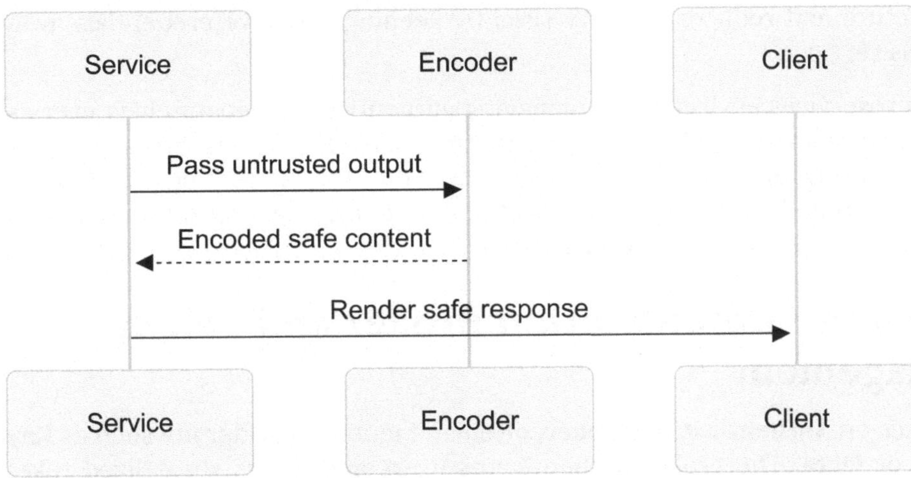

Figure 10.2: *Security Pattern - Output Encoding and Safe Rendering*

HTML Encoding with Spring Security

```
import org.springframework.web.util.HtmlUtils;
public class SafeRenderer {
    public static String encodeForHtml(String input) {
        return HtmlUtils.htmlEscape(input);
    }
}
```

Parameterized SQL with Spring JDBC

```
String sql = "INSERT INTO comments (user_id, text) VALUES (?, ?)";
jdbcTemplate.update(sql, userId, comment);
```

Trade-Offs

Output encoding and safe rendering come with both advantages and drawbacks. They prevent critical vulnerabilities such as XSS, SQL injection, and log injection, and are simple to apply consistently thanks to built-in support in most frameworks. However, they also introduce some overhead during rendering, and if the wrong context-specific encoding is used, security gaps may remain. In addition, we must remember to apply encoding at every output boundary to ensure full protection.

Authentication Broker and Token Management

Authentication is the process of verifying identity, and in distributed systems, it must be handled consistently across multiple services. Instead of letting each service manage credentials independently, an authentication broker centralizes the process, issues secure tokens, and delegates verification. This approach simplifies the architecture and reduces security risks by keeping sensitive credentials away from business services.

In a microservices environment, managing authentication separately in every service leads to complexity, duplicated logic, and inconsistent policies. Worse, services may end up storing or handling user passwords directly, increasing the risk of leaks. Without a unified system, it becomes difficult to enforce strong authentication, rotate credentials, or revoke access quickly.

Applying Authentication Broker and Token Management

Introduce an **Authentication Broker**, often an Identity Provider *IdP* such as **Keycloak**, **Auth0**, or **Okta**. The broker authenticates users and issues short-lived tokens like **JWT** or opaque tokens. Services then validate these tokens without ever handling raw credentials. This separation allows us to focus on business logic while relying on a trusted authority for identity management.

This diagram shows the Authentication Broker acting as the central authority, with services merely validating the tokens it issues.

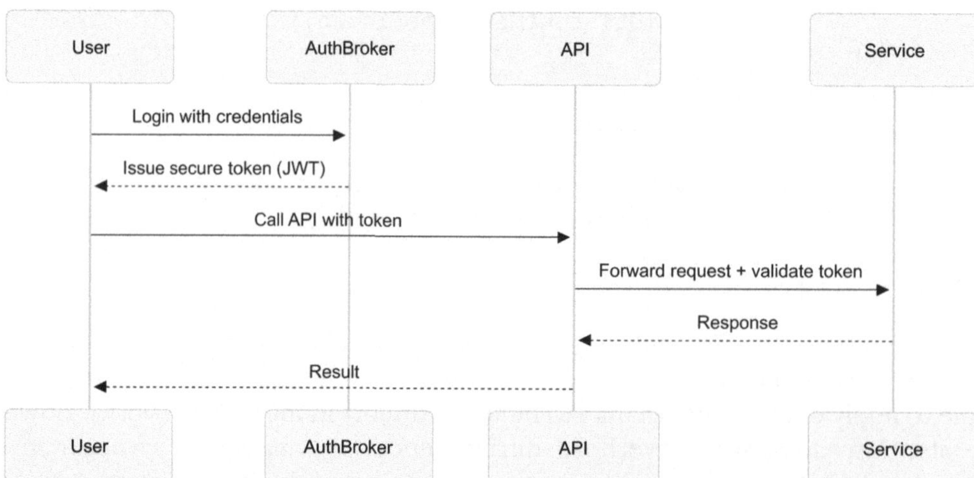

Figure 10.3: *Security Pattern - Authentication Broker and Token Management*

Using **Spring Security** to configure a resource server that validates JWT tokens

```
public class SecurityConfig {
    @Bean
    SecurityFilterChain securityFilterChain(HttpSecurity http)
throws Exception {
        return http
            .authorizeHttpRequests(auth -> auth
```

```
                    .requestMatchers("/public/**").permitAll()
                    .anyRequest().authenticated())
                .oauth2ResourceServer(oauth2 -> oauth2.jwt())
// Token validation
                .build();
    }
}
```

With this setup, the API does not store or process credentials. It only validates JWTs signed by the broker.

Trade-Offs

Authentication brokers and token management bring both advantages and challenges. On the positive side, centralizing authentication reduces duplication and inconsistency across services, keeps individual services free from handling sensitive credentials, and enables flexible control over token lifetimes, scopes, and revocation. On the other hand, this approach introduces a dependency on the broker's availability, which must therefore be highly reliable. In addition, mismanagement of tokens–such as granting overly long lifetimes or weak scopes–can still expose the system to vulnerabilities. Finally, establishing and maintaining a secure trust relationship between services and the broker requires careful configuration and ongoing oversight.

Authorization with Policy Enforcement Points

Authorization determines *what* a user or service can do after authentication. In distributed systems, policies must be consistent across many services, and enforcing them locally risks fragmentation.

If each service implements its own authorization rules, inconsistencies and privilege escalation become likely. Updating policies across dozens of services is slow and error-prone.

Applying Authorization with Policy Enforcement Points

Introduce **Policy Enforcement Points PEPs** within each service that delegate decisions to a **Policy Decision Point PDP**. Policies can follow **RBAC** role-based or **ABAC** attribute-based models.

This diagram shows the API acting as a Policy Enforcement Point, forwarding the request of the client to the Policy Decision Point, which evaluates the token and returns a permit or deny decision.

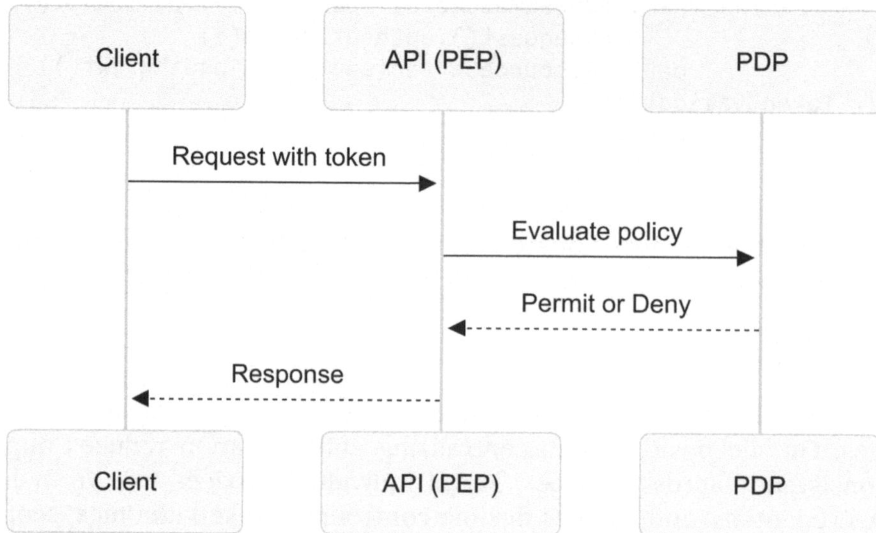

Figure 10.4: *Security Pattern - Authentication with Policy Enforcement Points*

The following example shows a simple **RoleBasedAuthorizationManager** that grants access only if the authenticated user has the role **ROLE_ADMIN**

```
public class RoleBasedAuthorizationManager
        implements AuthorizationManager<RequestAuthorization
Context> {
    @Override
    public AuthorizationDecision check(
        Supplier<Authentication> authentication,
        RequestAuthorizationContext context) {

        Authentication auth = authentication.get();
        boolean granted = auth.getAuthorities().stream()
            .anyMatch(a -> a.getAuthority().equals
("ROLE_ADMIN"));
        return new AuthorizationDecision(granted);
    }
}
```

Trade-Offs

Using a centralized Policy Decision Point (PDP) for authorization has clear trade-offs. On the positive side, it enables centralized policies, which simplifies auditing and ensures consistent enforcement across services. However, if the PDP is remote, every authorization check introduces latency. To maintain performance, caching mechanisms are often necessary to balance quick responses with up-to-date policy decisions.

Least Privilege and Scoped Tokens

The principle of least privilege ensures that users and services only receive the access rights strictly necessary.

Tokens with excessive privileges increase damage if stolen. A user token valid across all services is a high-value target.

Applying Least Privilege and Scoped Tokens

Issue **scoped tokens** with minimal privileges and short lifetimes. Services validate scopes before executing actions.

```
if (!jwt.getClaim("scope").contains("read:projects")) {
    throw new AccessDeniedException("Insufficient permissions");
}
```

Trade-Offs

Applying the principle of least privilege with scoped tokens comes with trade-offs. On the positive side, it limits the blast radius and reduces the risks associated with compromised tokens, since each token only grants narrowly defined permissions. On the downside, it introduces additional complexity in both token issuance and validation, as systems must handle more granular scopes and enforce them consistently.

Secure Communication and Abuse Prevention

In distributed systems, communication between services and clients is one of the most exposed surfaces for attack. Ensuring that services can trust each other, that requests are authentic, and that systems remain resilient under abuse is critical for maintaining availability and protecting sensitive data. Four key patterns reinforce this layer of defense: mutual trust between services, request signing, rate limiting, and idempotency.

Mutual TLS *m*TLS establishes strong two-way authentication, where each service presents a certificate proving its identity. Unlike simple API keys, which can be copied or leaked, mTLS relies on cryptographic certificates that are difficult to forge. This ensures that only trusted workloads within the infrastructure can communicate securely. The principle of zero trust builds on this by requiring continuous verification, never assuming that a service is inherently safe simply because it is inside the network perimeter.

Even with secure channels, attackers may try to intercept and replay valid requests. Request signing addresses this risk by attaching cryptographic signatures to each request, combined with nonces or timestamps to guarantee freshness. This prevents replay attacks and ensures that every request is provably authentic.

Another common threat is abuse through excessive calls. APIs exposed on the internet are vulnerable to brute-force attempts, denial-of-service DoS, or scraping. Rate limiting mitigates this by capping the number of requests per client or per tenant within a given time window. This preserves service availability and ensures fair usage of resources.

Finally, in distributed environments, retries are often necessary to handle transient failures. Without safeguards, retries can lead to duplicate operations, such as double charges in payment systems. Idempotency keys solve this by tagging each write operation with a unique identifier, allowing the system to detect duplicates and return the same safe result.

Together, these patterns form a defensive perimeter: services communicate only with trusted peers, requests are authenticated and fresh, abuse is throttled, and duplicate operations are safely managed.

This diagram shows how multiple safeguards work together: rate limiting at the gateway, request signing to prevent replay, mTLS between services, and idempotency keys to avoid duplicates.

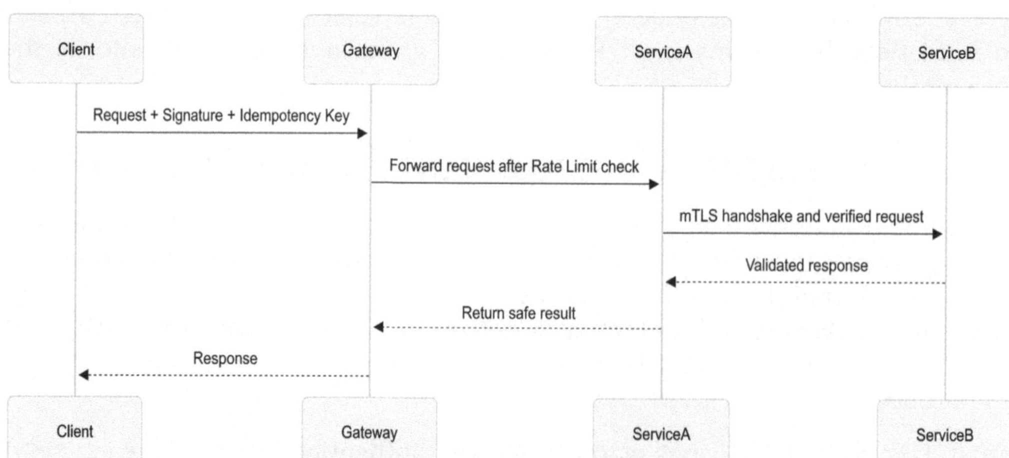

Figure 10.5: *Security Pattern - Combining Safeguards for Secure and Reliable API Communication*

These code snippets illustrate how signatures protect authenticity, rate limiters control abuse, and idempotency prevents harmful duplicates.

Request Signing HMAC:

```
String signature = hmacSha256(secretKey, payload + timestamp + nonce);
request.addHeader("X-Signature", signature);
```

```
request.addHeader("X-Nonce", nonce);
request.addHeader("X-Timestamp", String.valueOf(timestamp));
```

Rate Limiting (Guava RateLimiter):

```
RateLimiter limiter = RateLimiter.create(10.0); // 10 permits/sec
if (!limiter.tryAcquire()) {
    throw new TooManyRequestsException();
}
```

Idempotency Handling:

```
if (processedRequests.contains(requestId)) {
    return previousResponse;
}
processedRequests.add(requestId);
```

Data Integrity, Sessions, and Auditability

Beyond communication security, a distributed application must also protect the integrity of its data and maintain accountability. Three areas are particularly important: managing sessions and tokens safely, ensuring audit trails are reliable, and isolating tenant data in multi-tenant systems.

Secure session management remains a cornerstone of user-facing systems. Traditional server-side sessions risk hijacking if cookies are not protected, while stateless tokens such as JWTs bring challenges of revocation and rotation. A balanced approach is to use short-lived stateless tokens for scalability, combined with refresh tokens or revocation lists to maintain control. This way, applications benefit from performance while reducing exposure if tokens are compromised.

Audit trails are equally essential. Logs must capture what happened in the system, who performed an action, and when it occurred. Yet they must do this without leaking sensitive data such as passwords or credit card numbers. Proper audit logging includes structured formats, correlation identifiers for tracing requests across services, and tamper-evident storage that prevents manipulation. This ensures compliance with regulations and provides evidence in case of incidents.

Finally, in multi-tenant systems, strong data isolation is critical. Tenants must never access the information of each other. This can be enforced with row-level security in databases, tenant-specific encryption keys, and context propagation so that every request carries its tenant identity. Without such safeguards, a single vulnerability could expose the data of all customers.

This diagram highlights how tokens are validated, tenant context is enforced at the database level, and every action is logged for accountability.

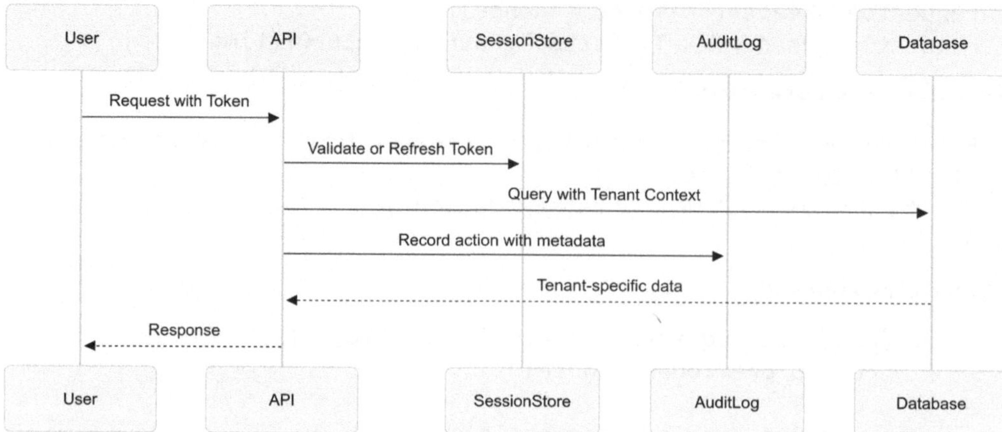

Figure 10.6: *Security Pattern - Token Validation, Tenant Isolation, and Action Auditing*

These implementations demonstrate how to secure sessions, maintain reliable logs, and enforce tenant isolation in multi-tenant systems.

Secure Session with Spring Security:

```
http
    .sessionManagement(session -> session
        .sessionFixation().migrateSession()
        .maximumSessions(1)
    )
    .oauth2ResourceServer(oauth2 -> oauth2.jwt());
```

Structured Audit Logging:

```
logger.info("User {} performed action {} on resource {} at {}",
    userId, action, resourceId, Instant.now());
Tenant Context in Repository:
public List<Project> findByTenant(String tenantId) {
    return entityManager.createQuery(
        "SELECT p FROM Project p WHERE p.tenantId = :tenant",
Project.class)
        .setParameter("tenant", tenantId)
        .getResultList();
}
```

Security design patterns provide a structured way to embed protection into distributed Java applications. Rather than patching vulnerabilities after they are discovered, these patterns ensure that safeguards such as input validation, output encoding, authentication and authorization, least-privilege tokens, secrets management, and service-to-service trust are consistently applied from the start. They also address abuse prevention with rate limiting, replay protection, and idempotency keys, while strengthening observability through secure logging and audit trails. By applying these practices, we reduce the attack surface, enforce clear trust boundaries, and guarantee that systems remain trustworthy even as they evolve and scale.

Scalability Design Patterns

Scalability design patterns are essential to ensure that applications remain responsive and reliable as workloads grow. Distributed Java systems must deal with unpredictable traffic, network failures, and uneven resource usage. Without a strategy, scaling often turns into a patchwork of fixes that collapse under stress.

These patterns provide structured solutions to recurring challenges such as handling sudden spikes in requests, avoiding cascading failures, isolating resources, and distributing data across nodes. By applying them, developers can design systems that not only perform well under normal load but also remain stable under extreme conditions.

The following subsections introduce key scalability patterns, each illustrated with practical examples and Java implementations.

Timeouts, Retries with Backoff, and Hedging

Distributed systems depend heavily on network calls to databases, APIs, or microservices. These calls can fail intermittently or even hang indefinitely. Without clear strategies to handle such failures, systems risk cascading outages.

If services wait indefinitely for responses, threads and connections pile up, eventually exhausting resources. Naive retry strategies can worsen the situation: multiple clients retrying simultaneously create synchronized *retry storms* that overwhelm the failing service.

Applying Solution

To improve reliability and resilience in distributed systems, several techniques can be applied:

- **Timeouts:** Set strict upper limits on how long calls can wait.
- **Retries with backoff and jitter:** Retry after progressively longer delays, with randomness to avoid synchronization.
- **Hedging:** Send the same request to multiple replicas and use the fastest response.

This diagram illustrates resilience strategies in action: a client request times out, triggers a retry with backoff and jitter, and finally issues a hedged request to a replica, which returns the fastest response.

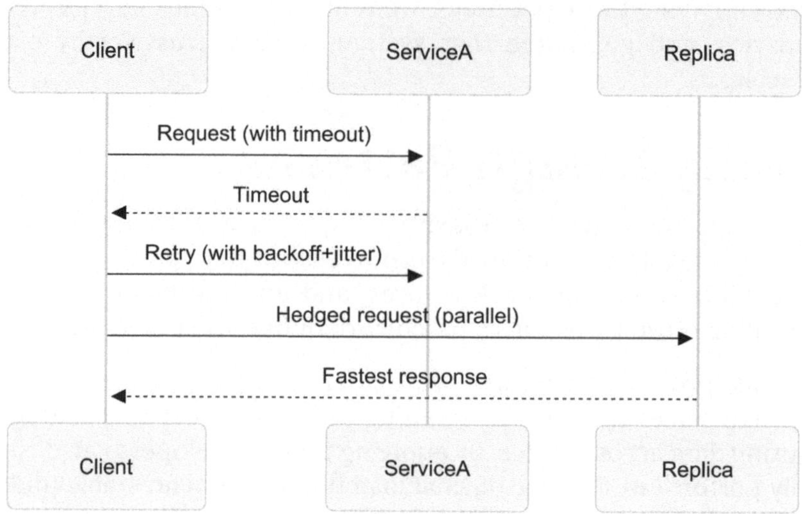

Figure 10.7: *Scalability Pattern - Resilience Strategies: Timeouts, Retries, and Hedged Requests*

The following code demonstrates how to configure and apply a retry mechanism with Resilience4j. It defines a retry policy with a maximum of three attempts and a wait duration of 300 milliseconds between retries. The external service call is wrapped with this policy, and a fallback value is returned if all attempts fail.

```
RetryConfig config = RetryConfig.custom()
    .maxAttempts(3)
    .waitDuration(Duration.ofMillis(300))
    .build();

Retry retry = Retry.of("serviceA", config);

Supplier<String> supplier =
    Retry.decorateSupplier(retry, () -> callExternalService());

String result = Try.ofSupplier(supplier)
    .recover(ex -> "fallback")
    .get();
```

Trade-Offs

Resilience strategies such as timeouts, retries, and hedging bring both strengths and challenges. On the positive side, they improve resilience by preventing indefinite waits and add flexibility through fallback paths. However, retries can increase system load if their limits are not carefully tuned, and hedging, while effective at reducing latency, duplicates requests and may waste resources if applied too aggressively.

Circuit Breaker Pattern

The circuit breaker pattern prevents repeated calls to unhealthy services, protecting the system from cascading failures.

Without a circuit breaker, failing services continue to receive requests. Each slow response ties up threads, leading to cascading failures across dependent services.

Applying Solution

Introduce a circuit breaker state machine:

- **Closed**: Calls flow normally.
- **Open**: After too many failures, calls are blocked.
- **Half-open**: After a cool-down, limited calls test if recovery occurred.

This diagram illustrates the states of the Circuit Breaker pattern, showing how it transitions between Closed, Open, and Half-Open based on failures, cooldowns, and recovery attempts.

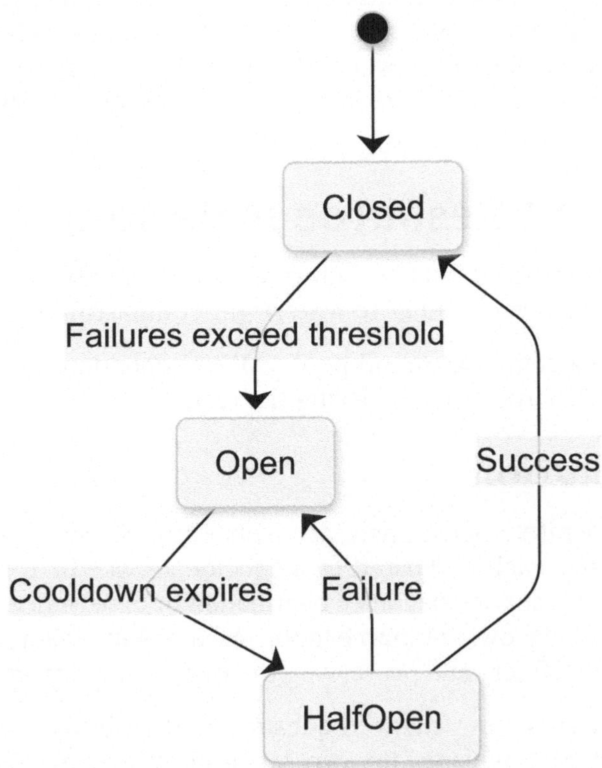

Figure 10.8: *Scalability Pattern - Circuit Breaker State Transitions: Closed, Open, and Half-Open*

The following code shows how to configure and apply a circuit breaker. A custom configuration defines the failure threshold and wait duration, then the **CircuitBreaker** is applied to wrap calls to an external service:

```
CircuitBreakerConfig config = CircuitBreakerConfig.custom()
    .failureRateThreshold(50)   // 50% failures
    .waitDurationInOpenState(Duration.ofSeconds(10))
    .build();

CircuitBreaker breaker = CircuitBreaker.of("externalService",
config);

Supplier<String> decorated =
    CircuitBreaker.decorateSupplier(breaker, () -> call
ExternalService());
```

Trade-Offs

The Circuit Breaker Pattern comes with important trade-offs. On the positive side, it prevents cascading failures across distributed systems and provides faster feedback when a downstream service is unavailable. At the same time, it has limitations: if thresholds are configured too strictly, the circuit may block calls prematurely, even when the service is capable of recovery. Moreover, it requires careful tuning of both thresholds and cool-down periods to strike the right balance between resilience and availability.

Bulkhead and Resource Isolation

Bulkhead isolation ensures that a failure in one component doesn't consume resources meant for others, similar to watertight compartments in ships.

If all services share a common thread pool or DB connection pool, one misbehaving service can monopolize resources, starving the rest.

Applying Solution

Resources are deliberately partitioned into isolated pools, such as thread pools and database connections, each dedicated to a specific service or tenant. This isolation ensures that when one service becomes overloaded or experiences failure, its impact remains confined to its own resource pool. As a result, failures remain isolated, preventing cascading effects and preserving the overall stability of the system.

This diagram illustrates how client requests are distributed across independent service pools. Each pool manages its own set of instances, for Service A, Service B, and Service C, ensuring that load, performance constraints, or failures affecting one service do not propagate to others. This approach enables controlled scalability, improved fault tolerance, and predictable system behavior under stress.

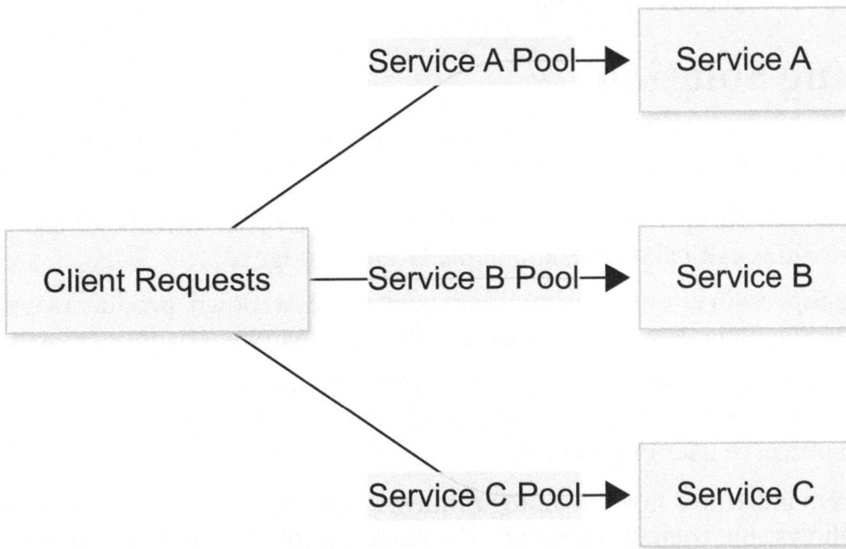

Figure 10.9: *Scalability Pattern - Client Request Distribution across Service Pools*

This example demonstrates how two services can run with separate thread pools. By assigning *Service* A and *Service* B to different **ExecutorService** instances, we prevent the workload of one service from exhausting the resources of the other, thereby improving fault isolation and resilience.

```
ExecutorService poolA = Executors.newFixedThreadPool(10);
ExecutorService poolB = Executors.newFixedThreadPool(10);
// Service A uses poolA, Service B uses poolB
```

Trade-Offs

The bulkhead pattern and resource isolation come with important trade-offs. On the positive side, they increase system resilience by isolating failures and ensuring a fair allocation of resources across components. At the same time, they introduce tuning challenges: if pools are under-provisioned, throttling and degraded performance may occur, while over-provisioned pools can lead to wasted resources.

Load Shedding and Backpressure

When demand exceeds capacity, a robust system chooses to degrade gracefully instead of collapsing. *Load shedding*, controlled rejection, and *backpressure* prevent unbounded queues, preserve critical resources, and protect overall user experience.

Traffic spikes can overwhelm CPU/threads/connections. Unbounded queues cause skyrocketing latency, followed by cascading timeouts. Without self-regulation, the entire system becomes unavailable.

Applying Solution

When systems are under heavy load, several resilience strategies can help maintain availability and protect critical functionality:

- **Load Shedding**: Reject requests early, HTTP 429 once thresholds are exceeded, prioritize critical traffic, and apply latency budgets.
- **Backpressure**: enforce bounded queues, slow down producers using pull-based mechanisms, and cut off the flow if consumers cannot keep up.
- **Graceful Degradation**: Return simplified or partial responses, without recommendations, rely on emergency caches, or provide approximate results to preserve user experience.

This diagram illustrates how incoming requests pass through an ingress, are queued if capacity allows, and then processed by the worker pool. When the queue is full, excess requests are rejected with an HTTP 429 response.

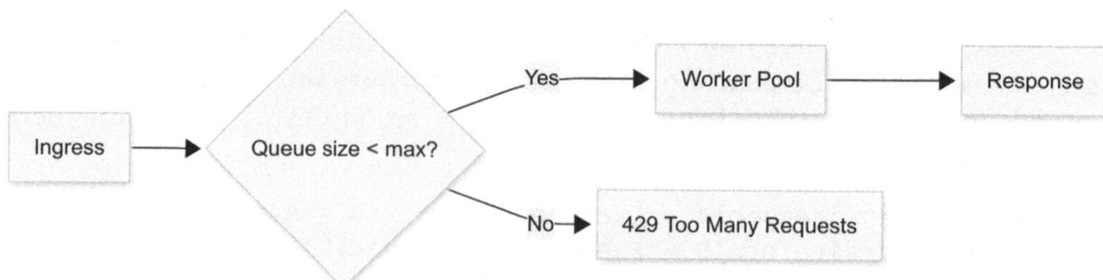

***Figure 10.10:** Scalability Pattern - Request Handling with Queue and Load Shedding*

The following example demonstrates how to combine backpressure with load shedding in a reactive pipeline. By bounding the request queue and applying timeouts, the system ensures stability under heavy load while rejecting excess requests gracefully:

```
// Bounded queue with backpressure and shedding
Flux<Request> incoming = requestStream()
    .onBackpressureBuffer(
        1000,
        dropped -> metrics.increment("shed"),
        BufferOverflowStrategy.DROP_LATEST
    );

incoming
```

```
    .flatMap(req -> handle(req)
        .timeout(Duration.ofMillis(300))
        .onErrorResume(TimeoutException.class,
            ex -> Mono.error(new TooManyRequestsException()))
    , 64)
    .subscribe();
```

Trade-Offs

This approach protects overall system stability and helps keep SLOs predictable, while also improving resilience against sudden traffic spikes. On the downside, clients must be prepared to handle rejections typically via HTTP 429 using retries with backoff, and selecting appropriate thresholds is non-trivial, it requires careful observability and tuning.

Caching Strategies

Caching reduces load on slow stores and dependencies. Properly used, it smooths spikes, improves p95/p99 latency, and lowers costs. Poorly applied, it introduces inconsistency and cache stampede problems.

Repeated reads on hot data overwhelm the database. Naive invalidation or poorly chosen TTLs lead to thundering herds on cache misses. Synchronous writes reduce throughput.

Applying Solution

Several caching strategies can be applied to improve performance and resilience while reducing database load:

- **Cache-aside**: The application first checks the cache; if the data is missing, it queries the database and then populates the cache.
- **Write-behind**: Writes are buffered in the cache and asynchronously flushed to the database.
- **Stampede Control**: Techniques such as single-flight, early refresh, TTL jitter, or versioned keys prevent cache stampedes under high load.
- **Coherence**: Strategies like adaptive TTLs, targeted invalidation, and a mix of soft and hard TTLs help maintain cache consistency with the underlying data.

This diagram illustrates the cache-aside strategy. The application first attempts to retrieve a value from the cache. If the key is present *cache hit*, the value is returned immediately. If the key is missing *cache miss*, the application queries the database, retrieves the value, and then stores it in the cache with a defined TTL before returning it to the client. This approach helps reduce database load while ensuring that frequently accessed data is served quickly.

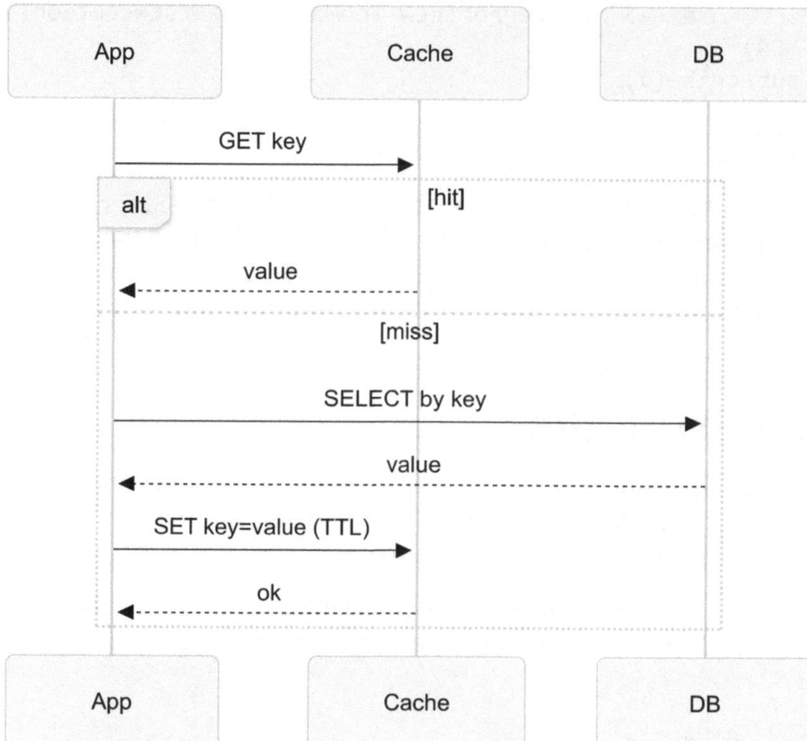

Figure 10.11: *Scalability Pattern - Cache-Aside Read Pattern*

The following implementation combines **the caching abstraction** of **Spring** with a **single-flight mechanism** to avoid cache stampedes. The **`@Cacheable`** annotation handles standard cache lookups, while the **`ConcurrentHashMap`** of **`CompletableFutures`** ensures that only one request for the same key triggers a backend call at a time.

```
@Cacheable(value = "product", key = "#id")
public Product getProduct(long id) {
    return repository.findById(id).orElseThrow();
}
// Single-flight to prevent stampede
private final ConcurrentHashMap<Long, CompletableFuture<Product>>
inflight = new ConcurrentHashMap<>();
public CompletableFuture<Product> cachedGet(long id) {
    return inflight.computeIfAbsent(id, k ->
        CompletableFuture.supplyAsync(() -> getProduct(k))
            .whenComplete((r, e) -> inflight.remove(k))
    );
}
```

Trade-Offs

This approach offers strong latency improvements and significantly reduces backend load. It can also improve perceived throughput when combined with write-behind caching strategies. However, it introduces eventual consistency issues and complicates cache invalidation. In addition, write-behind caching carries the risk of data loss if a flush operation fails, unless mechanisms such as a dead-letter queue DLQ or confirmation system are implemented.

Ensuring Consistency, Parallelism, and Edge Resilience

Scalability in distributed systems is not only about handling higher throughput but also about **preserving consistency and reliability at scale**. One of the foundational principles in this regard is **idempotency**. Idempotent consumers prevent duplicated messages from causing unintended side effects, such as double-billing or inconsistent states. By leveraging unique identifiers, processing logs, and the outbox/inbox pattern, systems achieve a pragmatic form of exactly-once semantics, which makes retries safe and predictable in message-driven environments.

Consistency is further reinforced through **Command Query Responsibility Segregation** or **CQRS** and the use of **read replicas**. By separating writes from reads, applications can optimize each side independently. Write models enforce strong domain invariants, while read models expose fast, denormalized projections to serve queries efficiently. Yet, distributed operations rarely succeed as atomic transactions. This is where the **Saga pattern** comes into play: by linking local transactions with compensating actions, sagas provide a way to maintain global coherence without relying on heavy two-phase commits. Together, CQRS and sagas highlight how scalability patterns must balance **performance with reliability**.

At the processing layer, **asynchronous messaging and work queues** allow systems to decouple producers from consumers, absorb spikes, and maintain elasticity. Brokers such as Kafka or RabbitMQ provide buffering, retry mechanisms, and dead-letter queues, ensuring resilience in the face of network failures or slow consumers. But when data volumes exceed the limits of a single node, **sharding and data partitioning** become necessary. Distributing records across multiple shards reduces contention and scales capacity, though at the cost of more complex routing and potentially expensive cross-shard queries.

Performance is also improved through **parallelism**, implemented with the **fan-out/fan-in pattern**. By splitting work into subtasks processed concurrently and then aggregating results, systems can drastically reduce latency for independent computations. However, parallelism introduces the challenge of coordination: certain tasks must only run once across a cluster. Here, **distributed locks and leader election** ensure exclusivity and designate a single primary node for critical operations. These mechanisms maintain **order and safety** in environments where concurrency could otherwise lead to duplication or corruption.

Finally, scalability extends to the **edge of the system**. The **API Gateway and Backend-for-Frontend BFF pattern** plays a vital role in protecting the core system. Gateways centralize cross-cutting concerns such as authentication, rate limiting, and monitoring, while BFFs tailor APIs to the specific needs of web, mobile, or IoT clients. This reduces network overhead, improves user experience, and provides a strategic control point for resilience features such as circuit breakers and caching.

Taken together, these patterns form a cohesive toolkit for scaling distributed Java applications. Idempotency ensures **safe retries**, CQRS and sagas provide **consistency at scale**, asynchronous messaging and sharding guarantee **elasticity**, fan-out/fan-in and distributed locks deliver **parallel efficiency with coordination**, and gateways ensure **resilience at the edge**. Scalability is therefore not merely about handling more requests; it is about doing so **safely, efficiently, and consistently** across every layer of the system.

Scalability design patterns make our distributed systems resilient under growth and stress. They provide the strategies we need to handle increased workloads, absorb traffic spikes, and coordinate distributed resources. Techniques such as timeouts, retries, circuit breakers, bulkheads, and load shedding protect against cascading failures, while caching, asynchronous messaging, sharding, and fan-out/fan-in improve throughput and latency. Patterns like CQRS, sagas, and idempotent consumers ensure that consistency is preserved at scale, while distributed locks and API gateways maintain order and resilience at the cluster and edge levels. Together, these patterns illustrate that scalability is not just about handling more requests; it is about ensuring that our systems do so efficiently, safely, and predictably.

Conclusion

Design patterns for security and scalability are not optional luxuries; they are the structural backbone of modern distributed Java applications. In this chapter, we saw how **security patterns** safeguard data and identities while reducing vulnerabilities, and how **scalability patterns** help systems stay responsive under growth and unpredictable stress.

Both families of patterns reinforce one another. Strong authentication, authorization, and secrets management mean little if the system collapses under load. Likewise, a perfectly scalable system without rate limiting or secure session, handling risks becomes an open door to attackers. Security and scalability are therefore two sides of the same architectural coin, and adopting their patterns systematically ensures that applications can both *survive threats* and *adapt to growth*.

In the next chapter, we take a step beyond the patterns of today and explore the **future trends in Java design patterns**. As technologies evolve, **reactive programming models**, **microservices practices**, **cloud-native infrastructures**, **AI/ML integration**, and next-generation security mechanisms, so do the design patterns that support them.

Points to Remember

- **Security patterns** such as input validation, PEP/PDP, mTLS, and idempotency keys protect applications against common vulnerabilities and enforce trust across distributed systems.
- **Scalability patterns** such as circuit breakers, caching, sagas, and sharding ensure resilience and performance even under heavy load or partial failures.
- Both security and scalability rely on **systematic enforcement**, not ad-hoc fixes.
- Effective design requires balancing trade-offs: strict validation vs. usability, retries vs. overload, centralization vs. distribution.
- Java developers have mature frameworks such as Spring Boot, Resilience4j, Reactor, Kafka, and so on that make implementing these patterns practical.

Multiple Choice Questions

1. Which of the following best describes the Circuit Breaker pattern?
    a. Encrypting sensitive data before storage.
    b. Assigning tokens with limited privileges.
    c. Separating read and write models for scalability.
    d. Blocking calls to failing services to prevent cascading failures.
2. Which of the following is the main purpose of an Idempotency Key?
    a. To ensure safe retries without duplicate side effects.
    b. To enforce least privilege access.
    c. To partition data across multiple databases.
    d. To prevent replay attacks.
3. Which caching strategy loads data into the cache automatically on a miss?
    a. Cache-Aside
    b. Read-Through

   c. Write-Behind
   d. Fan-Out
4. In Zero Trust architectures, which principle applies?
   a. Trust internal services by default.
   b. Use only session cookies.
   c. Never trust, always verify.
   d. Accept long-lived tokens for resilience.
5. Which scalability pattern coordinates long-running transactions with compensating actions?
   a. CQRS
   b. Saga
   c. Bulkhead
   d. Rate Limiting

Answers

1. d
2. a
3. b
4. c
5. b

Questions

1. How would you balance the trade-off between strict input validation and user experience in a public-facing API?
2. What strategies could you combine to defend against both DDoS attacks and brute-force attempts?
3. In what situations would you choose orchestration over choreography for sagas, and why?
4. How would you approach caching when data freshness is as important as performance?

5. Which scalability patterns do you consider most critical for cloud-native applications, and why?

Key Terms

- **PEP/PDP**: Policy Enforcement Point / Policy Decision Point, architecture for externalized authorization decisions.
- **Least Privilege**: A Security principle of granting only the permissions necessary to perform a task.
- **mTLS**: Mutual TLS, a protocol for authenticating both clients and servers in a secure channel.
- **Idempotency Key**: Unique identifier ensuring that repeated requests are processed only once.
- **Circuit Breaker**: A Scalability pattern that prevents cascading failures by blocking calls to failing services
- **Bulkhead**: A Resource isolation strategy to prevent one component's failure from exhausting shared resources.
- **Backpressure**: A Mechanism that prevents producers from overwhelming consumers by signaling capacity limits.
- **CQRS**: Command Query Responsibility Segregation, separates write models from read models for scalability.
- **Saga**: Distributed transaction pattern using compensating actions instead of global rollback.
- **Sharding**: Partitioning of data across multiple database nodes to achieve horizontal scalability.
- **BFF**: Backend-for-Frontend, an API tailored for a specific client application, such as mobile, web, or IoT.

Chapter 11
Future Trends in Java Design Patterns

Introduction

Design patterns have always been more than coding tricks; they are conceptual maps that guide us in tackling recurring challenges. In the early years of Java, patterns such as Singleton, Factory, and Observer were mostly applied within monolithic applications, where our main concerns were maintainability, reusability, and avoiding unnecessary coupling. Back then, the boundaries of design were largely confined to the JVM, and the environment was relatively stable compared to modern distributed landscapes.

Over time, however, the scope of Java systems expanded dramatically. What once lived inside a single process now spreads across clusters, APIs, and even global infrastructures. A modern Java application is rarely just *an application.* It is far more often a set of interconnected services deployed on cloud-native platforms, integrated with artificial intelligence services, and expected to deliver secure, low-latency responses under heavy load. In such a context, design patterns cannot remain frozen. They must evolve because the forces shaping software design have changed.

The central problem is therefore not whether patterns are still relevant, but how they are being reshaped by these new forces. Where we once chose Observer to decouple classes, today we may need a backpressure-aware variant to handle high-volume reactive streams. Where transactions were once confined to a local database, they now span microservices and require the reliability of patterns such as Saga or Outbox. Where a Facade once simplified library calls, it is now reborn as an API Gateway to manage cross-cutting concerns like security, routing, and throttling. Even the Proxy pattern has been re-imagined in the form of zero-trust gateways that enforce authentication and authorization across every network hop.

These evolutions are driven by five profound shifts in the Java ecosystem. First, concurrency models are no longer a single-thread-per-request affair; we now decide between lightweight virtual threads introduced by *Project Loom* and highly optimized reactive pipelines. Second, distribution is the norm, which means managing data consistency, coordination, and isolation across service boundaries is an everyday concern for us. Third, *cloud-native platforms* impose operational contracts such as health probes, autoscaling rules, and service mesh policies that deeply influence how we design applications. Fourth, *the integration of artificial intelligence* changes how our systems make decisions, introducing probabilistic workflows, model selection, and caching strategies that were absent from earlier generations. Finally, security has moved from a peripheral task to a pervasive principle, requiring us to embrace zero-trust networking, secrets management, and supply-chain integrity as fundamental aspects of design.

The purpose of this chapter is to explore how design patterns adapt to these realities. It focuses on five domains that are shaping the future of Java architecture: **reactive programming**, **microservices architectures**, **cloud-native development**, **the integration of artificial intelligence and machine learning**, and **security enhancements**. Each section will show how classical patterns reappear in new forms, how their trade-offs shift in modern environments, and how they continue to provide the shared vocabulary and design discipline necessary for building robust and scalable systems. The message is simple: patterns remain relevant not because they are static, but because they evolve alongside the technologies that we use to solve real problems.

Structure

In this chapter, we will cover:

- Reactive Programming
- Microservices Architectures
- Cloud-Native Development
- Integration of AI and Machine Learning
- Security Enhancements

Reactive Programming

The demand for responsive, resilient, and scalable systems has placed reactive programming at the center of modern Java design. Reactive approaches are not new; the Observer pattern has always supported asynchronous communication, but the scale and intensity of the current event-driven systems have transformed how this pattern is applied. Whether in financial platforms processing thousands of transactions per second, e-commerce websites handling flash sales, or IoT platforms ingesting sensor streams, we must control not only when and how events are delivered but also how many can be handled without overwhelming consumers.

Traditional multi-threaded models, where each request consumes a dedicated thread, break down under high concurrency. Thread pools saturate, context switches multiply, and latency spikes. Even asynchronous callback-based systems, while non-blocking, tend to devolve into tangled *callback hell* and provide limited control over resource consumption. Java developers need a model where **event flow is explicit**, **consumers control demand**, and **failure handling is first-class**. Patterns that once solved intra-application communication must now evolve to handle these new constraints.

Adapted Patterns

Reactive programming does not invent new design patterns from scratch; rather, it **reshapes classical patterns** to meet the demands of asynchronous, high-volume systems. The Observer pattern, once sufficient for decoupling publishers and subscribers, now faces challenges of flow control, error handling, and resilience. Similarly, structural ideas like Circuit Breaker or Bulkhead must evolve into non-blocking, stream-aware forms.

We shall explore how several well-known patterns are being **reinterpreted in reactive contexts**, each adapted to address a specific challenge such as backpressure, failure isolation, retry storms, or temporal constraints. These adaptations demonstrate that patterns remain vital tools, not because they are static recipes, but because they are flexible frameworks that absorb new technological forces.

Backpressure-Aware Observer

The classical Observer pattern assumed producers could emit freely, and subscribers would cope. In reactive systems, this is a recipe for memory exhaustion. Modern frameworks such as **Reactor** and **Mutiny** extend Observer semantics by allowing subscribers to request events in controlled batches. This transforms Observer into a **demand-driven relationship**, where the subscriber dictates pace.

Async Boundary with Bulkhead

Reactive streams chain operations across stages, but without careful boundaries, a slow stage can stall an entire pipeline. The solution is to introduce **explicit asynchronous boundaries,** for example, using `publishOn` in **Reactor** or `emitOn` in **Mutiny**, combined with dedicated schedulers. Each stage becomes a **bulkhead**, isolating failures or slowdowns from propagating upstream.

Idempotent Subscriber

Retry and replay are common in distributed pipelines. Without safeguards, subscribers risk applying the same event multiple times, causing incorrect side effects. The **Idempotent Subscriber** pattern requires consumers to track processed events via IDs or offsets and discard duplicates. The result is exactly-once *effects* built on top of at-least-once delivery.

Reactive Circuit Breaker with Retry Budget

In synchronous systems, the Circuit Breaker is well understood. In reactive systems, it must be non-blocking and account for retries. A **retry budget** prevents retries themselves from amplifying failure storms. If a downstream service fails, the breaker trips, retries are limited by policy, and the system fails fast instead of cascading.

Temporal Windowing

Reactive systems often enforce business rules across time. Instead of applying limits per event, we use temporal windows, sliding or tumbling intervals that group events. For example, a rate limiter might allow 100 messages per minute per user. This pattern blends Iterator semantics with time, turning an unbounded stream into bounded, analyzable segments.

Trade-Offs and Consequences

Reactive programming brings clear benefits: predictable latency under load, better resource utilization, and resilience against bursts. However, the trade-offs are non-trivial. Reactive APIs increase cognitive complexity; debugging chains of operators is harder than reading sequential code. Tooling support has improved, but developers must still weigh whether the performance gains justify the learning curve. Virtual threads, introduced by *Project Loom*, offer a simpler model for many request-response applications. In practice, the future is likely hybrid: **reactive at the edges** for event streams and data ingestion, **virtual threads in the core** for business logic that benefits from sequential readability.

This snippet brings together several adapted patterns: a **backpressure-aware observer**, an **asynchronous boundary** with **bounded concurrency**, a **fail-fast stag**e, and a **retry-budget policy**.

```
Flux<Integer> numbers = Flux.range(1, 1000)
    .log()
    .onBackpressureBuffer(50) // backpressure control
    .publishOn(Schedulers.boundedElastic(), 10) // async boundary
    .map(n -> {
        if (n % 100 == 0) throw new RuntimeException("Fail fast");
        return n * 2;
    })
    .retryWhen(Retry.backoff(3, Duration.ofMillis(200))); // retry
budget
```

```
numbers.subscribe(
    val -> System.out.println("Processed: " + val),
    err -> System.err.println("Error: " + err),
    () -> System.out.println("Completed")
);
```

Reactive programming demonstrates how even the simplest design patterns, like Observer, evolve under new forces. The need to manage flow, isolate failures, and tolerate retries reshapes classical structures into resilient, backpressure-aware designs. Yet, reactive programming is only a part of the story. When services are distributed across boundaries, new challenges emerge around coordination, consistency, and client interaction. These are addressed by the next domain: **Microservices Architectures**.

Microservices Architectures

Microservices have become a defining architectural style for modern Java applications. Instead of one monolithic deployment, systems are composed of autonomous services, each focused on a bounded context. These services can scale independently, evolve separately, and further can be deployed without affecting the entire system. The promise is agility and resilience, but the reality is that decomposition introduces new problems: distributed transactions, coordination overhead, and the constant risk of inconsistency.

In a monolithic application, patterns such as Transaction Script or Repository ensured consistency because everything ran within a single database transaction. Once a system splits into microservices, that guarantee disappears. A payment service, an order service, and an inventory service may all need to update the state as part of one logical business action. Network failures, partial updates, or retries can easily break assumptions of consistency. Without adapted patterns, systems risk becoming brittle and incoherent despite their modular promise.

Adapted Patterns

To manage these complexities, familiar patterns have been **extended and reshaped** for distributed environments. Concepts like transactions, observers, and facades are not abandoned; instead, they re-emerge in new forms designed to handle network boundaries, partial failures, and service autonomy. The following adaptations illustrate how classical ideas continue to guide microservice design in Java, but at a scale and scope that requires fresh implementations.

Saga: Orchestration versus Choreography

Sagas extend the idea of transaction management across services. Instead of one atomic commit, a business process is broken into steps, each with a compensating action. In the orchestration style, a central coordinator commands each step and triggers compensations. This provides global visibility and simplifies error handling but introduces a new point of control. In the choreography style, services react to domain events without a central controller, increasing autonomy but making it harder to see the big picture. Both approaches highlight the trade-off between visibility and flexibility.

Outbox Pattern

One of the most fragile points in microservices is ensuring that domain events are reliably published when a local state change occurs. The Outbox pattern addresses this by writing events into a dedicated table within the same transaction as the state change. A relay process then publishes those events to a message broker. In Java, frameworks like Spring Boot or Quarkus and Debezium simplify implementing Outbox, ensuring events are never lost even if the service crashes immediately after updating its database.

CQRS: Command Query Responsibility Segregation

CQRS separates the models for writing and reading data. Commands mutate state in a write-optimized model, while queries retrieve projections optimized for read efficiency. In microservices, this separation allows read models to evolve without destabilizing writes and enables scaling read traffic independently. Combined with the Outbox pattern, CQRS ensures that projections are always updated consistently, even in asynchronous pipelines.

API Gateway and Backend-for-Frontend

The Gateway pattern reappears in microservices as a single entry point that handles cross-cutting concerns like authentication, throttling, and routing. In Java systems, Spring Cloud Gateway or Quarkus API Gateway extensions fulfill this role. For client-specific needs, the Backend-for-Frontend pattern provides tailored endpoints for mobile, web, or partner applications, reducing chatty calls and preventing domain services from becoming overloaded with presentation concerns.

Service Mesh and Sidecars

At scale, some concerns are too repetitive or complex to handle in every service. Service meshes externalize concerns like mTLS encryption, retries, and service discovery. In this sense, the Mediator pattern resurfaces at the infrastructure level. However, developers must still decide what resilience logic belongs in code, such as business-aware circuit breakers versus what can be safely delegated to the mesh.

Trade-Offs and Consequences

Microservices offer autonomy, scalability, and technological diversity. But they also introduce higher operational costs, more complex failure modes, and the need for robust observability. Saga and Outbox patterns address consistency, but at the cost of more moving parts. Gateways and service meshes centralize concerns but may become bottlenecks if overburdened. The art is not in applying microservices blindly but in tailoring them to business capabilities and adopting patterns that balance autonomy with coherence.

Microservices demonstrate how patterns adapt when consistency and coordination move beyond a single process. Transaction management becomes Sagas, Observer turns into event-driven choreography, and Facade reappears as API Gateway. Yet microservices alone are not enough. As organizations move toward cloud-native deployments, patterns must also reflect the operational realities of dynamic, containerized environments. This is where the next section on **Cloud-Native Development** takes us.

Cloud-Native Development

The shift from static servers to dynamic cloud platforms has redefined how Java applications are built and operated. Instead of designing systems for a fixed runtime environment, we now create applications that are ephemeral, scalable, and observable by default. The rise of Kubernetes and container orchestration means that many operational practices–such as scaling, rolling updates, and fault recovery–are now automated by the platform. Design patterns in this space must therefore bridge the gap between application code and platform behavior, ensuring that Java systems are reliable citizens in cloud-native ecosystems.

Traditional Java applications often assumed long-lived servers, manual configuration, and static scaling. Such assumptions break down in cloud-native environments, where instances may start and stop rapidly, workloads fluctuate unpredictably, and resilience must be guaranteed without human intervention. Without adapted patterns, we risk creating applications that technically run in containers but do not behave well under orchestration. For example, a service that ignores health probes may be marked as healthy by Kubernetes even while failing to process requests, or a system without readiness checks may accept traffic before it is fully initialized.

Adapted Patterns

To address these challenges, design patterns must evolve in tandem with **platform contracts**. Familiar structural and behavioral ideas such as Facade, Mediator, or Strategy now reappear in the way services expose health, manage configuration, and roll out new versions. The following adaptations illustrate how cloud-native practices are reshaping Java design patterns to ensure applications are not only correct but also operable, observable, and resilient in a dynamic environment.

Operator Pattern

In Kubernetes, the Operator pattern embodies a control loop that continuously reconciles desired state with actual state. Written in Java using frameworks such as the Fabric8 Kubernetes Client or the Java Operator SDK, operators act as domain-specific controllers. For instance, an operator may provision databases, manage tenants, or enforce compliance policies. This pattern echoes the classical Controller but at the infrastructure level, giving us a programmable interface to operational automation.

Blue-Green and Canary Releases

Releasing new versions of a Java service in production requires caution. Blue-Green deployment keeps two environments–one active, one idle–allowing instant switches. Canary releases gradually expose a small percentage of users to the new version before full rollout. These approaches modernize the Strategy pattern: different deployment strategies are selected at runtime depending on risk, user base, and error budgets. Tools such as Argo Rollouts or Flagger integrate directly with Kubernetes to support these workflows.

Service Mesh Integration

While introduced in microservices, service meshes take on new importance in cloud-native systems. By externalizing service discovery, retries, and mTLS encryption, a mesh embodies a **distributed Mediator**. For Java developers, this means focusing application-level code on business resilience, such as handling compensations in Sagas, while letting the mesh manage low-level transport concerns. The consequence is a clearer separation of responsibilities between application patterns and infrastructure patterns.

Trade-Offs and Consequences

Cloud-native patterns make Java applications more robust in dynamic environments, but also shift some control away from developers. Relying too heavily on the platform may mask poor application design; conversely, resisting platform features can lead to duplicated effort. Operators simplify automation but add another moving part to maintain. Canary and Blue-Green deployments reduce risk but require sophisticated observability to detect regressions early. The challenge is to balance code-level responsibility with platform-level capabilities, ensuring neither is overburdened.

Cloud-native patterns highlight how design extends beyond source code into the platform itself. By aligning with Kubernetes operators, release strategies, and service meshes, Java applications embrace resilience and operability as design-time concerns. Yet cloud-native deployments are not the final frontier. Increasingly, Java systems must also integrate **intelligence** from predictive models to conversational AI, requiring new adaptations of classical design patterns. That is the focus of the next section: **Integration of AI and Machine Learning**.

Integration of AI and Machine Learning

Artificial intelligence is no longer confined to research labs. From recommendation engines to conversational assistants, AI and machine learning have become **first-class features** in modern applications. For Java developers, this represents a shift from deterministic workflows where algorithms follow predefined logic to probabilistic workflows where outputs are generated by models that adapt from data. Integrating these capabilities requires design patterns that balance the flexibility of AI with the reliability expected from production systems.

AI services are powerful but unpredictable. A machine learning model may return results that are biased, incomplete, or inconsistent. Latency can vary widely depending on model size, input complexity, and provider load. Costs also accumulate rapidly if every request triggers a full inference on a large model. In addition, organizations often rely on multiple providers for redundancy or compliance reasons. Without structured design patterns, we risk creating brittle integrations where models are tightly coupled, results are unchecked, and errors cascade through the system.

Adapted Patterns

Rather than inventing entirely new approaches, we are discovering that classical design patterns adapt naturally to AI integration. The Strategy pattern, long used for algorithm selection, now governs the choice between models. The Adapter pattern connects diverse AI providers through a unified API. Composite and Facade appear in **Retrieval-Augmented Generation** pipelines, while **Proxy re-emerges in guardrails** that mediate and validate model output. These adaptations show that the principles of design patterns remain relevant even when facing the uncertainty of machine intelligence.

Strategy-Based Model Selection

AI workloads often require choosing between multiple models: a small model for quick responses, a large model for accuracy, or a domain-specific model for compliance. The Strategy pattern enables dynamic selection based on latency, cost, or quality requirements.

Adapter for Multi-Provider Integration

AI APIs vary widely in authentication, input formats, and output schemas. An Adapter layer standardizes these differences, allowing the application to switch providers without rewriting business logic. For example, a Java Adapter might translate a generic `GenerateText` request into provider-specific payloads for OpenAI, Mistral AI, or a local model.

Retrieval-Augmented Generation Pipelines

To ground model responses in reliable data, Retrieval-Augmented Generation RAG combines retrieval from structured sources with generative synthesis. This pipeline can be modeled as a composition of smaller patterns: a **Repository** for indexed data, a **Chain of Responsibility** for retrieval steps, and a **Facade** for the orchestration layer.

Inference Cache

Because repeated queries are common, caching results by semantic fingerprint reduces both latency and cost. This adaptation of the **Flyweight pattern** ensures that identical or similar prompts reuse cached results, while expiration policies handle staleness.

Guardrails and Proxy Controls

Before outputs are passed downstream, a guardrail layer acts as a **Proxy** that validates, redacts, or reformulates results. This ensures compliance, prevents leakage of sensitive data, and enforces business rules.

Trade-Offs and Consequences

Integrating AI patterns brings new strengths, adaptability, personalization, and predictive power, but also new risks. Strategy-based selection prevents vendor lock-in but requires careful monitoring of performance trade-offs. Adapters provide flexibility but can mask provider-specific optimizations. RAG pipelines improve reliability but increase architectural complexity. Inference caches cut costs but raise questions of freshness and cache invalidation. Guardrails protect integrity but add latency. The key is to design with **observability and feedback loops**, ensuring AI-enhanced systems remain predictable in practice.

This simplified **Model Gateway** shows how Strategy *choosing a model*, Adapter *standardizing* APIs, and Facade *centralized access* work together to provide a flexible AI integration layer in Java.

```
public interface ModelClient {
    String generateText(String prompt);
}

public class OpenAIClient implements ModelClient {
    public String generateText(String prompt) {
        // Call OpenAI API...
        return "...";
    }
}

public class MistralAiClient implements ModelClient {
    public String generateText(String prompt) {
        // Call Mistral AI API...
        return "...";
    }
}

public class ModelGateway {
    private final Map<String, ModelClient> clients = Map.of(
        "openai", new OpenAIClient(),
        "mistralai", new MistralAiClient()
    );

    public String respond(String prompt, String strategy) {
        ModelClient client = clients.get(strategy);
        return client.generateText(prompt);
    }
}
```

The integration of AI and Machine Learning demonstrates that patterns are resilient, not rigid. They extend their reach from deterministic algorithms into probabilistic workflows, ensuring Java applications can safely embrace intelligence while staying reliable. But intelligence alone is not enough. In an era of zero-trust networking and supply-chain risks, **security** has become the cornerstone of sustainable design. That is the focus of the next section: **Security Enhancements**.

Security Enhancements

In the past, security was often treated as a separate concern, added late in the development cycle or delegated entirely to infrastructure teams. That approach is no longer sustainable. In the contemporary landscape of microservices, cloud-native deployments, and AI-powered applications, **security is architectural**. Every pattern must embed mechanisms for authentication, authorization, confidentiality, and integrity. For Java developers, this means that design patterns cannot be considered complete unless they incorporate security by default.

As systems grow more distributed and interconnected, traditional assumptions of trust quickly collapse. Within a monolith, trust was implicit: if code could access an object, it was considered safe. In a microservices architecture running on the cloud, every network call is a potential attack surface. Without embedded security, patterns such as Saga, Outbox, or Gateway risk exposing data or operations to unauthorized actors. Moreover, supply-chain attacks–compromising libraries, containers, or build pipelines show that security cannot be limited to runtime but must span the entire software lifecycle.

Adapted Patterns

Classical patterns like Proxy, Facade, or Builder reemerge in security contexts, but with new semantics. The Proxy becomes a zero-trust gateway mediating every request. The Facade appears as an API Gateway that enforces authentication and rate limits. Builder is mirrored in CI/CD pipelines that construct signed artifacts. These adaptations illustrate how the language of design patterns continues to evolve, ensuring that **security is not an afterthought, but rather a structural principle**.

Token Exchange and Session Scope

Tokens are now short-lived, context-specific, and sometimes proof-of-possession rather than simple bearer credentials. This approach extends the Chain of Responsibility, where tokens evolve through different layers of trust, exchanged for narrower scopes as they propagate. Spring Security and MicroProfile JWT support these exchanges directly.

Secrets Vault

Configuration once handled by properties files now requires strong protection. A Secrets Vault externalizes secret management, rotating keys dynamically, and removing sensitive data from code or configuration files. In Java, Vault clients or Kubernetes secrets integrations follow the Repository pattern, abstracting secure storage behind a stable interface.

Supply-Chain Integrity

Attacks increasingly target the pipeline, not just the runtime. The Builder pattern reappears here; builders must produce artifacts that are signed and verifiable. Generating a Software Bill of Materials SBOM becomes part of the artifact, ensuring downstream systems can validate dependencies. For Java, tools like JReleaser and Sigstore integrate this step into Maven or Gradle pipelines.

Cryptographic Agility

No cryptographic algorithm can be assumed permanent. The Strategy pattern applies here; applications should encapsulate cryptographic choices behind interfaces, allowing algorithms to be swapped as new standards emerge, for example, moving toward post-quantum cryptography.

Trade-Offs and Consequences

Embedding security patterns strengthens resilience but comes at a cost. Zero-trust models increase latency and operational complexity. Token exchange and short lifespans add administrative overhead but minimize exposure. Secrets vaults reduce risks of leakage but add dependencies on external systems. Supply-chain integrity improves trust but requires changes in tooling and process discipline. Developers must accept that security is not free; it is a set of **deliberate trade-offs** balancing performance, usability, and protection.

Security enhancements reveal how patterns extend beyond code structure to encompass the entire lifecycle of software. Proxy becomes a gatekeeper, Builder secures the pipeline, and Strategy governs cryptography. Taken together, these adaptations show that the future of Java design patterns is not just about scaling or distributing applications but about **ensuring that they remain trustworthy**. With security embedded into every layer, we are ready to consider how all these forces, reactive, microservices, cloud-native, intelligent, and secure, combine in a unified case study.

Conclusion

The journey through future trends in Java design patterns shows that **patterns are not static recipes but adaptive tools**. As we have seen, the essence of classical ideas such as Observer, Proxy, Strategy, Facade, and Builder remains intact, but their **applications evolve** under new forces. Reactive programming adapts Observer to handle backpressure. Microservices extend transaction management into Saga and Outbox. Cloud-native environments introduce patterns such as Operators, health probes, and progressive delivery. AI integration brings Strategy, Adapter, and Facade into play for model orchestration, caching, and guardrails. Security, now woven into every layer, reshapes Proxy, Builder, and Strategy into zero-trust gateways, artifact pipelines, and cryptographic agility.

The lesson is not to memorize a list of patterns, but instead, to understand **why do patterns change**. They evolve in response to concurrency pressure, distribution, platform automation, probabilistic intelligence, and pervasive security. For Java developers, this adaptability is a sign of strength: patterns remain a shared vocabulary that bridges technical shifts, ensuring design literacy across generations of tools and frameworks.

This chapter closes the book with a simple truth: the real value of patterns is not in their code examples but in the discipline of design thinking they instill. Whichever technologies the future holds, new platforms, new concurrency models, and new AI paradigms patterns will continue to evolve, subsequently, guiding us to build systems that are robust, scalable, and trustworthy.

Points to Remember

- Patterns are **adaptable frameworks**, not fixed templates.
- Reactive programming reshapes Observer into **backpressure-aware pipelines**.
- Microservices transform transaction patterns into **Saga and Outbox**, with **CQRS** enabling scalable read/write separation.
- Cloud-native environments embed patterns like **Operators, health probes, and canary deployments** into everyday practice.
- AI integration uses **Strategy for model selection**, **Adapter for multi-provider APIs**, and **RAG pipelines** for reliable outputs.
- Security is structural: **zero-trust proxies, token exchange, secrets vaults, supply-chain integrity, and cryptographic agility** ensure trust.
- Patterns survive because they evolve with technology, preserving a **common design vocabulary**.

Multiple Choice Questions

1. Which adaptation of the Observer pattern ensures resilience in reactive streams?
    a. Backpressure-aware subscription
    b. Temporal Windowing
    c. Outbox relay
    d. Service Mesh integration

2. The Outbox pattern is primarily used to:
    a. Cache inference results
    b. Manage deployment rollouts
    c. Guarantee reliable event publication with state changes
    d. Provide guardrails for model outputs
3. In cloud-native environments, the Operator pattern is best described as:
    a. Cache-Aside
    b. Read-Through
    c. Write-Behind
    d. Fan-Out
4. Which combination illustrates AI integration patterns in Java?
    a. Builder + Prototype
    b. Singleton + Flyweight
    c. Observer + Iterator
    d. Strategy + Adapter + Facade
5. Which practice strengthens supply-chain integrity in Java systems?
    a. Health and readiness probes
    b. Secrets vaults
    c. Artifact signing and SBOM verification
    d. Circuit breakers with retry budgets

Answers

1. a
2. c
3. b
4. d
5. c

Questions

1. In your current systems, where could backpressure-aware reactive streams prevent bottlenecks?
2. If you were decomposing a monolithic Java application, which bounded context would you extract first and why?
3. How would you balance Kubernetes platform features with code-level resilience in your own designs?
4. What strategy would you use to integrate multiple AI providers without creating vendor lock-in?
5. How can you embed zero-trust principles into your software lifecycle, beyond runtime authentication?

Key Terms

- **Backpressure:** Flow-control mechanism preventing producers from overwhelming subscribers.
- **Saga:** Distributed transaction pattern with compensating actions.
- **Outbox:** Ensures reliable event publishing alongside state changes.
- **CQRS:** Separates command (write) and query (read) models for scalability.
- **Operator Pattern:** Cloud-native controller reconciling desired vs. actual state.
- **Canary Release:** Deployment strategy exposing a small portion of users to new versions.
- **Retrieval-Augmented Generation (RAG):** AI pipeline combining data retrieval with generative synthesis.
- **Inference Cache:** Cache for AI outputs, reducing latency and cost.
- **Guardrails:** Validation layer controlling model outputs before downstream use.
- **Zero-Trust Proxy:** Enforces authentication and authorization on every request.
- **Secrets Vault:** Secure, centralized management of sensitive configuration values.
- **Supply-Chain Integrity:** Assurance that artifacts are signed, verifiable, and free from malicious dependencies.
- **Cryptographic Agility:** Ability to swap cryptographic algorithms without disrupting system design.

Index

A

B

C

F

H

I